W9-BQL-647

IMPROVING
THE URBAN HIGH SCHOOL
What Works and Why

IMPROVING
THE URBAN HIGH SCHOOL
What Works and Why

KAREN SEASHORE LOUIS   MATTHEW B. MILES

Teachers College, Columbia University
New York & London

Carrie Rich Memorial Library
Campbell University
Buies Creek, NC 27506

Published by Teachers College Press, 1234 Amsterdam Avenue
New York, NY 10027

Copyright © 1990 by Karen Seashore Louis and Matthew B. Miles

All rights reserved. No part of this publication may be reproduced or transmitted in any
form or by any means, electronic or mechanical, including photocopy, or any information storage and retrieval system, without permission from the publisher.

Figures 9.1, A.1, and C.1 were prepared by Estela Morales.

Library of Congress Cataloging-in-Publication Data

Louis, Karen Seashore.
    Improving the urban high school : what works and why / Karen
  Seashore Louis, Matthew B. Miles.
      p.   cm.
      Includes bibliographical references (p. 325).
      ISBN 0-8077-3022-X (alk. paper). – ISBN 0-8077-3021-1 (pbk. :
  alk paper)
      1. Education, Urban – United States.   2. High schools – United
  States – Case studies.   3. Urban schools – United States – Case
  studies.   4. School improvement programs – United States – Case
  studies.   5. Educational surveys – United States.   I. Miles. Matthew
  B. II. Title.
  LC5131.L64   1990

370.19′348′973 – dc20   90-31068
                                                                              CIP

ISBN 0-8077-3021-1 (pbk.)
        0-8077-3022-X

Printed on acid-free paper

Manufactured in the United States of America

97   96   95   94   93   92   91   90   8   7   6   5   4   3   2   1

Contents

21080290

Preface

This book is written for people closely involved with high school improvement, especially those in America's cities. We are speaking to principals, assistant principals, department heads, teachers, district office staff, consultants, local board members, and citizens and parents who care about better schools. Over the past four years, we've learned a great deal about what makes for successful reform in urban high schools, and want to get this report of our experience where it can do the most good.

WHY THIS BOOK?

The current educational reform movement calls for dramatic increases in student achievement, restructuring toward school-based decision making, and improvement of curriculum and teaching. Effective schools and effective teaching programs abound. But there are many strikes against *real* school change, and the risk of failure is large. The energy and enthusiasm for change we've seen in many schools may come to little or nothing in the end, unless we do it right. Such failure will only breed depression and cynicism. School improvement is at a critical point. We all need to get better at leading and managing change.

This book grew out of our own long experience in watching and documenting, and sometimes directly helping with, school improvement. There is a good deal of research knowledge about what makes some schools better than others. And researchers know a lot about the change process, after several decades of research on topics from organization development in schools to the implementation of externally funded programs and dissemination of information. But the missing crucial piece for most school people is *how to get there*: how to lead and manage the process of school reform. While there is a growing literature on the management of change, most of it deals with relatively small-scale innovations, or has been developed outside educational settings.

Furthermore, much current writing on change in the private sector seems caught up in a romance with leadership. In most schools, the ability of any one individual "at the top" to create dramatic turnarounds is radically constrained. Even if principals and superintendents had the same authority as chief executive officers of corporations (which they do not), urging school administrators to take on the mantle of strong and charismatic leadership is unrealistic. It is one thing to call abstractly for "new leadership" and another to locate enough new movers and shakers to staff the 16,000 school districts and 84,000 school buildings in the country.

And so we have felt challenged to write a book for real people struggling with the steady work of school improvement — a book that would help to clarify how ordinary schools like theirs have actually dealt successfully with the exigencies, crises, routines, and flow of change.

WHAT WE DID

Though both of us have been involved with schools over the past two decades, we decided to take a new close-up look at school improvement efforts, to form a solid grounding for what we were to write. We wanted to find out how successful school improvement really worked.

We deliberately chose to look at urban high schools, the most difficult settings for improvement we could think of. They're often crowded with students from poor, minority, and immigrant backgrounds, whose families live in sometimes appalling circumstances — students who are seriously underachieving and dropping out in terrible numbers. In many cases, city school buildings are decaying, equipment is missing, teachers are frustrated and discouraged with an outmoded curriculum and school structure, administrators are too harried to think straight, parents are desperate, and children are short-changed out of any pretense at equal educational opportunity. We believed that if we could understand how real improvement takes place in such settings, the lessons could be useful in less difficult schools.

So to ground our work we did five in-depth case studies of high schools that were improving in Boston, New York, New Jersey, Cleveland, and Los Angeles. And we did a national survey of 178 big-city high school principals whose schools had been carrying out serious improvement efforts for one to four years. We were able to draw conclusions, across our five cases and from the survey, that made sense. We are basically researchers, and we used methods of data collection and analysis that we are confident about from long experience.

There are many books in the business management literature focusing on leading and managing change. But many of them advise strategies based on an image of organizations that does not fit well with the reality of life in schools, which are more bureaucratic than a typical private-sector organization, and yet less hierarchical and tightly linked together. We wanted to adapt the best of this literature, add what is known about school improvement, and connect it to what we had found, reflecting on the core issues of leading and managing change.

We also wanted to write about what really had worked (not just describe a thousand ways to fail), in practical language that would resonate with the efforts of the many good people now hard at work on reform. Improving big-city high schools is a long and difficult process, and we had no illusions that we could — or should — provide recipes or offer panaceas. Yet we did want to point to ideas and practices that would succeed without requiring a miracle worker to manage them.

Our effort to ground our work, link it to the change literature, and draw implications hasn't been easy. Most chapters expanded well beyond our original estimates. We've worked hard to present results that reflect the authentic complexities of life in urban high schools, in reports that didn't talk down, yet were straightforward enough to be useful. Above all, we wanted to avoid the researcher's frequent conclusion: "More research is needed. . . . "

THE BOOK ITSELF

This book is *not* a collation of specific "how to's." It's not a polemical review of how bad city high schools are, or a technical discussion of what to do about "at-risk" students. Nor is it a general treatise on school improvement, a technical research report, or advice on "how to deal with people."

It *is*, first, a clear summary of what we found in our survey and case studies of improvement efforts. We've looked at what urban high schools are doing to improve, how they're going about it, and what makes it more likely for them to succeed.

Second, it makes connections between our schools' experience and the larger literature on school improvement, and the leadership and management of change. And third, it suggests what understanding these connections may mean for people who want to improve schools. Though we took urban high schools as our focus, we believe the ideas are generic enough to be relevant to schools at other levels, in other settings.

Though we are writing for people most closely involved with local school improvement, we can hardly object if the book is read by researchers, university teachers, or state department of education people. If they are seriously interested in school improvement, there is much here for them.

Acknowledgments

We have been aided in this task by the support of many wonderful colleagues, both researchers and school people.

Our case studies and survey were conducted with Sheila Rosenblum, Tony Cipollone, and the late Eleanor Farrar. Together, we collected data, wrote case studies, and produced the preliminary analysis on which the structure of this book is based. Without their many analytic insights, this book could never have been written. Our colleagues didn't always agree with all the specific conclusions we have drawn from the data, but they have never been shy in challenging our assertions, and calling us to task to ensure that our results were based on systematic and accurate analysis. Tony's contributions, in addition to data collection in the Agassiz case, included assistance in the survey data analysis. We are particularly grateful for Sheila and Eleanor's direct contribution as co-authors of the chapters based on their case studies of Alameda and Burroughs. With Eleanor's death in 1989, we lost a loved and valued colleague.

Clearly our work would never have seen publication without the strong support of other colleagues: the administrators and teachers in the schools that were covered in our cases. Their energy and commitment to improvement were amazing. Not only did they spend many hours talking to us, but they tirelessly read drafts of our case studies to ensure that they were accurate, both in fact and in interpretation. Where they challenged our interpretations (which was relatively rare), we incorporated information about the nature of their disagreement into the text. Since our cases are presented with pseudonyms, we must refrain from giving them the personal and professional recognition they truly deserve.

The original case studies and survey were carried out with support from the Boston Foundation, the Conrad N. Hilton Foundation, the Fund for New Jersey, the Regional Laboratory for the Northeast and Islands, the Far West Laboratory for Educational Research and Development, and the New Jersey State Department of Education. We were aided in the final preparation of the book by the support of the North Central Educational Laboratory. We are very much indebted to these organizations for their steady encouragement as well as financial support. Our conclusions, of course, do not necessarily reflect the views of any of these agencies.

We would also like to acknowledge the support of the Center for Survey Research, at the University of Massachusetts/Boston, and the Department of Educational Policy and Administration, University of Minnesota, both of which contributed unreimbursed financial and endless collegial support for data analysis and production of this book. Two doctoral candidates at the University of Minnesota — Melissa Anderson and Ismael Abu-Saad — helped us with many details of bibliography and final computer runs.

Because of the advent of word processors, it turns out there are no unsung secretaries to thank. We keyboarded it all ourselves. Thus it remains only to thank each other for our energy, forbearance, good will, and bright ideas in a project that has been tough, exciting, and very satisfying. The collaboration has been seamless, and our names appear in alphabetical order to symbolize that.

K.S.L.   &   M.B.M.

Part I

INTRODUCTION

We begin with a look at the territory: What will it mean to reform the urban high school? What challenges, opportunities, and risks lie ahead? How much do we really know, and what are some of the core issues that need to be faced?

Chapter 2 describes our general model. We make the case for rethinking the way we look at schools, and organizing for *change*, as contrasted with only organizing for stability. Leading and managing change are two distinct but intertwined processes. We examine and debunk some of the "conventional wisdom" about leading and managing change. And we focus on key "action motifs" for change leaders and change managers that will be reviewed in depth throughout the rest of the book.

Chapter 3, through our survey data, provides an overview of sustained improvement efforts in urban high schools across the country. We summarize what the schools we surveyed were like; describe the change programs they were involved in; and look carefully at the issues of planning, the problems of implementation, and the results achieved.

1

Reforming the Urban High School

A Look at the Territory

A recent study argues that U.S. high schools are organized as "shopping malls" rather than serious educational institutions.[1] If we extend this image, urban high schools seem more like the dilapidated commercial intersections that dot our inner cities than the chromed, glassy, interior-landscaped versions in suburbia. Run-down and overpriced, they often present a limited selection of shoddy goods for their customers.[2] In the suburban shopping mall the customer may be king, but in the inner-city mini-mart the customer is often poor and usually has neither the resources to go elsewhere in search of better merchandise, nor the assertiveness to demand improved service.

THE CHALLENGE

Urban education has deteriorated badly over the past twenty years. Facilities are decaying, dropout rates have increased, achievement is down, and student employment and further education are at lower levels. Fingers can be pointed at many causes—changing demographic patterns, political corruption, rigid and old-fashioned administration, poor or burned-out teachers—but few solutions seem to be in sight. Research findings indicating that larger school systems are less effective than smaller ones in educating lower-income or disadvantaged students increase concerns about the viability of urban education (Friedkin & Necochea, 1988). Some argue (mostly privately) that the only way to improve urban education is to tear it all down and start over. But that solution is a fantasy, given the current (and foreseeable) pressures on urban high schools to "do more with less," as Oakes (1987) points out.

Based on our experience, teachers and administrators who inhabit urban schools believe that the overwhelming disciplinary problems of the mid-'70s are under control. But absence of tension in the hallways and a relatively calm atmosphere in classrooms do not add up to positive educational experiences. When we recently asked a class of juniors in a large New York high school to tell us what they liked most about school they replied, "When it's time to leave." What do they want more of? "Exciting classes." "Teachers who know something." But even when teachers have attended the best pre- and in-service programs, those bound for urban high schools are still prepared in the same way as suburban ones, despite evidence that urban schools need a different breed (Corcoran, Walker, & White, 1988; Haberman, 1988).

OPPORTUNITIES AND RISKS

Yet this is a time when there are serious opportunities for reforming the existing system. Much recent energy has gone into a wide range of commission and research reports that delineate the problems and provide clear images of excellence.[3] There is strong motivation to act on these reports at state, regional, and local levels, and many states and districts are enacting massive educational reform efforts that require improved performance and offer support as well.[4] Furthermore, spokespeople for educational reform have attracted serious public attention for the first time in several decades: Education is, at least temporarily, on the political agenda and visible in the public press (Kaplan, 1985). Above all, we are well past the stage of good intentions: There is a substantial batch of tools in the form of well-documented, research-based "effective schools" and "effective teaching" programs that are being implemented in an increasing number of elementary and secondary schools (Corcoran, 1985; Kyle, 1985; Neufeld, Farrar, & Miles, 1983; Purkey & Smith, 1983).

Even so, changing high schools is not well charted. Most of the studies of planned educational change have emphasized the elementary school. There is clear consensus in the literature that approaches that work in elementary schools may fail when transferred to the more complicated and turbulent environment of high schools (Neufeld, Farrar, & Miles, 1983). Although we have "images of excellence" for high schools, we lack clear images of implementation — how an ordinary high school can move through the procedures of improvement to become excellent.[5] Recommendations to secondary school administrators about how to manage an improvement program are often simply borrowed from private-sector models, such as the popular *In Search of Excellence* (Peters

& Waterman, 1984), although we know that management problems in the public sector — especially in schools — are often quite different.

Thus, there *is* a serious risk: The images put forth in the books and reports, and the emerging public consensus around the need for change, may inspire us, but never become reality (Chubb, 1988). Lack of clarity in how to approach the improvement process may cause frustration among the high school staffs, district office personnel, and state officials who are struggling to achieve something new. Faced with small failures and unserviceable plans, the tendency to return to "business as usual" while mouthing the rhetoric of improvement will be inevitable.

This risk is particularly great for urban high schools, which are much more complex social, administrative, and political settings, and have intense educational disadvantages such as low-income student populations, outdated physical plants, and limited discretionary resources. Locating a program or a set of principles for improving school performance is only a tiny first step in such settings. The hard work of improvement comes in negotiating the difficult path of getting new practices and ideas into the real life of the school.

We must avoid the risk of failing to achieve excellence, and the risks of cynicism, superficial rhetoric, and despair that will follow in its wake. We need to learn from success in the difficult task of improving the urban high school. Along with images of excellence we need practical guidelines drawn from the experience of real people who have transformed ordinary high schools into outstanding ones. These need to be communicated clearly to people who care and can do something: principals, school staff members, parents, and policy makers at the district level.

This book is our answer to this challenge. It does not provide a blueprint for school reform. It differs from previous reports and studies by dealing concretely with leadership and management for change in urban high schools: not *what* is to be done, but *how* it can be done. It is based on the day-to-day work of typical administrators and teachers, and focuses on the problems of designing and implementing major improvement programs at the secondary school level. It also reflects the complex reality of daily life in schools: We do not propose an approach to reform based on locating and pushing the right buttons, because that is not the way schools (or other organizations, for that matter) are really administered. Rather, we have used the efforts of real urban high schools that are *trying* to become excellent to illuminate actual leadership and management issues — the issues facing any school that is working on getting better.

KNOWLEDGE AND PRACTICE: WHERE ARE WE NOW?

By now most people with an interest in high school reform have learned that neither the "images of excellence" from the commission and study reports nor the research on effective schools and effective teaching is robust enough to serve as a road map to urban secondary school improvement (Corcoran, 1985). This is not, in our view, because of flaws in research methodology[6]; the weaknesses of individual research designs are offset by the consistency in findings across many studies in different settings. Nor is it because the literature lacks clear causal connections between school characteristics and effectiveness; a number of recent studies have begun to remedy this problem (Fullan, 1988; Rosenholtz, 1989).

More problematic is the lack of attention to some critical factors that affect school improvement efforts (such as the relative importance of the individual characteristics of the teachers and students in the school)[7] and contradictory data about other actors — for example, the role of the principal in an effective school (Austin, 1979; D'Amico, 1982; Rutherford, Hall, & Hord, 1985). And, as noted above, most research on effective schools has been conducted in elementary settings, which, because of the political and organizational differences between the two, renders the research less useful to those searching for detailed guides to high school improvement.[8]

Despite the limited literature on high school improvement, some districts and individual schools are heeding the current concern about high school quality presented in the various commission reports and national studies mentioned above. However, the movement toward comprehensive improvement is far from a mad rush to get on the train. It is estimated that only 10 percent of American high schools have mounted a comprehensive improvement program (Purkey, Rutter, & Newmann, 1987), which leaves considerable room for expansion of effort. Urban high schools, however, are under more pressure to improve, even though they lack guides to lead them in the right direction. Of the approximately 1,260 high schools located in urban settings, 34 percent (428) were estimated to be attempting a comprehensive program as of 1982 (Purkey et al., 1987).

How have they fared? We can't really tell, but we believe from the survey we conducted in 1985 (see Chapter 3) that the problems of frustration and backsliding that concern us may already have begun. When we asked a large number of knowledgeable people for nominations of urban high schools that were seriously implementing an improvement program based on the principles in the effective schools and effective teaching literature, we could locate only 279, of which only 178 had been implementing a comprehensive program for at least a year.

The 1982 and 1985 figures are not strictly comparable and we would not conclude that the number of schools involved in such efforts has declined a lot.[9] However, neither is there evidence that the numbers are swelling, and it seems possible that many of those who reported involvement in 1982 joined the ranks of high schools whose commitment to reform is in a file drawer rather than embedded in daily activities.

And we also know that even those schools that are moving toward improvement face many barriers along the way. As we'll see in Chapter 3, our 1985 survey of the 178 schools implementing improvement programs indicates that major and minor problems littered the wake of their progress. The most frequent major impediments were lack of teacher time and energy and lack of resources — problems that are hardly unique to high schools or urban settings. However, a substantial number reported problems that were directly related to the complexity of their organizations and settings. These included adult–student tensions, conflict with special interest groups, political pressures or tensions, conflicts with the district office, and problems in reaching agreement among the staff over the desirability of the reform effort's goals.

Researchers have speculated on the differences between high schools and elementary schools that must be considered when improvement programs are initiated at the secondary level (Farrar, Neufeld, & Miles, 1984; Firestone & Herriott, 1982). We turn now to a discussion of high school characteristics and how they bear on improving high schools, before moving on to discuss how these issues will be addressed in the remainder of this book.

CAN HIGH SCHOOLS BE IMPROVED? SOME RECURRING ISSUES

What Goals? Whose Goals?

One problem in high schools is the diversity of purposes and objectives. Yes, we all can agree that the goal is to educate students — but in what, and for what? In elementary schools, achieving a unified view of what the schools should (and can) achieve is relatively easier (Firestone, Herriott, & Wilson, 1987). We tend to believe that we know what the "basics" are for young children, and we are agreed that schools are also to place strong emphasis upon personal and social development.

But at the high school level even the commission reports disagree about what an excellent high school should look like: Should the emphasis be on a classical academic education? On preparing children for the complex, critical thinking skills that may be needed in the next century? On making sure that they have basic skills needed to move into the world of work? And how much attention should be paid to individual guidance and social development? Are sports and extra-curricular activities an important part of the educational experience, a reward for academic achievement, or a frill? Should students be regularly tested and held back if they don't make the grade, or urged to move on to prevent discouragement and early dropout? And how about vocational education: Is it central to the role of today's high schools, or an outmoded concept that should be abandoned?

The school improvement literature urges schools to develop a school-wide consensus on school purposes or school mission, and many improvement initiatives being proposed at state levels define these purposes in terms of improved student achievement (largely in Math and English). Yet, when we move to individual schools the conflicts among goals are magnified as differences of opinion arise between and among parents, staff, and students. An analysis of goals for high schools, for example (Sirotnik, 1983), revealed that more than half of the teachers, parents, and students surveyed at the secondary level viewed the social, personal, and vocational purposes of high schools to be more important than cognitive or intellectual development.

Thus it is hardly surprising that administrators in high school need to manage this goal diversity actively if they plan to carry out significant improvement programs. In the first flush of concern about developing a reform, it may be relatively easy to get staff to commit themselves to a relatively vague plan of action. However, when the reform is actually implemented, conflicts that were not previously discussed may surface. In our study, only a few principals reported that getting staff to agree to a plan for change was difficult, but 43 percent said that maintaining consensus over improvement goals among the staff was a problem.

Complicated and Lonely Places

Several structural features of high school organization also influence reform efforts: size, organizational complexity, student movement about the school, and tracking by ability. For example, large size makes every intervention logistically more difficult and expensive, and the department structure encourages conflicts and competition over students and resources (Powell, Cohen, & Farrar, 1985). Internal competition may, under the right conditions, increase innovativeness in private-sector organizations (Kanter, 1983; Peters & Waterman, 1984). But this finding is hard to translate to a public high school, where the "innovative projects" that may bite the dust as a result of friendly competition between the Math and Social Studies departments are student careers!

Ability groups, another persistent feature of high schools, are problematic because they often create divisions in high schools over the curriculum and how it is taught. Tracking also encourages social divisions in the school, which make goals and procedural consensus harder to forge. Curricular and social divisions take on greater significance in light of findings suggesting that high schools are more "loosely coupled" than elementary schools, and authority more decentralized. Issues of curriculum and tracking are therefore more difficult to resolve, although they are clearly basic to any real change in high school performance. In fact, even many successfully changing schools simply skirt this issue; only 37 percent of the schools in our study indicated that curriculum changes were central to their program—the lowest percentage indicated for any reform objective other than individualizing instruction. We question whether real reform can occur until these issues are addressed frontally.[10]

Where Are the Leaders?

The role of the principal also complicates high school improvement efforts. The school improvement literature views the principal's role as pivotal, both as manager of reform and as instructional leader. However, few high school principals are qualified to supervise faculty in departments and disciplines beyond the ones they once taught in (and high school principals are often drawn from the ranks of coaches and gym and health teachers rather than from the academic disciplines). Instructional leadership in terms of curricular reform and teacher supervision is also difficult because of the large number of courses and teachers found in most high schools. Moreover, even if principals were able to do close substantive supervision, they hardly have time. The instructional leadership role urged on principals by improvement programs encounters considerable competition from other responsibilities, including overall management of the organization and serving as the front line of contact with a variety of outside constituents.

Reorganizing the responsibilities of principals may be essential to the success of most improvement efforts. On this point, preliminary findings on change in high schools suggest that leadership for school improvement does not necessarily reside in principals, nor do department heads show much indication of assuming a leadership role (Hall &

Guzman, 1984). Instead, most of the impetus for change comes from outside the school, usually from the district office. Most urban districts (75%, according to our survey data) have a reform initiative of their own, and district central office staff typically have a strong influence on the design of school programs (see also Farrar, 1987a).

The issue is not just who gets things started, because the principal is always accountable for how changes are carried out (Lipman & Ranking, 1982). In urban settings with complicated district offices, however, principals are caught in a real Catch-22: They are given responsibility for making a real difference in achievement, dropout rates, or other performance factors, but they often lack authority to lead effectively. Fifty-eight percent of the principals we surveyed indicated that lack of autonomy created problems for them in carrying out their plans for reform. Early reports on "school-based management" efforts in many settings indicate that in larger districts accountability is often decentralized without an accompanying increase in school-level authority over key staffing or curriculum decisions. Clune and White (1988) found across-the-board satisfaction with school-based management programs, even in those districts that had not decentralized. We interpret this to mean that any effort to give schools more autonomy can improve principal morale. The real issue is what can increase initiative taking and change at this level.

Schools Are Places Where People Work

Lots of things happen in the day-to-day life of high schools, but most of them are directed toward work. That work is largely carried out by teachers and students, whose characteristics and problems are important issues in reform. High school teachers view their work differently than elementary teachers (Firestone et al., 1987). They are more likely to view themselves as subject matter specialists, and less likely to see themselves as having responsibility for the "whole child," a task that is delegated to administrators and guidance specialists. Because they are attached to departments, they often feel a greater loyalty to their immediate work group than to the school as a whole (Hall & Guzman, 1984). This has profound implications for school reform efforts: One recent study found that school-wide planning (a key ingredient of many proposed reform efforts) does not take root easily in secondary schools because it is viewed as foreign (Berman & Gjelten, 1984).

Furthermore, because each teacher meets between 120 and 150 students daily, many students are anonymous and emotionally detached from their high schools (Firestone & Rosenblum, 1988; Sizer, 1984).

Teachers often don't have the friendly attachment to students that characterizes elementary schools: Twenty-two percent of the principals in our survey indicated that negative staff attitudes about students seriously hindered the development of any plans for reform. Under these conditions, building student commitment to school improvement is difficult, even if it is considered essential. The influence of students on high school reforms is difficult to anticipate and is as yet largely unreported. A rare exception is Metz (1988b). But some of the reforms that are aimed primarily at stricter rules and raising standards may lead to higher dropout rates. Since academic performance and school retention are highly correlated, we surmise that school improvement programs face a tough challenge to raise standards without leading some discouraged or resistant students to drop out. Teachers and students may bargain with each other to reduce work in return for compliant behavior (Sedlak, Wheeler, Pullin, & Cusick, 1986). At best, alienated students will stay in school, but will contribute to more overt tension between adults and students in the school. This is bound to lead to problems with reform efforts: Such tensions caused implementation problems for one-third of the urban high schools in our survey.

Urban Is Different

The problems faced by urban high schools differ from those in other settings not so much in type as in scope and intensity. Most of the differences revolve around the vast diversity of the student body and in the local environment.

All teachers of adolescents comment upon the range of developmental levels that can be found within a typical high school. Consider what this may mean in an urban high school, where one can often find students from age 12 to 20, representing a full range of pre- to post-adolescent behaviors. Developmental diversity is only one dimension: Skill diversity is another. According to Powell et al. (1985), the typical high school is composed of three major groups of students. Fifteen percent belong to a group that might be labeled superior both in motivation and performance. Another 15 percent have skill deficiencies or learning disabilities that require special attention. The remaining group—the large majority—perform at or slightly above national norms. In the urban high school this distribution takes a different shape: In the median school in our sample, for instance, 35 percent of the students performed one or more grade levels below national norms on standardized reading tests. It is not uncommon for faculty to estimate that 25 percent or more of the students have serious learning disabilities, although federal and local regulations often prevent classifying so many students in that category. Finally, each school also harbors talented students of exceptional promise, and programs must be devised to fit them as well.

As the proportion of students who require highly individualized help increases, the tensions are simply increased. Many teachers who are trained to teach average students find it difficult to adjust, and suffer profound frustration. One teacher we recently interviewed commented without thinking that 80 percent of the students in his classes couldn't do the work assigned. One cannot help but be struck by the helplessness of this situation, in which both teacher and student fail each other on a daily basis.

Cultural diversity is a fact of life in almost all urban high schools. The typical teacher is white, while the typical student is a member of a minority group. Minority–majority differences are compounded by the presence of many students who come from very poor backgrounds (a quarter of the student population of the schools in our sample come from a family where no adult is employed) or who do not speak English well or at all. Bilingual programs create additional complexity in schools that are already divided by departments; where there are multiple lingual groups the subdivisions among students and faculty increase vastly. (Many urban areas are legally required to serve 30 or more groups with bilingual programs.)

But fragmentation of the school's program and structure is only one aspect of the problem. More importantly, the normal gaps between adult and adolescent, between teacher and student, are magnified. As one administrator with whom we spoke put it, "No matter how hard they [faculty] try they just can't understand the problems these kids bring to school. . . . "

The environmental diversity facing the urban high school is, in most cases, far beyond that in suburban or rural schools. First, there is a large number of constituencies to which the school must respond: the courts (many urban schools are either under court-ordered desegregation or involved in other litigation dealing with equal educational opportunity), special interest groups in the community, and militant unions. Second, there is the broader environment of urban politics, which is often turbulent. In chaotic urban settings, education is less focal than in rural areas, where schools are often viewed as the cultural or social center of the community. In suburbia, even those who have no children are in favor of high quality education because of its positive effects on property values: Good education is a good investment. But in cities, only the transient poor may have children in public schools, and property values are unrelated to the question of education. Thus, schools lack economic and social meaning to most residents.

Environmental diversity often seems to lead to a sense of fatalism: No matter what the school does, the outside world seems to be battling over and controlling its fate. To give a poignant example, in one of the districts we recently visited, a high school recognized by the Ford Foundation and acknowledged to be among the most rapidly improving, was slated for closure, while other low-performing schools remained open and unaffected by district cutbacks.

This leads us to a final, but critical, point: The urban high school is a complex organization embedded in an even more complex organization—the district. All high schools exist in districts, of course, but in most suburban and rural settings the district office is small and schools have a relatively high level of autonomy. Urban district offices, however, are large bureaucracies, often employing hundreds of people. In many cases the middle-level personnel are deeply entrenched specialists and administrators who have worked their way out of the schools in the same district. Most have little direct contact with schools, and little or none with teachers.[11] The layers of red tape are similar to those in any large bureaucracy that is dealing simultaneously with regulations from federal, state, and local levels. The superintendency tends, on the other hand, to be a revolving door: The average tenure of superintendents in both urban and suburban settings is increasingly short—less than three years—as the educational environment becomes more turbulent and the pressures greater.

Finally, there are strong pressures for school uniformity. Big districts tend to have wide variations in the quality and performance of schools within their boundaries, but, for a variety of reasons, often treat them as if they were all the same. Policy makers at the state level also tend to treat all schools in the state as if they were the same, paying little attention to the differing needs and problems that are encountered at the level of school and classroom (Elmore & McLaughlin, 1988). Research suggests that this press toward uniform treatment of very different schools may be counterproductive (McLaughlin, 1988; Oakes, 1987).

With each policy change at the top come new policies, programs, and regulations to replace those that the school may have just begun to incorporate. Too often the result is a series of failed or aborted efforts to improve, which causes even the ablest at the school level to eye new district reform efforts with a very jaundiced eye. The principal, if he or she is to be effective, must be simultaneously a supreme politician, negotiating special resources and exemptions from "the rules," and an outlaw who is willing to spend time covering up unauthorized deviations from policy.

But Tomorrow Won't Be the Same as Today

Although the discussion above seems to imply that schools — especially urban schools — are in an organizational gridlock that effectively prevents change, the pressures to do something different are increasingly urgent. According to a recent article,

> Today's . . . organizations face an era of turbulent change, the sources of which are varied, often unpredictable, and difficult to understand. In the last decade, [they] have had to deal with such traumas as dramatic technological shifts . . . economic uncertainty, fast growth, increased . . . competition and major shifts in demography and values. (Barczek, Smith, & Wilemon, 1988, p. 16)

The same language could certainly apply to public education. One educational futurologist has predicted that the demands for change bombarding us are just beginning — that by the end of the century we will see: interactive technologies creating an explosion of off-campus learning; the replacement of "hard textbooks" with computer texts; an increasing role for vocationalism (job training) in secondary schooling; the inclusion of "non-traditional students" who are older, minority, or non-native English speakers as legitimate clients of public schools; and a reduction of fiscal support as the proportion of the population that is retired nears 40 percent (Cetron, 1985).

Others have noted that the issue of "global competitiveness" will increasingly involve the educational sector. While school administrators may now worry about how good their school or district looks compared with one a few miles away, policy makers at state and federal levels are talking about comparing performance with more distant (and often very different) systems.

Finally, many private-sector executives are presenting new challenges to public education. They argue that we are in the middle of dramatic restructuring of industry and agriculture, which demands a new kind of education. Rather than assuming that literacy and citizenship are the basic attributes needed in an effective work force, they contend that we need a population of workers who can be problem solvers, who can adapt to rapidly changing workplace conditions and new technologies, and who can contribute more actively to improving the productivity of our business and the quality of our products.

Nowhere are these pressures for massive change and adaptation more evident than in urban districts, where the gap between expectations and performing often seems the widest.

HOW CAN THIS BOOK HELP?

We may conclude that the research base for helping urban high schools to improve is rather limited, while the issues and demands facing the schools are great. Where do we go from here? How might this book be useful to people who want to improve the urban high schools they work in?

There are many ways to approach the implementation of a reform. If we look at private industry, for example, we see a number of successful strategies to promote rapid "turnaround," but few are relevant to public high schools. School systems cannot, for example, engage in massive changes in top- to mid-level leadership in order to ensure that changes in policy are carried out, as Lee Iacocca did at Chrysler (Iacocca & Novak, 1984). Even if there were no administrator unions, there are simply not enough qualified and seasoned replacements available. Nor can districts cut back on unprofitable products or diversify to acquire more productive ones: Their line of business is set by law, and they must deal with existing constituencies. Massive attempts to change organizational culture and goals are also found in industry, but these rely heavily on the deployment of resources for training and internal consulting that seem beyond the possible in the public sector.[12]

Some recent recommendations for dramatic structural reforms in education, such as abandoning curriculum requirements aside from a small number of basic disciplines, and instituting a voucher system for the last two years of high school, have been made (Berman, 1985), but it is very unlikely that any state legislature will pass untested proposals of this magnitude. In our view, dramatic turnarounds may be desirable, but are unlikely to occur in most schools.

We have come to think of school improvement as a braid in which a collection of reform programs and plans becomes melded with the existing political and cultural setting: At best, changes are based on steady and patient efforts to work within the school as it exists, while maintaining a vision of what can be. It is a slow process that depends not on flashy leadership, but on dogged tenacity and skill at coping with the inevitable crises that occur in any evolving program of change. In our case studies, we have sought to document the day-to-day work of improvement to show what is really needed.

Most school leaders—principals, other administrators, and teachers—are not trained to be change managers. They are often faced with requirements (or internally generated desires) to reform, but have no real idea how such an effort should be organized. In many schools we have visited in the past, change efforts failed because of problems that could have been anticipated and mistakes that could have been avoided. We believe many of these mistakes would not be made in many private-sector organizations because their managers have been exposed to the principles of leadership and management of change through university courses, management development programs, or the popular management literature. And case studies of change are usually a key part of such learning.

In this book we will generate some practical principles of change leadership and management for high schools. Our focus is on urban high schools, but the discussion is relevant for any secondary school that exists in a complex setting or has "urban-like" features. Our principles of change leadership and management are data-based, drawn from a national survey of urban high school administrators (which we have already referred to in the preceding sections); strongly grounded in our five in-depth case studies; and linked to theories of organizational change derived from both the public and private sector. The aim is to look at what urban high schools are doing to improve, how they are going about it, and what makes it more or less difficult for them to succeed.

In Chapter 2 we briefly describe our model and assumptions about the change process in schools. In Chapter 3 our survey data provide an overview of urban high school reform efforts. They set the stage for a discussion of the generic dilemmas of guiding change in high schools, and illustrate both the problems and promise of making high schools more effective.

Part II of the book describes the process of managing change even more concretely. Chapters 4 through 6 present case studies of five high schools that are managing the change process with greater or lesser promise for ultimate success.[13]

In Part III this information is synthesized. We identify five key issues that cut across the case studies and the survey — issues that must be considered in any serious effort to improve a big-city high school. Chapter 7 looks at issues in the school's local and historical context. Chapter 8 discusses the planning of improvement efforts. Chapter 9 is focused on "vision," empowerment, and the ownership of change efforts. Chapter 10 examines key resources, and how they are garnered and used. Chapter 11 looks at the day-to-day problems of the change process, and how they can be coped with successfully. Chapter 12 summarizes our conclusions about leadership and management of change.

What is involved in making change happen? We turn to this problem in the next chapter.

NOTES

1. The study by Powell, Cohen, & Farrar (1985) goes far beyond sheer metaphor; their close-up descriptions of high schools document just how teachers and students strike bargains that let students opt out of learning and demand little work from teachers.

2. Corcoran, Walker, & White (1988) present extensive data showing that the resources available for teachers and students in urban high school settings are grossly inadequate to support teaching and learning.

3. The most influential reports have been Boyer, 1983; Goodlad, 1983; National Commission on Excellence, 1983; Sizer, 1984.

4. For analysis of state and local reform efforts, see Anderson & Odden (1988) and Odden & March (1988).

5. Fullan (1988) reviews 10 recent studies of the change process in high schools, concluding that we need to know much more about processes of institutional change on a long-term basis. See also Clark, Lotto, & Astuto (1984).

6. For critical discussion of such flaws, see Huitt, Caldwell, & Segars (1982); Frechtling (1982); and Ralph & Fenessey (no date).

7. Metz (1988a) discusses effects of student socio-economic status (SES) on teacher motivation and job satisfaction, but implies that there is little potential for improving the situation in schools serving middle- or low-SES students.

8. The best secondary research includes the classic study of effective inner-city high schools in England (Rutter et al., 1979); an analysis of high schools "recognized" as effective by the Department of Education (Wilson & Corcoran, 1988); a study of large urban high schools in Canada (Fullan & Newton, 1988); and an examination of secondary reform efforts in California (Odden & Marsh, 1988).

9. The estimates by Purkey et al. (1987) are extrapolated from a random sample survey where the actual number of urban high schools was 46. Our figure is based on a sample of urban high schools nominated by knowledgeable experts as having an implemented program, with some visible progress.

10. See Houston (1988) for a discussion of what serious restructuring of high schools to avoid curricular and social divisions might look like.

11. Louis & Dentler (1988) found that district office personnel rarely send information directly to teachers, even when that information is intended for use in the classroom.

12. One major firm, for example, spent about $70,000 per work group for initial training in a work redesign program for customer service representatives; maintenance costs were $3,000 a week, not including added training. Materials development costs were additional (Montgomery, 1986). Many large firms maintain large training departments that operate as small universities for middle- and senior-level managers. Funding at this level is not inconceivable for

urban high schools, where million-dollar dropout reduction programs exist—
but the funds typically go for various student-focused programs rather than
staff training and development.

13. Methodological details about both of these data collection efforts can
be found in Appendix A.

2

Making Change Happen
Leading and Managing

There is uneasiness in the general administration and management literature with the dominant models of how to organize. Throughout the '70s
and '80s, theorists have been pointing out that most organizations — and
particularly schools — do not look like the rational, predictable, well-
controlled settings that the textbooks on planning and administration tell
us they should be.[1] Others, like Ouchi (1981) and Kanter (1983), emphasize that although organizations can be manageable, those that are now
emerging as most effective and adaptive organizations are designed very
differently from the norm of even the recent past.

If we believe that new ways of organizing will work better, we can
also predict that tried-and-true administrative practices probably won't
lead to effectiveness in the 1990s, much less in the twenty-first century.
New words are entering the literature, words not much used in the post-
World War II days: "leadership," "organizational culture," "empowerment," and "visioning." Few, however, have discussed how these new
ideas relate to school systems, or how they may affect the role of the
school administrators.

LEADERSHIP AND MANAGEMENT

The basic argument of this book, which we will lay out briefly in
this chapter, is that creating more effective schools requires a significant
change in patterns of *leadership* and *management* at the school level.
While this change may be felt most dramatically by the principal, it will
also have significant implications for the roles that other administrators,
specialists, and teachers play in the school.

The distinction between leadership and management is a hoary one
in the literature on administration. The terms are both complementary
and distinctive: Leaders set the course for the organization; managers
make sure the course is followed. Leaders make strategic plans; manag-

ers design operational systems for carrying out the plans. Leaders stimulate and inspire; managers use their interpersonal influence and authority to translate that energy into productive work. From the perspective of this book, "effective managers keep the system on keel and headed in the direction that has been set. Leaders on the other hand . . . make new things happen" (Egan, 1988).

The character of the person in the top leadership position is often believed to be *the* most important factor in improving organizations. There is a tendency to become impatient with the mechanics of running a school, and turn to the person at the top as a scapegoat or a savior: "Get the right person in the principal's office, and your problems will be solved." This image of leader as wizard is reinforced in popular books like *Iacocca* (Iacocca & Novak, 1984) and in many news stories about "turnarounds" in business and education.

But management is also celebrated in recent books: Peters and Waterman (1984) argue that, in successful companies, people in positions of authority are on top of the details of what is happening in the organization, are close to the real action and work, and manage by walking around rather than remaining remote in their offices. The grandfather of many current ideas about administration, Chester Barnard, said that in his tenure as a vice-president of New Jersey Telephone he rarely made more than a few important decisions a year. He claimed that the real functions of the executive were to oil the communication system and to work on socializing and selecting the right people for the organization (an almost classical definition of management) as well as to articulate new agendas that motivate people (Barnard, 1938). Egan's (1988) description of what good managers do in industry almost sounds as if it were drawn from the research on effective schools. His "management task cycle" involves six steps: setting goals, developing clear work programs, facilitating the execution of work programs, providing feedback, making and monitoring adjustments, and rewarding performance. And Egan's five-step "leadership task cycle" helps us see how it differs from management: creating visions of how things could be done better, turning visions into workable agendas, communicating agendas so as to generate excitement and commitment in others, creating a climate of problem solving and learning around the agendas, and persisting until the agendas are accomplished.

What About Schools?

The leadership–management distinction is also embedded in our thinking about school administrators. As a recent popular introductory educational administration text indicates, "At the heart of the debate about the principalship is the question of whether the principal leads or maintains the school" (Sergiovanni, Burlingame, Coombs, & Thurston, 1987). However, the authors go on to say that this dichotomy is really inadequate for capturing the complexities of the principal's job. Rather, there is a continuum of demands: Good school leaders must understand and be able to cope with the *regularities* and inevitable small crises of daily life, make *situational adjustments* (for example, adapting to new state curriculum requirements), and deal with *change* (addressing a significant challenge, such as revitalizing a "burned out" staff, or a dramatic influx of new students and teachers as a consequence of a school closing).

We agree, and emphasize that school administrators need both leadership and management skills to deal with change *and* with "ordinary circumstances." A principal is a manager of many issues larger than late buses, and leadership is required in many situations where the problems are less profound than a major demographic shift in the student population. In other words, leadership and management are difficult to segregate in the actual daily work of schools.

One added point: As we'll see shortly, just as the line between leadership and management is hard to draw, the skills for making change happen are not located exclusively in the principal's office, but are often distributed throughout the school.

ORGANIZING FOR CHANGE

This book is mainly focused on the *change* side of what leaders and managers do in schools. In this section, we discuss old and new models of organizing, and then show how they relate to the general problem of making change happen in schools.

The Old Model: Organizing for Stability

The dominant perspective on how to organize — whether the organization is a manufacturing plant or a school — has been a bureaucratic one since roughly the turn of the century.

> It is almost second nature to organize by setting up a structure of clearly defined activities linked by clear lines of command, communication, coordination and control. Thus, when a manager designs an organization he or she frequently designs a formal structure of jobs into which people can then be fitted. (Morgan, 1986, p. 33)

The main ingredients of the bureaucratic model are as familiar to educators as hot dogs and apple pie, and their applicability to the way
schools are supposed to operate is clear.[2]

First, bureaucracies operate under the assumption that there is a
clear *division of labor* among people in different roles. In U.S. schools,
this typically means that teachers work with children on cognitive tasks,
counselors deal with socio-emotional issues, other specialized teachers
deal with various forms of remediation, and administrators coordinate,
schedule, and protect the teachers from interference with classroom
activities caused by disciplinary problems, parents, and unreasonable
demands from the district office.

Second, there is a clear *hierarchy.* People know to whom they
report, and to whom they may give orders. It is now quite commonplace
to note that schools are more "loosely coupled" than other kinds of
bureaucracies, because the hierarchy traditionally permits moderate
levels of autonomy for teachers within classrooms and gives schools
some latitude in developing policies of their own (Weick, 1976). Nevertheless, there is an assumption that important policies are made "at the
top" by the superintendent and/or the school board, while those in the
middle (principals) and at the bottom (teachers) carry out the policies.
As one district superintendent in New York recently put it, "Creative
flouting of the rules is essential to getting anything done around here —
and I hope that my principals are doing it."[3] But the structure and the
rulebook reflect centralization.

Older models of organizing emphasized the need to establish control and accountability through clear, standardized operating procedures. At an extreme, a school system would have thick manuals of rules
to cover everything from curriculum to purchasing. The rules and procedures served a very important function: They permitted relatively
limited on-site supervision of most employees; supervisors and policy
makers needed to become involved only when there were clear exceptions to normal procedures. The rules also served to protect employees
against exploitation by supervisors.

This model "worked" in schools for a long time, and had some
notable advantages over less formal arrangements: Few questioned the
fact that it created a productive, goal-oriented climate in business and
social services. Theories of administration based on the model permitted
growth of increasingly larger schools and school systems and sustained
the demand for accountability. Above all, the old model focused on
efficiency, which was a decided virtue during a time when many more
students were entering school and staying longer.

But, though the old model didn't prohibit leadership at the school
level, it certainly didn't encourage it. It is safe to say that most princi-

pals, under these conditions, chose to emphasize their role as maintainers rather than leaders. Lightfoot's (1983) study of six *effective* high schools suggests that only three of them had a principal who balanced leadership and management functions. Most principals' days are spent maintaining order by buffering the school against small intrusions. Leithwood and Montgomery (1986), for example, estimate that no more than 10 percent of the principals in Ontario emphasize an active problem-solving and change role. If that is so, one may understand—although not admire—a principal who recently claimed that he preferred having no say over the teachers who were assigned to his school: "If the central office sends teachers to me, at least I don't get blamed for poor teaching."[4]

Newer Models: Organizing for Change

In Chapter 1 we discussed several trends in urban education. What are their implications for organizations, including school districts and schools? One clear consequence is a change in what is expected of schools: If the old demand was for *efficiency* (doing things in ways that minimized cost and led to standardized learning procedures and outcomes), the new demand is for *effectiveness* (producing the best possible learning outcomes given variable student characteristics and needs, changing resources, and a dynamic definition of what should be taught). Newer models of organizing also imply a very different way of thinking about how schools should be structured. Rather than a bureaucratic model, we need a newer *adaptive model*. We suggest that some of the following characteristics may be critical for schools.[5]

Vision-Driven

Effective schools must be able to adapt to their changing environment; they must be planful, and not simply react to crises or pressures. In order for schools to be future-oriented, they must be vision-driven, not only goal-directed. This distinction is critical: A vision relates a school to its place in society and gives larger meaning to the work that is being done by administrators, teachers, and students; goals only deal with desired ends inside the organization. Schools will always need goals—but they are not enough.

Guided by Judgment, Not Rules

For effectiveness, schools must become more "professionalized." The main difference between a professional organization and a bureaucratic organization (whether or not it employs professionals in the strict sense of the word) is in the expertise required in non-administrative jobs, which require a broad set of skills and more adaptive problem solving. In the adaptive school, teaching is viewed as a highly skilled craft rather than as a predictable technology that can be predetermined and managed via rules.

Judgment orientation is sometimes referred to as "empowerment" in the reform literature, because the underlying assumption is that teachers may contribute to more decisions than in the past. However, the term "empowerment" is used in so many ways (from referring to the "right" of one group versus another to make decisions, to feelings of being influential) that we prefer to focus here on the underlying need of the school to draw upon the best judgment of all of its members.

Accountability-Based

Where rules and external standards drive the organization, evaluation is usually made on the basis of how well the rules were followed. In a judgment-guided organization, however, individuals and groups must be held accountable for *performance*, not procedures. A sense of responsibility and accountability must be owned by members of the organization rather than simply imposed from outside. Learning and improvement of performance will occur only from serious peer and group assessments of how well their own judgments are working.

Team-Focused

Effective organizations, including schools, must be designed around the team concept, not around a hierarchical concept. The old ideas about professional autonomy for individuals (teachers behind their classroom doors) must make way for collective problem solving. Teams are not necessarily permanent, nor are they always coterminous with departments; they must be organized around shifting needs and problems to solve.

Network-Based; Semi-Autonomous

Organizations will increasingly be regarded as "loosely linked" groups, not as rigidly connected hierarchies (Firestone, 1980; Weick, 1976). Although schools are nested within districts and are connected by common regulations in some areas (for example, hiring, salaries, testing), until recently they have actually operated quite autonomously in others (for example, scheduling, *de facto* curriculum, guidance). During the 1980s, there has been a tendency to decrease the autonomy of the individual school through state, federal, and local regulation. We predict that effective school systems will move away from this form of regulatory coordination, and increasingly emphasize coordination through communication, and the development of joint cooperative tasks at all levels. This may be referred to as "school-based management," but this term is too often used to indicate only the decentralization of authority and accountability within an otherwise unchanged bureaucratic model. We, on the other hand, are arguing for a pervasive shift in models of organizing that treats the school as part of an interconnected web of relationships, not as a cog in the bureaucratic machine.

Multi-Specialized

Without eliminating specialization from the organization, individuals in an effective organization must become more versatile, more able to carry out different functions and activities. Teachers will perform activities that have been traditionally defined as administrative, and many of the functions currently staffed by "specialists" may be shared among faculty. Schools will come to resemble the Japanese model of organization, in which individuals are trained to be able to perform well in multiple roles and departments, thus increasing organizational flexibility and adaptiveness (Ouchi, 1981). Authority to carry out tasks will be based on ability, and not on position (Sergiovanni, 1987).

Involved with the "Whole Person"

Strict specialization is declining in part because we realize that specialization means a loss in our ability to deal with "the whole person." In medicine, there is a revival of the family practitioner or general internist, and an increase in demand for "one stop" health plans where health care is coordinated by professionals, not by the patient. In education, we are beginning to realize that specialized intervention by isolated counselors, reading teachers, disciplinary vice-principals, and so on, cannot prevent at-risk students from slipping through the cracks. And, as educators are beginning to understand, most students are at risk at some point in their educational career. Whole-person involvement means individualized treatment of students, in and out of the classroom.

Furthermore, schools are increasingly accepting the social responsibility to coordinate multiple services for children and adolescents, not simply to provide them with an opportunity to learn. As the proportion of our at-risk students grows, the pressure to develop new, more holistic models for organizing schools to meet the needs will increase.

Implications for Leadership and Management

If an adaptive model like the one sketched out here is to replace the bureaucratic model as the ideal for schools, we will clearly need more leadership. There will be visions to be identified, agendas to be built, new ways of working together to be designed, and climates of problem solving and learning to be nurtured — among the many other major tasks. But there will be a need for better management as well. The adaptive school will be a more complex organization than the bureaucratic school, and more day-to-day interventions will be needed to make sure that necessary coordination occurs, that required decisions are made, and that the relevant teams have the resources to function effectively. Although the roles of teachers may expand and develop considerably, the principal's role will be no less central. All principals — not just principals of poorly performing urban schools — will need to become better versed in the skills of leading and managing change.

LEADERSHIP AND MANAGEMENT FOR CHANGE

The underlying theme of the adaptive model is the need for constant learning and evolution to improve the basic functioning of the school. As we noted in Chapter 1, the effective schools research has spelled out many of the characteristics of schools that do particularly well in raising children's test scores, but it tells us relatively little about how to get there, except to exhort the principal to somehow exercise "instructional leadership."

In the old days, the most treasured principal competencies were the ability to design and enforce a student discipline system, to keep parents off the teachers' backs, and to keep the district office out of everybody's hair. These are clear management or maintenance tasks, and do not require a great deal of leadership. To make change happen, however, the principal — and others in the school — must possess additional leadership qualities and management skills.

But before we turn to the positive, it may be useful to analyze why school improvement endeavors fail, often because of decisions made at early stages. Later chapters will talk about how to do things more effectively. We will begin with summarizing and debunking some of the conventional wisdom about change—much of which ensures that major change programs will not get off the ground. We'll show why many usual approaches don't work, citing our own and others' research.

The Conventional Wisdom: What Doesn't Work, and Why

1. *"Design the change program in the district office using specialists who really know what they are doing and have time to spend— then hand it over to the faculty who are to do it."*

This strategy typically fails because implementation is a "user-dominant" process: It stands or falls on what local people actually do, no matter what the central office mandates (Berman, 1981). For success, people who implement changes need ongoing assistance, and the opportunity to actively steer and redesign the change program. The idea for innovation can originate in the central office—if the local school people who will implement it are empowered to make significant choices about the details of design and action, and get central office support as they proceed (Cox, French, & Loucks-Horsley, 1987; Crandall, Eiseman, & Louis, 1986; Huberman & Miles, 1984).

2. *"Make sure the new program has enough resources: Fund it with add-on grant money, which can be used to pay a new staff member who can direct it."*

This strategy doesn't work because it lets local schools off the hook. They—and districts—would prefer not to rearrange *existing* resource allocations to include new program costs. But when the soft money goes away, so will the program. The very act of prioritizing to include program costs on a "hard line" creates commitment. This also has implications for operations (integrating major innovations with existing functions) and continuation. Where schools and districts have made real commitments of their own resources from the beginning, they are more likely to nurture an innovation until it is really part of the school's procedures (Louis, Rosenblum, & Molitor, 1981; Miles, 1983).

3. *"Save limited resources to fund implementation: Let the program planning activities be carried out by volunteers."*

This conventional wisdom practically ensures later difficulty. If time, assistance, and funds are not provided for planning, the message is clear: This is not a high priority. Effective planning requires at least moderate support: a facilitator for initial meetings; travel to visit other programs or similar organizations; or extra released time to help gather data (Kell & Louis, 1980). A combination of support and pressure from the district and building leadership is important for getting the job done (Huberman & Miles, 1984) and is an important intangible resource as well, because it indicates that what teachers are doing *is* important.

4. *"Make sure that people who are involved in planning the program agree with one another and the central office perspective, since this will speed up the pre-implementation phase and ensure that the plans will be acceptable to key figures. It's important to have a small unified team."*

This does not work because it soon creates an in-group of believers and an out-group of resisters. Such polarization can easily slow down or block improvement (as we'll see in some of our cases). For success, the time to involve those who may be passive or active resisters is during planning (Kell & Louis, 1980). If resisters are on the committee (typically in the minority, but accessible) they are more likely to be part of the solution than if they are left alone in their own out-groups.

5. *"Make sure you focus on problems that you know that you can solve: After all, the literature says that more major innovations are less likely to be adopted."*

This conventional wisdom is simply false. Trivial, easy innovations are also less important by definition: "Easy in, easy out." Studies have found that efforts to address more major, difficult problems, and to create more changes at the same time tend to be more successful (Berman & McLaughlin, 1977; Louis, Rosenblum, & Molitor, 1981). People will easily agree to trivial innovations, but they become committed only to bigger ones. Nevertheless, in some circumstances it is important for school leaders to generate a few visible "early wins" to demonstrate the efficacy of the school in its efforts to become successful.

6. *"Don't bother to look around for what other schools or school systems are doing: We all know that programs designed by people inside the system work better than those coming from outside."*

False again. People can learn to love an adopted child just as much as one that they "grew themselves" (Crandall et al., 1986). Major programs often build an elements or ideas that came from elsewhere. When it comes to educational program innovation, the author of Ecclesiastes was right: Most good ideas have already germinated. An exhaustive search is impractical, but a reasonable amount of effort in looking at what others are doing is stimulating, and will improve the change effort — even if planners finally do decide to design the program "from scratch."

7. *"Go for the best: Pick a well-known national program to replicate and make it the centerpiece of your efforts."*

This doesn't work because there is no "magic bullet" to reform secondary schools, and putting all or most of the eggs into a particular consultant's or program's basket may gain little. Just because a program is widely distributed, or is backed up by research, a dynamic consultant, and field testing, does not ensure that it will match local needs (Firestone, 1981). The safest form of program design is to design a major change effort around a variety of interrelated components: If a single component is not successful, it can be abandoned without jeopardizing the whole effort (Rosenblum & Louis, 1981).

8. *"Make sure you don't disrupt the system too much; do a pilot project in only one part of the organization. After all, what if it doesn't work?"*

This strategy fails because pilot projects can go away very easily. Isolated efforts that affect only some faculty or some parts of the school lack visibility. Although they may be less controversial in the beginning, they are also much easier to drop without controversy (Berman & McLaughlin, 1977). And, if the problems aren't visible, neither are the successes. For success, try multiple pilots or a steadily expanding strategy — and for a program with a good track record, consider a substantial, even school-wide, implementation from the beginning.

9. *"Make sure to spread the planning process out — you wouldn't want to rush into things too fast, and you need time to build support."*

This maxim doesn't work because excitement generated during planning is easily lost if action does not occur within a reasonable period of time (Kell & Louis, 1980). Creating change involves momentum. It is helpful to set clear milestones if the planning process is to take more than a few months. Even though planning itself is a process that can lead to significant empowerment and commitment, it appears that planning for longer than a school year without significant action outside the planning group is self-defeating. Furthermore, support and commitment cannot all be built in advance: They tend to develop *after* people have intensive, successful experience with the change, not before (Huberman & Miles, 1984).

10. *"Get an evaluation of the program in place so that you can show success after a year or so of implementation: This will help to build support."*

This is ineffective for two reasons. First, people rely much more on their own experience of success with an innovation than on "research" (Huberman & Miles, 1984). Second, successful innovation — particularly a large-scale change effort — does not bear fruit rapidly. The first year of innovation is often a period of disorganization, as teachers and administrators confront their uncertainties about their ability to acquire new skills or do things in a new way (Hall & Hord, 1987).

For effective change, it seems that the best strategies are to celebrate small wins and day-to-day successes, as well as to maintain a patient long-term time perspective. Even small-scale changes require up to two years for good stabilization (Huberman & Miles, 1984), and a five- to ten-year perspective is typical for more substantial reforms (Louis, 1986; van Velzen, Miles, Ekholm, Hameyer, & Robin, 1985).

We believe our debunking of these conventional beliefs about the planning of change is well based on our own and others' research. But just knowing what doesn't work is not enough, particularly when it comes to the ups and downs of implementation. As our examples suggest, positive leadership and management of change are much more subtle processes than leadership failure and mismanagement.

In the remainder of this book we will be highlighting a number of key action motifs, first for change leaders and then for change managers. They emerged from the case studies (Chapters 4 through 6) and our cross-case analyses (Chapters 7 through 11).[6]

Action Motifs for Successful Change Leaders

Three forms of action seem to be especially important in motivating a school's staff to engage in significant change: articulating a vision, getting staff to believe that the vision reflects their own interests, and the use of evolutionary planning strategies.

Effective Change Leaders Articulate a Vision

Effective school leaders are able to talk about what they want for the school — and talk about it with sufficient commitment that others understand that they are serious. Such a vision doesn't have to be tightly defined, or reducible to a slogan. However, it is not "pie in the sky": the principal of an inner-city high school does not motivate staff for serious and realistic change efforts by imagining that the curriculum and achievement of the school's at-risk students should be modeled on those of academically selective schools in the district. Instead, a solid vision is grounded in an understanding of the historical strengths of the school and its staff, in realistic (but high) goals for pupils, and in an understanding of how past strengths may be tied to future performance. A clear example of a vision comes from our case study of Alameda High School, whose principal sold her staff on the ideal of a school that maximized learning opportunities and personal growth for all — teachers as well as students ("We're not only a school for students, but a university for teachers").

Change leaders are also able to help people develop images of "how to get there" — which we call *process themes* — so that action is directly tied to the vision. This is not the same as a detailed plan for implementing change: Rather, it ties the vision of the school's future to a general strategy for change. In the Alameda case (Chapter 4), the principal's process themes included early physical and climate improvement, then extensive staff development and teacher involvement in curriculum design and innovation, tailored to the low-income, largely Hispanic population of the school.

Effective Change Leaders Get Shared Vision Ownership

Real ownership means sharing influence and authority. Even where the initial ideas spring from the principal (or even the district office), teachers, department heads, and school-based specialists need to know they can influence the vision (and its actualization) in significant ways. Sharing the vision is not just a matter of exhorting staff to believe, but of sharing responsibility and accountability. And staff have to be rewarded for suggesting and trying new things, not only for succeeding (Kanter, 1983). Change leaders must also be willing to protect and buffer, to take the rap in case innovative projects begun without permission or situated outside of regulations or local customs are attacked. Resources need to be rearranged to support teacher-initiated projects; success stories need to be shared among the entire staff to reinforce the belief that change and achievement of the vision are possible.

Effective Change Leaders Use Evolutionary Planning

It is hardly novel to claim that administration involves planning, and practical manuals for changing organizations often devote most of their space to the planning phases of a new program. We believe, however, that the image of planning presented in many books about change is inappropriate.

The traditional approach to planning emphasized the development of long-range master plans based on demographic and economic projections, and goals set by each unit in the organization. In education, these goals were often expressed either in a narrowly quantitative fashion (the Boston Compact, for example, set goals as annual percentage increases in various performance indicators, such as decreased truancy, increased applications for college, increases in standardized test scores, and so on), or in rather vague generalities.

In recent years, there has been advocacy of strategic planning emphasizing external adaptation, setting medium-range goals (two to three years), doing assessment and evaluation through the judgment of the leaders rather than precise statistical models, and focusing on the broad participation of members (McCune, 1986; Steiner, 1979). The newest iterations of this approach have begun to dismiss references to planning at all, preferring the concept of "strategic management," where the emphasis on intuitive, judgmental approaches to making decisions is even greater.

Effective planning for serious change in schools is more like the latter models, in the sense of avoiding a grandiose "blueprinting" approach, but it has something else as well: a strong evolutionary character. Both the change program and the school develop steadily, driven by the change themes and the shared vision. New opportunities are sought or appear fortuitously; data on the progress of the improvement effort suggest detours or new avenues; new capacities develop and permit more ambitious efforts than anyone had ever thought of. Evolutionary planning is not a hand-to-mouth approach, but coherent, intelligent adaptation based on direct experience with what is working toward the vision and what isn't. It's not living "a day at a time," but through a stream of examined experiences.

Action Motifs for Effective Change Managers

When it comes to the management of change, the five case studies reveal another set of actions that seemed to promote change: continuous monitoring of the school's environment, with a particular eye toward finding additional resources, and repeated efforts to cope with potential and actual problems facing the school to protect innovative efforts.

Effective Change Managers Negotiate the School's Relationship with Its Environment

The environment of the school consists of both a *demand* system and a *resources* system. The demand system has multiple constituencies competing to ensure attention to their values and aspirations for students. The resource system is composed of individuals, groups, and organizations (often the same as those making demands) that are passively or actively available to provide assistance and support (Beckhard & Harris, 1987).

School administrators have traditionally been pushed toward a narrow view of their role as managers of the environment. Effective principals are urged to be instructional leaders (Purkey & Smith, 1983), staying on top of new research and practice developments in curriculum and pedagogy. They should search the environment for new information, and facilitate the same behavior on the part of their teachers (Louis, Chabotar, & Kell, 1981). In addition, the principal is supposed to buffer teachers from unnecessary intrusion into their instructional time (Rossmiller, 1989).

Our research suggests that the role of environmental manager needs to be defined more broadly. First, effective school change requires being proactive — grabbing, getting, and taking advantage of potential resources rather than waiting for them to be provided. This style is not "opportunism," in the sense that resources are being acquired with no thought given to change goals. Rather, it suggests a down-to-earth image of the school leader as a garage sale junkie, able to browse and find what the school needs in the most unlikely places.

Second, environmental managers need to think constantly of assistance, training, and support as a master resource that will help other staff. Many change efforts founder because teachers (and administrators) simply have not been provided with the opportunities to acquire new skills they need; frustration rather than resistance becomes the silent disease undermining the planned activities (Crandall et al., 1986).

Third, environmental managers must think very broadly about resources. Change is often avoided or starved because people believe they do not have enough money. But, though all of the schools we studied did have some extra resources to support their improvement activities, in the more successful schools the resources were not only additional dollars, but involved reallocations of time, people, materials, existing equipment, and assistance. Our most successful case study schools had *fewer* dollar resources than the least successful, but were more effective in putting them where they could make a real difference.

Finally, managing the environment requires extending the traditional teacher-buffering activities of principals to include a more active negotiating stance in relation to the district office. While district offices are a source of support, ideas, and money to support major change efforts, the urban district's relationship with its schools is increasingly complex. Many districts, responding to environmental pressures of their own, are moving into more regulatory, standardizing postures. Although many districts claim to be involved in school-based management, our observations suggest that the scope of decentralization is often very limited (Alexander & Louis, 1989). Many regulatory efforts may be sound, but some (for example, personnel assignment or the development of district-wide standardized testing programs) may well interfere with school-based efforts to turn around. Principals must be ready to anticipate conflicts between district policies and school agendas, and to develop solutions that preserve the main priorities of the school.

Effective Change Managers Have Coping Skills

Major school improvement efforts, no matter how well planned, will constantly encounter a wide range of problems at all stages. Some of these are small and easy — so routine, in fact, that they may not even be perceived as problems. Others are more severe, demanding acknowledgment and action.

Thus, there is a major need to *coordinate or orchestrate* the evolution of the program within the school, and deal with problems appropriately. Any change effort that is more than trivial, or that involves many parts of the school, becomes a set of management issues. Which department should take on the responsibility for administering a new student self-esteem program? When district office staff members show a new interest in the school, how should their talents best be utilized? Who should write the required annual report on the project? Questions such as these probably require *relatively* little time on the part of a change manager — if he or she believes that dealing with them is part of the job, and a top priority. The issue here is one of priority setting amidst the constant press to get things done in a school. None of the above decisions may be monumental, nor, in most cases, is there only one correct decision. But a cumulative backlog of unmade decisions — poor orchestration and coordination — can lead to serious logjams.

Some issues are not trivial, however, but require *deep coping*. Key personnel leave the school and a component of the change effort is left leaderless; a new state mandate is passed that distracts staff from their own programs; a serious student discipline problem undermines a campaign to increase positive community involvement; after a review, staff believe that a major component of the program does not "fit" the school. Although often unpredictable, events of this magnitude are also virtually inevitable. The tendency of solid change managers is to constantly search for, confront, and acknowledge serious problems when they first appear, and to act rapidly to make major adjustments to solve them.

Less effective change managers use only *shallow coping* techniques that are more appropriate for small or transient problems. For example, in response to an urgent need to have teachers in a specific program activity meet and plan, the shallow coper may postpone making a decision ("we'll deal with that in next year's schedule"), or avoid a structural solution in favor of exhortation (urge the teachers to meet after school voluntarily). The deep coper, on the other hand, might rearrange the school's schedule or negotiate with the district to provide a stipend for weekend work.

Coping also involves enormous *persistence and tenacity*. Good copers choose their targets for long-term action, and stick to them. If lack of school control over personnel assignments affects the change program, they will attack this problem from every possible angle over a period of months (or even years). If staff need new skills, but many don't yet perceive this, the good coper will recognize the need for a long time line, modeling of the desired behaviors, training, or technical assistance — and will muster all possible resources to address the problem.

The ability to be a deep coper requires change managers to have a high tolerance for complexity and ambiguity. Good coping is difficult for principals who like to have all of the *i*'s dotted and *t*'s crossed, because all of the needs cannot be foreseen. Copers exhibit a willingness to live with risks, as they try various ways to solve persistent issues. (Oddly enough, risk takers usually get more latitude from the district and parents than those who are more cautious.)

LOOKING FORWARD

As we proceed through this book, these key themes of leadership and management will be played out repeatedly. In Chapter 3, we examine the results of our national survey of urban high school principals and note how the themes surfaced repeatedly.

In Part II, Chapters 4 through 6, we look at five case studies of schools with a range of success in their improvement efforts. In the two more successful sites, Agassiz and Alameda, we can see how the key motifs for leaders and managers of change worked out, and how "recipes for failure" were avoided. In the two moderately successful sites, Bartholdi and Burroughs, we can see a different balance: leadership and management efforts, though quite strong, did not get as far. And in our final case, Chester, we see a change effort that did not work because the odds against it were too high, and the key success motifs were not sustained.

Part III, Chapters 7 through 11, goes into depth on our key motifs, looking across all five cases to draw conclusions about what works and why, covering in turn the context of school improvement, evolutionary planning, vision building, resource management, and coping skills.

Finally, in Chapter 12, we provide an integrative review of leadership and management for change, summarizing major issues and suggesting implications.

NOTES

1. Useful recent critiques of traditional views are Firestone (1980); Bolman & Deal (1984); Morgan (1986); and Patterson, Parker, & Purkey (1986).

2. On the applicability of bureaucratic models to schools see Firestone (1980) and Bachrach & Conley (1986). For a review of the special characteristics of schools as organizations, see Miles (1981).

3. Mary Ann Raywid of Hofstra University provided this quote from an interview she conducted.

4. This quote was provided by Richard Rossmiller of the University of Wisconsin.

5. This section incorporates ideas of many other writers, as well as our own. For readings that advocate alternatives to a bureaucratic school structure see Firestone (1980); Miles & Ekholm (1986); and Sergiovanni (1987).

6. Although these themes grew out of our research on urban high schools, they correspond rather closely to the change leadership themes developed by Egan (1988) based on private industry.

3

Reforming the Big-City High School
An Overview

As we noted in Chapter 1, despite much current discussion of the need for reform in urban high schools, there is limited movement toward comprehensive and substantial improvement efforts. And, as we saw, the impediments to change can feel very substantial to those who are involved in big-city schools. Still, we are left with questions: Why do so few urban schools report successful turnarounds? And why is there so much anecdotal discussion about discontinuity and great expectations that come to little? Is there a lack of interest and commitment, or are there other factors?

We know from other studies of change in school settings that any effort to move toward improvement faces many major and minor impediments (Berman & McLaughlin, 1977; Huberman & Miles, 1984; Louis, Rosenblum, & Molitor, 1981). In this study we have made two assumptions about reform efforts in schools. First, we believe that many of the implementation crises that occur in high schools are difficult to anticipate, and cannot really be managed according to the principles put forth in textbooks on administration.[1] This non-rational side of the process of change is due both to the inherent structure of schools as "loosely linked" organizations (Weick, 1976) and to the difficulty of controlling relationships between the school and its immediate environment, which includes the community, the district, and the local political system (Patterson, Purkey, & Parker, 1986; Pfeffer & Salancik, 1978). Because schools are public organizations with only limited control over the access of clients (students) to the system, and because they are staffed by unionized professionals who are used to substantial amounts of autonomy in their work, these non-manageable conditions are very prominent.

Our second assumption is that schools are *not* totally ungovernable, nor are the processes and outcomes of change totally random. We know from dozens of previous studies of change in schools that effective diagnosis of the school's needs, and relatively detailed planning for the implementation process will positively affect the success of change efforts (Crandall, Eiseman, & Louis, 1986).

These assumptions led us to our investigation of the process of designing and implementing major "effective schools" programs in urban high schools, and to a set of more specific questions that will be answered in this chapter.

- What kinds of program emphases are found within urban high schools that attempt reform? What implications do the reported program emphases have for the potential efficacy of the change programs?
- What kinds of planning processes are used? What are the implications for program success?
- What kinds of problems are encountered during planning and implementation? To what degree are these "manageable" by actors in the school, or "non-rational" in the sense that the school cannot anticipate or control them easily?
- What evidence is there that change efforts based on effective schools programs will improve the quality of education in urban high schools?

To answer these questions, we initiated two separate data collection efforts. The first, which is the primary basis for this chapter, was a national survey of urban high school principals involved in effective schools programs. Our methods are described in Appendix B: In brief, we carried out one-hour structured phone interviews with the principal or a designated administrator. The second part of our effort was a set of five case studies, based on multiple visits over a year, and a follow-up visit two years later, which will be reported in Chapters 4 through 6. We will link findings from survey and case studies throughout the book.

THE SCHOOLS: A QUICK PICTURE

Through our survey, we wanted to develop some empirically supported generalizations about the problems facing urban high schools when they implement effective schools programs, and the way in which these problems affect improvement outcomes. Previous studies (Purkey, Rutter, & Newmann, 1987) have described what urban high schools are doing in terms of comprehensive improvement, but they lack any data about the process and outcomes of change. Our process of finding and surveying schools, described in Appendix B, resulted in our locating 279 schools in cities with populations of at least 70,000, and that were attempting a major reform program based on the effective schools literature. Of these eligible schools, 207 agreed to speak with us, and were far enough along in the planning and implementation process to respond to our questions.

The typical school in the sample is medium-sized, with 1,540 students, 82 teachers, and 11 non-teaching professionals (Table C.1, Appendix C). Most are comprehensive, four-year schools with a relatively stable and experienced staff. One-fifth of the schools could be rated as very stable, with 75% or more of the faculty having 10 or more years of experience in that school. Another fifth are quite unstable, with fewer than a third of the staff having been at the school for 10 or more years.

They are also schools with recognizable urban problems. The average school has 35 percent of the students one or more grades behind national norms in achievement, and serves a somewhat transient population, losing more than 11 percent of students from September through June. More than half the students are minorities, and a large proportion of them come from economically disadvantaged backgrounds. Forty percent of the students qualify for subsidized food programs; twenty-four percent are from families on some form of public assistance.

The five case study schools that we will describe in later chapters are quite representative of this broader group, with the exception of Burroughs, which serves junior high school age students. Table 3.1 presents a quick overview of their characteristics. As can be seen at a glance, the five schools come from different types of urban communities, ranging from a smaller, decaying city in the Northeast (Chester) to the urban sprawl lying just outside Los Angeles proper (Alameda). The size ranges are considerable, and include a very small high school (Agassiz) along with several large high schools. Minority and special needs populations predominate at all schools, but the mixture of minorities varies from Alameda (a true contemporary melting pot of ethnic subgroups, the largest of which is Hispanic) to Chester and Agassiz (where black students clearly dominate within the student population). In all of the schools, the lingual minorities and special needs children form substantial proportions of the population; in all schools, there is a majority of students eligible for free or reduced-price lunches.

THE PROGRAMS

Change theory suggests that two characteristics of a change effort will affect the probability of success: whether the planned change is

Table 3.1   Case Study Sites and Improvement Programs (1985)

School	Location	Grades	Size	Population	Improvement Program
Agassiz	Boston, residential neighborhood	9–12	750	70% black 25% bilingual 31% special needs	Business–school collaboration; school-based planning; evolving since 1982.
Alameda	Los Angeles, urban sprawl	9–12	2,100	35% Hispanic 23% other minority 30% limited English	State school improvement program (SIP) plus heavy staff development; since 1978.
Bartholdi	New York, deteriorated poor neighborhood	9–12	2,100	70% Hispanic 29% black 12% special needs	Comprehensive dropout prevention program; since 1985. [Effective schools work since 1983.]
Burroughs	Cleveland, working-class/poor neighborhood	7–9	600	67% black 25% whites bused in	Middle schools planning program (1981), then effective schools program (1982) and movement toward team teaching.
Chester	New Jersey, working-class neighborhood	10–12	2,300	78% black 12% Hispanic 13% special needs	Comprehensive programmatic planning, plus effective teaching program; since 1985. [School-based planning and effective schools work 1981–83.]

large or small in scope, and whether there is broad participation in developing the change programs (Berman & McLaughlin, 1977). These two issues can be addressed in the survey data.

Components of Urban Effective Schools Programs

Principals were asked whether 15 components from effective schools research were included in their schools' programs. Of these, nine were judged to be core elements because they were included in 75 percent or more of the high schools (Table C.2, Appendix C). These focus on aspects of *school climate* and structuring of *higher expectations* for students — consensus on goals, increasing expectations for student academic performance and discipline, creating more structured work settings, and increasing parental involvement. Most also claim to address the *work of teachers* through staff development, a focus on classroom management, and increasing feedback to students about their performance.

Common components (addressed by 50 to 75% of the schools) focus more on strengthening the student's role in the school: increasing opportunities for student leadership, improving working conditions, and paying more attention to frequent testing and assessment of achievement. Another common component is enlarging the principal's role as an instructional leader.

Infrequently mentioned components (addressed by fewer than 50% of the schools) focus on the teaching-learning process: individualizing instruction and increasing individual help to students.

CONCLUSION: These results suggest that many of the programs that meet our criterion of addressing effective schools findings may be superficial. They may fail to confront the learning environments of classrooms, or to deal centrally with teacher–student relationships in learning settings.

Creating high expectations for students will probably have little impact unless the quality of the teaching-learning process is confronted, or the meaning of being a student is changed; yet these program components are least likely to be central. Other survey items point to this as a potential problem. For example, fewer than 50 percent felt that the original plan for the program dealt with specific plans for classroom-level changes "to a great extent."

Our case study data confirm this concern: The five case study high schools were chosen because they were regarded by people inside and outside the district as especially promising. Yet, in two of them we observed some real difficulties in developing a core program that reflected the real meaning and heart of effective schools research: a frontal attack on the nature of teaching and learning for disadvantaged students. In these two cases (Bartholdi and Chester), the program had not really affected what went on "behind the classroom door," but focused more on improving the safety of the school, ensuring that students were actually in attendance, and increasing attention to surface climate issues.

Whose Programs Are They Anyway?

Research shows that school improvement efforts are most likely to succeed where there is a combination of internal commitment to and incentives for change, and external pressure and support (Huberman & Miles, 1984; Louis & Dentler, 1988). In addition, we know that commitment to an educational change program often comes about through involvement in planning or decision making for change (Crandall, Eiseman, & Louis, 1986). Thus, the issue of who is involved in and influences the development of the program may be a crucial one.

The data (Table C.3, Appendix C) suggest that effective schools programs in urban high schools are, for the most part, stimulated by *outside pressure*, either from the district or from state mandates. Most schools had large planning teams, composed of 10 to 14 people, which were broadly representative of the schools' constituencies.

Despite this stimulus, it is people *inside* the school who have the greatest *actual influence* over the nature of the plan. The major actor is the principal. The finding of principal centrality may be partially due to response bias (principals were usually the respondent), but it is supported by the five case studies.

Department heads are the next most influential group (although they were actually members of the formally designated planning team in only 34% of the cases). Individual teachers, assistant principals, and district office representatives also exert influence in slightly more than half the schools. All other groups — parents, state department members, unions, or school boards — have influence in only in a fraction of the schools.

CONCLUSION: Comprehensive change planning in urban schools is characterized by a "management team" approach in most schools. Although there are representative planning groups in most instances, the real work gets done by a kitchen cabinet composed primarily of administrators and department chairs.

This observation is corroborated in our case study schools, all of which had a small group of people who exercised real influence over the emergence of a plan, outside of the operations of a planning group. In the three most successful schools, principals were central to the development process: All staff acknowledged their contribution and leadership. In these schools, ownership of the program was also clearly located at the school level, even where there was a state or district stimulus. In the two less successful schools, district and state roles were stronger, sometimes overshadowing the role of school staff. In addition, the principal was not necessarily the driving force underlying the program within the school even where s/he was committed to the effort.

PLANNING: MOSTLY ECSTASY—A LITTLE AGONY

Principals report that the planning process was generally a positive experience with relatively few significant problems (Table C.4, Appendix C). Most felt highly supported by school staff and the district office; support was engendered by a consensus on the need for action. They also expressed enthusiasm for the outcomes of the planning process: 70 percent indicated that it resulted "to a great extent" in a *shared understanding* among all staff of the school's problems and a school-wide *consensus about the goals* for improvement; 65 percent indicated that "to a great extent" the plan produced was *realistic* — it corresponded well with what the teachers in the school were willing and able to do. Strong teacher *commitment* and specific *plans for administrative changes* were also mentioned in nearly 60 percent of the schools.

An open-ended question that asked for additional information about problems in the planning process revealed some potentially serious *barriers to developing commitment*. First, 33 percent mentioned some difficulties in sustaining teacher interest in planning: This was due either to initially low morale, open resistance, or lack of staff skills and experience in change programs. Furthermore, 22 percent indicated that "staff attitudes about students" interfered with planning. Thus, while overt teacher resistance to change is not necessarily a problem, low interest and motivation will clearly affect the success of effective schools change programs.

Second, 32 percent mentioned the chronic problem of all high school improvement programs: difficulty finding appropriate *time*, and enough time, for broadly participatory planning activities. This problem probably accounts for the actual influence of the principal and department heads, who have greater flexibility in their schedules, and may also account for some of the problems of resistance found among teachers.

Finally, 21 percent mentioned that there were problems in dealing with the district office, ranging from low support to conflict between what the school wanted to do and the district's "official" improvement program. Again, our case study materials show that conflicts with the district office were pervasive elements during planning in four out of the five high schools.

Interestingly, resources (in terms of dollars) were not a big issue during the planning period: Only 12 percent mentioned lack of money as a problem. This finding stands in stark contrast to the often-voiced concern of educators that "we can't do it because we don't have the money."

CONCLUSION: Moving from an administrator-dominated planning process to one which is more broadly participatory is a significant problem in urban high schools. For a variety of reasons, ranging from attitudes to scheduling conflicts, involving teachers at the beginning is a major challenge.

REALITY IN THE CHANGE PROCESS

If planning typically went relatively smoothly in the surveyed high schools, the path of implementation was considerably stonier. Although the most common problems are not necessarily difficult to deal with, a substantial group of schools encountered much greater impediments to change.

Chronic Implementation Problems

When principals were asked which of a list of 18 problems were major, minor, or "not a problem," the average principal indicated that three or four had caused major implementation difficulties, while several more had caused minor difficulties (Table C.5, Appendix C).

What kinds of problems are most frequently found to be serious? We can best approach this question by looking at three different sources of problems (Table 3.2): the change program itself, the people inside and outside the school who could influence the course of the change program, and the characteristics of the school or district setting. Those mentioned as a source of major or minor problems by at least 50 percent of the principals are included in the table.

Table 3.2   Sources of Implementation Problems

THE CHANGE PROGRAM

Maintaining communication about the project*
Lack of staff skills that were required
Slow progress in reaching goals
Staff disagreement over the desirability of activities
A project plan that was too ambitious

THE PEOPLE

Teacher time and energy*
Maintaining staff interest and involvement*

THE SETTING

Money, resources*
Arranging for staff development*
Constraints of the physical plant*
Unanticipated crises that detracted from the program
Competing requirements from other change programs

---

*Indicates that this was a major problem for at least 20% of the schools. The others listed are minor: those that over 40% called minor, and less than 20% called major.

We can see that setting problems are frequent, and most often seen as major. They are also relatively intractable, difficult for school-based actors to solve themselves. People problems are less frequent, while major. Though program problems are frequent, the only major one is "maintaining communication."

Not surprisingly, the chronic concerns of change managers everywhere are at the very top of the list of major problems: *lack of time and energy on the part of teachers, and lack of money*. It is easy to dismiss these as straw men. But look at one of our *successful* cases. Even there these problems were acute.

■ In Agassiz, the problem of teacher energy (and morale) was viewed as so critical by the principal that the first two years of the program focused primarily upon providing teachers with evidence that the program could affect the quality of the school before any effort was made to ask for high levels of teacher participation. In the same school, a new focus on decentralized planning and goal setting for student achievement was fully implemented in only one department: The planning process required extensive meeting time for the whole department, and the only way to locate it within the complex school schedule was to eliminate homeroom duties for the English faculty.

Unlike the planning phase, implementation implies a resource crisis. In all of the five schools, program operations were dependent on substantial "soft money" allocations ranging from several thousand dollars a year to over a million dollars for the program. In the three programs in existence for more than three years, key activities were slowly transferred to hard budget lines. However, the problems of maintaining the program were particularly severe in the case of two schools where key program staff were funded through grants. The problem of how to deal with program continuation and institutionalization was even more apparent in the two newer programs, both of which were funded at very high levels for three years.

Among the schools we surveyed, relatively few were dependent on large amounts of soft money: In contrast to the resource-rich case studies, the average amount devoted to the project over and above the normal budget was only $800. Herein lies a problem. We question very seriously how an urban school can engage in major reform activities without any additional resources to pay for training, consulting, inservice, and other costs usually associated with significant change efforts. The low investment is, perhaps, reflective of the problem of superficiality we have pointed to above. If all that is being done is to improve discipline and attendance, or to introduce small-scale positive reward systems, perhaps $800 a year is sufficient. But will this actually make the school effective in terms of student achievement?

The time/money problem is also reflected in another of the serious problems mentioned in the survey: difficulty in arranging for staff development. This is a serious problem for most high schools, where providing extra training to staff requires a substantial budget for released time/substitutes, or complex rearrangements in the schedule.

■ In Chester, the time/money problem for staff development was particularly severe, because the district claimed total control over the contract's mandated staff development days despite its verbal support for the high school's program.

Another common problem cited in the survey was the quality and characteristics of the physical plant. This also appears an easy excuse, but it can be critical in older urban districts.

■ In two case study schools, the physical plant problems were serious
enough to substantially affect the course of the program. In Agassiz,
a Ford Foundation reviewer told the principal she doubted that a
student could learn in the building because its condition was so depressing. In Bartholdi, the closing of a school annex building resulted
in severe overcrowding which seriously affected teacher morale, and
increased problems with the schedule, making it even more difficult
for staff to meet. In the first case, the improvement of the physical
plant became a precondition for implementing a truly effective
schools program. The district was under court order to improve the
building, so the funds did become available (although it took a battle
on the principal's part to have some of the monies allocated to critical
cosmetic improvements). In the latter there has been no real solution
to the problem.

CONCLUSION: To a large extent the major problems involve
barriers to improvement that are either inherent in the setting
itself (physical plant), at least partly outside the immediate
control of the school (availability of teacher time, money), or
deeply embedded in the culture of the school (teacher morale,
resistance to change). Only one – maintaining communication
about the project – deals directly with the management of
change. Surmounting these difficult problems usually requires
active and deep coping skills on the part of school leadership, a
topic that will be addressed in Chapter 11.

Lesser Implementation Problems

Chronic problems that were not perceived as major seemed quite
different, however. Except for "unanticipated crises" that detracted
from the change program, and competing requirements from other
change programs, these are almost exclusively concerned with change
management issues. These include maintaining staff interest/involve-
ment, a project plan that was too ambitious, staff disagreement over
program goals, lack of staff skills, and slow progress in reaching goals.

Based on our case studies, we would argue that these problems are
not minor in the sense that they have no critical importance to program
effectiveness. Rather, they are minor because they are considered tractable: They can be managed and even solved. In contrast, the problems

listed previously must be coped with on a continuous basis, and are often considered intractable.

Rare But Intractable Problems

Some problems were encountered by only a few schools, but are more basic and difficult to solve. They arose from the external setting: turnover in the district office (mentioned by only 40%); conflicts with the district office (33%); political pressures or tensions in the city (27%); and conflict between the school and special interest groups in the community (23%).

These problems are relatively intractable and difficult to deal with. Among the infrequently occurring problems, only adult–student tensions (35%) can be dealt with primarily through internal staff efforts. We are, however, cheered to find that they seriously affected program implementation in only 2 to 8 percent of the schools.

Increasing, Decreasing, or Staying the Same?

Some argue that the problems of implementation are worst at the beginning of a change effort (Hall, 1979). Others indicate that the most serious difficulties occur later, when accumulated threats often result in "downsizing" (Huberman & Miles, 1984). Thus we looked at whether the types and frequency of implementation problems changed over the duration of program operation.

We found only one time-based difference. Programs that had been in operation at least three years were more likely than more recently initiated efforts to report that "competing requirements of other programs" were *not* a problem. This may reflect the fact that state and district reform activity had increased over the recent period. It's also possible that the older reform efforts had stabilized before new change programs were mandated. Thus, coordinating them may have proved less problematic.

CONCLUSION: Overall, there is no reason to believe that implementation problems ever go away (at least within a four- to five-year time perspective), or that they accumulate. They are a fact of life for school administrators, as predictable and as regular as the seasons.

OUTCOMES AND EFFECTS

The implementation of an effective schools program has visible payoffs rather quickly in urban high schools—at least in some areas. Even discounting the "halo effect" of having the program manager report the program's results, some indicators of improvement show real promise. Rapid (and sustained) change is shown in student behavior, student attitudes, staff morale, the image of the school in the community, staff communication over educational issues, and inter-department collaboration (Table C.6, Appendix C).[2]

On the other hand, some important results are rarely achieved no matter how long a program has been in operation: Dropout rates and employment seem to be difficult to attack through such programs.[3] Still others take a long time to effect. Programs implemented for less than three years show significantly less impact on student achievement, student attendance, teaching methods, new teacher skills, and student-faculty relations than those that have been in place longer.

If we look only at those programs that have been implemented for three or more years, the conclusion that effective schools programs have greater impact on the cosmetic and administrative side of schools than on the teaching-learning process and student achievement is almost inescapable. Indicators of quality schooling that are least affected are employment, dropout rates, achievement, and new teacher skills.

While the reform efforts have had real impact (according to the principals), they fall short of a renewal in education in many of the schools. Given the comments made earlier in this chapter about the possibly superficial focus of the programs, this may not be surprising. Also, real improvements in areas such as attendance, student and teacher attitudes, and teaching methods may, in fact, have payoffs in the longer run that cannot yet be observed.

Perhaps because they realize that change comes slowly in an urban high school, 68 percent of the principals who have been implementing programs for three or more years anticipate that their efforts will go on for at least five more years. Fewer than 50 percent of the principals whose programs have been in place for two years or less see a need to maintain their efforts for this amount of time.

CONCLUSION: *Really* changing schools takes a long time, but time can build a strong investment in achieving the initial goals of the reform among those schools that persist. The longer

schools have been involved in a change program, the more
likely they are to indicate a long-term commitment to their
efforts.

Urban administrators who are not already veterans of a major
internally designed reform effort clearly need a more realistic view of
what will change rapidly, and what problems will require a "generation" or two of students to solve. As one department chair in Agassiz
High School reported, "We'll only see the benefits (of the new district
curriculum) when we graduate our first class of seniors who have come
through the whole program since seventh grade." For most teachers and
administrators (as well as policy makers), a time perspective of this sort
may be realistic, but it is difficult to accept (Louis, 1986).

SUMMARY AND IMPLICATIONS

This analysis of our survey data is brief. We will return to survey
data in Chapters 7 to 11 to illustrate and support points that emerge
from the case studies. Nevertheless, we may summarize the main implications of this chapter as follows:

- Among the minority of American high schools implementing
  programs based on effective schools principles, many do not appear to be attacking basic elements of the school's teaching and
  learning process.
- Planning is energizing to the school, is well supported both inside
  and out, and generally creates ownership of the program at the
  school level even where it is stimulated by a mandate at the
  district or state level.
- Implementation, however, is characterized by an increased number of real problems, many of which are severe and difficult to
  deal with because they represent dilemmas inherent in the setting
  or deeply embedded in the culture of the school.
- Less severe problems typically reflect implementation or change
  management issues, and are potentially amenable to interventions by the principal or other change agents within the school.
- Relationships with districts can be a modest and continuous
  source of implementation problems for schools, despite the reported high level of "support" for improvement from this source.

- Schools implementing effective schools programs are changing. Image and "climate" seem to change rather rapidly in response to the programs; other aspects change more slowly, while some, such as employment and dropout rates, may be affected in only limited ways by effective schools programs.
- Producing real effects takes time; many programs that are in the early stages of implementation are apparently too optimistic about the time frame.

These data support our two initial assumptions about reform efforts in urban high schools. First, many implementation crises are difficult to anticipate, and cannot be easily avoided no matter how effective and thorough the planning process. As we suggested at the beginning of this chapter, this non-rational side to the change process is, to some extent, inherent in the nature of schools. However, as we also pointed out, many of the issues facing schools *can* be coped with—if there is both will and skill on the part of change leaders and managers (Miles, 1987). An increasing number of articles and books outline sensible steps for managing change that are well grounded in extensive research (Crandall et al., 1986; Fullan, 1982; van Velzen et al., 1985).

But often administrators simply don't know what to expect. They estimate that a program will take a few months to put into place, or cost them a few hundred dollars a year, when in reality time and resources should be multiplied many times.

Now as we turn to the more detailed reports of five case studies, the reader should keep in mind the implications we have drawn from the survey data, in addition to the themes and issues for change management and leadership outlined in Chapter 2. In combination, these will set a frame for a sharper glimpse of how "real change" happened (or did not happen) in these schools.

NOTES

1. For conceptual analysis of this view, see March & Olsen (1976). Patterson, Parker, & Purkey (1986) apply the ideas to school systems.

2. This list of outcomes is based on two criteria: At least 35% of both early- and later-implementing schools reported the outcome was "greatly improved," and no more than 15% reported no improvement at all.

3. The criterion for rare outcomes was that more than 25% of early implementers reported no improvement.

Part II

CASE STUDIES

In this part of the book, we report five case studies with differing amounts of success. We think it is important to examine success stories carefully, because they are a prime source of practical advice. Nothing succeeds like success – it has actually worked. Failure as such only tells us what *not* to do – and there are usually dozens of different ways to fail, so we learn less. But making careful comparisons with success can be helpful.

Chapter 4 reports successful efforts in Agassiz and Alameda, to which we have given "A" pseudonyms. Chapter 5 reviews two somewhat less successful "B"-level efforts – Burroughs and Bartholdi – and Chapter 6 describes the "C"-level improvement effort in Chester that didn't really work.

As the accounts unfold, the reader can reflect on the A-B-C differences, as we did, and form a stronger, more valid idea of how – and *why* – successful school improvement works. What's present in our A sites, weaker in B sites, and absent in our C site? Or, what negative factors are conspicuous in Chester, less evident in Burroughs and Bartholdi, and blessedly absent in Agassiz and Alameda?

The names of people and schools are pseudonyms. The only exceptions are public figures such as mayors, governors, and well-known superintendents. We are extremely grateful to the school people in our five cities who let us into their working lives, told us what was on their minds, and helped us be sure we had the story right.

We have used the same basic structure for all five cases to make comparisons easier. The structure is built around some basic ideas, as discussed below.

A PICTURE OF THE SCHOOL IN 1985. After a quick overview, we describe the school as we met it in 1985, when we first visited. It's described in "now" language for vividness, so the reader can get a feel for the school.

THE CONTEXT.   We believe it is very important to describe the pressures from the school's local and state environment, as well as the "deep history" of the school's prior efforts to improve. This social and historical context is an important determinant of the progress of any change effort.

THE IMPROVEMENT PROGRAM.   Next we turn to the main change effort itself. What the reform *is* makes a difference. Programs that emphasize curriculum, or teaching practices, or organizational climate, or target special groups such as dropouts are chosen for different reasons, and make rather different demands on the school. Most schools are working on a "braid" of several such efforts, lasting for a number of years.

THE STORY OF IMPLEMENTATION.   School improvement is a complex process. Many different individuals, roles, and groups are involved over a long time, both inside and outside the school. It's important to get the chronology clear, warts and all, so we can see what led to what.

Implementation is never problem-free. We describe the main problems encountered, and, more important, how they are coped with. Good coping can spell the difference between success and failure.

PRELIMINARY RESULTS.   Our case data were mostly collected during 1985–86. We provide a preliminary view of how well the effort was carried out; what its results appeared to be at the end of 1986, in terms of outcomes for students, faculty, administrators, and the school as a whole; and the prospects for continuation.

EPILOGUE.   We returned to the schools two years later, in 1988, to see what had been happening. We report subsequent key events and changes, describe the current status of the change effort, and review the outcomes as of 1988.

WHY DID THIS HAPPEN? A REFLECTIVE REVIEW.   Up to this point, the case has essentially described *what* happened, inviting the reader to draw conclusions as to *why* it happened that way. A final section of the case gives our reflections on why things happened as they did and how we might explain the degree of success that was accomplished.

For an account of how the case study data were collected, written up, and analyzed, see Appendix A.

4

On the Move
Two Success Stories

KAREN SEASHORE LOUIS   SHEILA ROSENBLUM
MATTHEW B. MILES

We begin our case accounts with a look at what works. In two of our schools, Agassiz and Alameda, change programs produced substantial impact. After a sustained, well-implemented improvement effort, teachers were teaching more effectively, the school's climate and functioning were stronger, and there were discernible effects on student learning, behavior, attitudes, and attendance. How did all this happen?

AGASSIZ HIGH SCHOOL:
THE SLOWER YOU GO, THE FASTER YOU GET THERE

The teachers here lacked self-confidence. It was so bad that one teacher told me that working as a Kelly girl in the summer had improved her self-image.

During our darkest hours we gravitated toward collegial networking. We had a hard basis of caring and respect to see us through. We could share our goals, support each other. . . .

When he first started, I'd talk to him about curriculum issues and he'd say, "No, I've got to get discipline under control first," or, "I've got to get the building renovated first." . . . Naturally I didn't believe him. . . . But this was because I really didn't know him (yet). . . .

Louis Agassiz High School,[1] named for the great Harvard zoologist, is small for city high schools: 750 students. Located in one of the largest residential communities in Boston, the East End, it serves a mostly minority population. The East End is still racially mixed, but the neighborhood around the school is all black. The population of Agassiz High

School has shifted from 70 percent white in the early 1960s to officially 70 percent black. However, most visitors will see no more than a handful of white students in attendance.

Over the past few years, Agassiz has been involved in a complex program aimed at real improvements in student experiences and achievement. Much of the program was part of the system-wide "Boston Compact" school–business collaborative improvement effort, and it has opened out to a broader attack on problems of structure, climate, organization, and roles. The needs of students lie at the heart of this evolutionary, school-designed reform. The innovations include attendance, discipline, and dropout prevention programs; a junior ROTC; a health careers program; a self-esteem training program; and others. Many of the ideas behind these programs, and the participatory planning approach, are drawn from the research on what makes schools and teachers effective. The work at Agassiz is based on the belief that to become better, schools need to be more self-analytic, to set meaningful goals, and to hold high performance expectations for students and teachers alike.

Agassiz has come back from a bad low point in the early '80s. The school is more orderly, the climate is caring yet demanding, and student and staff energy and morale are up — along with student achievement. The results at Agassiz have been very promising, and have been sustained since our first contact in 1985. But the story also shows that the road of school-initiated reform is traveled slowly, and often feels more like an obstacle course than an interstate highway.

A Picture of the School in 1985

Agassiz High's physical plant dates from the 1920s. It sits back from a street of run-down, two-family wooden houses, surrounded by a parking lot. Even with recent renovation, it has the institutional feeling of many such buildings: high ceilings, long cold corridors, depressing stairwells, and a concrete-floored cafeteria on the first floor.

One is greeted by a single door monitor (sometimes an on-duty teacher) who signs in visitors and checks IDs for late-arriving students. There is the usual glass case full of athletic awards, many of them very recent. The walls are decorated with student and teacher art, and posters urging the importance of education. Bulletin boards show awards for homerooms with the highest attendance rate for the previous week.

Two things stand out for a visitor. First, the students look active and happy; they seem to lack that quality of sullen passivity one often sees in urban high schools. Second, the school is unusually orderly and quiet even during class changes. A classroom where a teacher is out for a restroom visit can be quiet enough for the proverbial pin drop.

Although Agassiz has lost many teachers in recent years because of city-wide attrition and cutbacks, the school is fairly well staffed. Seventy teachers are organized in seven departments (Mathematics, Language Arts, Humanities, Science, Bilingual Education, Special Education, and a Career Education cluster including vocational education, business, and other subjects), each headed by a non-teaching administrator. A central administrative team consists of headmaster Mark Cohen, three assistant headmasters with responsibility for discipline and guidance, and a development officer in charge of special programs and public relations. Additional support staff include 2.5 guidance counselors, a nurse, librarian, psychologist, and assorted non-professional staff; altogether 120 adults work at Agassiz.

Mark Cohen (who was a health teacher and basketball coach at Agassiz until he was promoted) is in his early forties. His manner is friendly, but brisk. In a school where most teachers dress casually, if not sloppily, he wears a well-tailored suit. He is in effect what he was: a good coach. He sets high standards, is supportive, and expects his team to come through. He also has an unusual ability to mobilize people and resources. And he's responsive.

> He keeps his door open and listens to people . . . he admits he's not a curriculum person, but he'll listen to people who know something about it and keep the school moving.

As in most Boston schools, the teachers tend to be middle-aged; many have been in the school for 15 or more years. More than a few teachers live in the East End, and some actually grew up there. Some of the older teachers talk nostalgically of the traditional Agassiz High of 30 years ago, when there was "a dress-code with jackets and ties — if you forgot your tie you could rent one for a nickel." But it was hardly a "golden age": the top graduates of those days had trouble getting admitted to Boston University because the school's standards were seen as so low.

Agassiz's curriculum is a rather traditional one; the basics are emphasized and innovations in the curriculum are mostly designed to attract or retain students who might otherwise go to one of the city's magnet programs or a parochial school. The curriculum does cover a full range of tracks: college preparatory, business education, general, and special needs. Vocational students attend Agassiz for their academic subjects, and a city-wide vocational center for the rest of the day.

The Context

Agassiz needs to be understood in its social and political context, including the community, school district, and state. Its historical context, especially in relation to prior innovation efforts, is crucial as well.

The Community

If you ask Boston residents where they live, they are more likely to tell you the name of their neighborhood than to say "Boston." East Enders still think of Agassiz as "their" school, despite the crosstown busing that accompanied court-ordered desegregation.

Though Boston is still a mostly white city (nearly 75% in the early 1980s, and 60% by 1985), the East End is more racially mixed (50% white), but with a fair amount of residential segregation. Boston is also an economically mixed city. In the early 1980s, about a third of the population had a median family income of under $10,000, but over 10 percent made $30,000 or more. Although there are some areas of extreme poverty, such as Roxbury or South Boston, and areas of equally extreme wealth, such as Back Bay and Beacon Hill, the East End is economically mixed. Some parts are poor and run-down, with deteriorating three-decker wooden houses, and others are middle class, with large and gracious Victorian homes.

Approximately 60 percent of Boston residents are Catholic, and there is a long history of parochial school use. In 1970, for example, only half the families with school-age children in Boston sent them to public schools. Despite "white flight" (63% white students in 1972 and 24% in 1981), recent figures are not too different. In 1981, 25 percent of black families with children and 45 percent of white ones did not use the public school system at all.

Though the Boston system is not large by urban standards (57,000 students), many outside commissions and observers since the 1930s have judged it as poor. The schools mostly serve working-class and lower-class students; the only middle-class enclave is the prestigious Boston Latin School, once a feeder school for Harvard. Nevertheless, most white parents were not considered pressure points for change until the dramatic desegregation conflicts of the mid-1970s. The bitterness of that experience for both blacks and whites has been well documented on TV and in print. (See Dentler & Scott, 1983; Lukas, 1985; and Lupo, 1977.)

Busing created much parental dissatisfaction with the schools. It had other important impacts too. First, since the school district went into receivership under judge Arthur Garrity, the system's failings—the physical disrepair of its buildings and the poor quality of its curricula and teaching — were exposed to public attention. Second, the role of the Boston School Committee changed: It could no longer dispense patronage jobs, and was under much public pressure to "do something about education."

Most important of all, the intense negative publicity during the busing and violence galvanized Boston's business community to improve the city's image. They believed that improving the city's education system would keep it from becoming another Newark. Behind the concern with quality lay the economic demands of the current business boom: Recent expansion has created a pressing need for qualified entry-level workers, which the crumbling school system could not fill.

The business community was an architect of the Boston Compact, a novel venture that involves an agreement between local businesses and the school system to provide jobs in return for agreed-upon increases in school performance in attendance, scores on standardized basic skills tests, student retention, and placement in jobs and college.[2]

Since 1983, business has been joined by the city government. When Kevin White was mayor, there was little interest in the quality of public education in Boston — perhaps because only 25 percent of families actually had school-age children. White also wanted to avoid being tarnished by the desegregation crisis, not to mention the cronyism and corruption of School Committee scandals. The new mayor, Ray Flynn, was elected on a reform platform emphasizing education, and more resources and interest are evident.

The School District

In the mid- to late '70s, the central office (known informally as "Court Street") was in turmoil. Although some of the worst-managed components of the system were being brought to order under the court's jurisdiction, top leadership was virtually non-existent. Superintendents served at the pleasure of the School Committee, which cycled them in and out so fast that they had little time to develop or support improvement programs.

For example: Superintendent Leary initiated a strong effort in participatory curriculum development; his successor, superintendent Fahey, abolished the program and the department. Robert Wood, who came next, revived it. By the end of this period, schools had learned to ignore central office initiatives, and do as they wanted.

But in 1981, the School Committee made an unprecedented decision to appoint a real outsider, Robert "Bud" Spillane, who came with a three-year contract. Spillane was a strong leader, not afraid of confrontation with the Committee, prepared to tell the truth about the quality of education in Boston, and determined to pull Boston's image up. Spillane was not always popular at the school level: He demoted a number of headmasters, and made uncomplimentary public statements on teaching quality and the Boston Teacher's Union.

However, Agassiz's relationship with Court Street had never been poor, and, as we'll see, headmaster Cohen saw much of value in the programs Spillane immediately began to initiate. Three were central to school change: School-Based Management, intended to decentralize some of the budgetary and personnel decisions to the school level; the School Improvement program, based on the emerging effective schools literature; and the Boston Compact, the school–business collaboration. The first two programs were optional, and the Compact was required of all schools. Cohen decided to use the Compact as a vehicle for designing a comprehensive change program for Agassiz.

The State

The Massachusetts constitution places the state in a weak position regarding the schools, and there is a long tradition of local political and fiscal autonomy. Even though this traditionally hands-off stance has been changing recently (a mainstreaming law for special needs students, desegregation compliance monitoring, school capacity building, and minimum standards efforts), the state has had little impact on the improvement activities in Agassiz.

Because of a state-mandated tax cap and the low Boston tax base, the city goes almost yearly to the legislature for extra funds. Each year there are battles between non-urban legislators who wish to punish profligacy and corruption, and the chronically short-of-funds school department.

Innovation History

The history of change efforts is important at Agassiz High, particularly the story of what happened in the late '60s to mid-'70s.

The culture and improvement-oriented style of Agassiz High are intimately intertwined with the careers of the "class of '69," as it was dubbed by Frank Levesque, chair of the Math Department. Around 1969, many new strong figures arrived simultaneously in the school: Levesque; Bob Murphy (then a business teacher and now the development officer responsible for managing the Compact program); headmaster Mark Cohen; Curt Litton, the man who was to be head-master (off and on) until 1980, and whom Cohen calls his mentor; and others.

This group seemed to share a personal affinity and a common view of how education should work at Agassiz. They favored a humanistic approach that stressed individualization of learning experiences. The natural friendship bonds were strengthened in 1970 when, with support from New England Telephone Company (their school–business partner) and the Sloane School of Management at MIT, key administrative and teaching staff received T-group training. As Bob Murphy put it, "This gave us a core of people who knew how to react, to form committees, to take hold of change." During the mid-'70s, these skills were to come in handier than anyone would have foreseen. And just as important in the intervening years was the reinforcement of common professional interests, along with mutual trust and support.

EARLY INNOVATION.   In 1970 Court Street, anxious to innovate, initiated a "flexible campus" program, which provided for alternative out-of-school educational experiences. At Agassiz, the Flexible Campus was designed by the staff and enthusiastically coordinated by Bob Murphy, who described it as "a whole shopping list of programs that we thought would be good for our students." Even today Bob's office says "Flexible Campus Coordinator" rather than Development Officer. Murphy, a large, talkative man, speaks openly and with affection about everyone in the school, and has often hosted faculty picnics at his house.

RACIAL ISSUES AND DESEGREGATION.   As another staff member put it, "Our curriculum then was a reflection of the '70s. We were constant-ly expanding, adding new courses." But the innovation of the early '70s came to an abrupt halt in 1974. The neighborhood surrounding the school had been changing rapidly from racially mixed to black-domi-nated. Race relations in Boston were deteriorating, as southern black immigration increased, and lower- and working-class whites began to feel threatened (cf. Lukas, 1985).

This pattern played out in the East End in a race riot, which occurred across from the school, though its source was a neighborhood fracas several blocks away. As Murphy put it,

> I couldn't believe it when I went outside and saw the blacks lined up on one side of the field and the whites on the other, throwing rocks at each other; I thought, "This is insane." I felt like Count Pierre in *War and Peace.* . . .

But, as he put it, "School went on . . . some kids didn't come. Those who did didn't seem affected by it."

But it was to be the end of an era. The fall of '74 brought court-ordered desegregation. Although Agassiz was spared the intense racial incidents that occurred in Charlestown and South Boston, perhaps in part because of the group and communication skills of its core team, the school reverted to a state of crisis management rather than purposeful innovation. One staff member stated that "everything but safety took a back burner."

Many of the programs that worked well in a fairly stable school just couldn't be carried out under conditions of threats of violence. In addition, the students themselves needed stability, not innovation; because of student assignments under the court order, the average student who arrived at Agassiz during the mid- to late '70s had already been in six different schools in the system.

LEADERSHIP. The mid-'70s were also a period of instability in leadership. Curt Litton was called to Court Street during the early days of desegregation. John Shannon was appointed headmaster, and Mark Cohen became his vice-headmaster. Litton came back after three years, but stayed for only two-and-a-half years — a period when he taught Cohen a good deal about how to deal with Court Street — before being moved back to the central office. Cohen was appointed acting headmaster, but after six months was "bumped" by an elderly headmaster whose school had been closed (Boston has a rather strong administrator union).

As Cohen put it, "That year was very hard on staff." Morale, already low, dipped further in the absence of any leadership. Fortunately, because of the court order, the superintendent realized the need to have stronger leadership at Agassiz, and Cohen was re-appointed as acting head in the fall of 1982.

THE DOWN SIDE. By this time the school was different from the forward-looking, innovative one of the early '70s. During desegregation Agassiz was classified as a "district" school. As one person put it, that "puts us at the third tier in terms of perceived quality — the best students go to Latin or Tech [the exam schools]; the other motivated students go to a magnet school."

Agassiz's reputation, never very high within the system, had slumped further, because of the publicity from racial incidents at the school (most of which, staff said, were created by outsiders in the neighborhood) and slipping scores. Agassiz's reading and math scores were among the lowest in the city. In 1981–82, the ninth grade math scores were at the 18th percentile, as compared with a system median of 32nd percentile. In reading, the school's ninth grade placed at the 20th percentile, compared with a system average of the 42nd. In 1983, 29 percent of the ninth graders who took a state-required listening test failed.

Figures on student behavior were notoriously unreliable in Boston in the early '80s. But staff mention serious problems, including low attendance (73% in 1981–82), misbehavior in the halls, and minor vandalism. Dropout estimates are vague, but estimates based on the changing size of the current senior class come to perhaps 50 percent. In the ninth grade alone, dropouts were as high as 22 percent in some years.

Although in 1981 the city officially listed Agassiz as having 31 percent special needs students (well above the system average), some staff claimed that many more who should have been receiving special needs assistance were not, because of state caps on the allowable percentage. Bilingual students, a small minority in the early '70s, now represented 25 percent of the student population, many of whom were also served by other special needs programs.

The school building itself was deteriorating badly. When the winds blew hard from the east, the classrooms on that side could not be used because the windows were so loose; paint was peeling from walls and ceilings; the lockers had not been replaced since the 1930s. A visitor from the Ford Foundation in early 1982 flatly said that the building was not a place in which students could learn.

Staff morale in Agassiz, as in most of the Boston schools, was at an all-time low. Along with day-to-day crises, in 1980–81 they were faced with massive layoffs as declining enrollment drove cutbacks. The deep cuts in the faculty were painful, as was the public perception that Agassiz was among the worst of the high schools in Boston. As Ginny Fiske, the liaison from New England Telephone Company put it,

> The teachers here lacked self-confidence. It was so bad that one teacher told me that working as a Kelly girl in the summer had improved her self-image.

A key staff member commented,

> In '81 this was a dead school. We had a winning basketball team, but when we played English High they would fill their side of the gym and we would have just a few students turn out. There was no identity — not among students, not among the staff.

The problems were compounded by the increasing social distance between the staff and the students.

> A lot of teachers just aren't aware of the real world that these kids face. They have their head in the sand.

Overall, other teachers in the system viewed an assignment to Agassiz as a dead end. As one new (minority) staff member put it,

> The school had a bad reputation. It was in a very bad neighborhood and safety was a big issue. Reportedly, there were a lot of fights in the school and a lot of weapons. Academically the reputation was that the school was not strong.

Many of the teachers were just hanging on: One faculty member with 20 years' experience said,

> I [have] union protection and good benefits. . . . I kept myself going for years by teaching night school to adults — that was a lot more enjoyable.

Another long-timer noted that most couldn't see any real alternative.

> You have to realize that there weren't many other places to go. We could transfer, but transfer to what? We were still going to be teaching the same students.

There was, at this point, no strong central office curriculum effort; policies had shifted, over the course of 10 years, from "very loose" (the period of the Flexible Campus) to "back to the basics," to "adjusted loose." At Agassiz, curriculum was largely the responsibility of the department heads, and was highly variable in quality and essentially traditional.

THE PLUS SIDE.   But the school had several things going for it, despite the erosion. Since 1970, it had a relationship with its industrial partner, New England Telephone Company, whose new president was extremely interested in upgrading urban education. Although this pairing had been fairly strong during the '70s, it was to take on increasing importance after 1982.

And during the period of desegregation, each district in the system was paired with a local university to encourage the influx of improvement resources. Agassiz was lucky to be linked with UMass/Boston, whose chancellor also had a strong commitment to community service and active involvement. The liaison faculty member from the UMass staff was personally committed to the school.

Finally, most of the "old team" had hung on through the bad years, in part because of interpersonal loyalties.

> During our darkest hours we gravitated toward collegial networking. We had a hard basis of caring and respect to see us through. We could share our goals, support each other. . . .

Another teacher said,

> The faculty who remained were people who enjoyed teaching. And we enjoyed teaching city kids. We felt comfortable here.

This stability in the cohesive "class of '69" was in large measure a matter of luck, because the instability in the school system during the desegregation period led to high levels of turnover and reassignment of many Boston public school staff. In a single year, Agassiz lost 40 of 120 teachers, and was reassigned 30 new, mostly younger, ones.

The Improvement Program

The Boston Compact was variously seen as a "high school assistance office" (by the Compact's executive director), as a "collective bargaining agent for kids" (by the head of the system's education and employment office), as a "forum for educators, business, and college representatives to talk about problems" (by the Teacher's Union president), and as a "political coalition builder" (by superintendent Spillane).

Though it was district-mandated, it was really a partially filled vessel into which locally developed school plans were to be poured. Program *goals* were established, but each school had to figure out how to get there. It's also important to remember that other improvement efforts were going on at Agassiz already (for example, physical plant improvement through desegregation funds).

Why This Program?

For superintendent Spillane, the main incentive was building a political coalition to support the dying, deeply eroded system; he turned to business as a more powerful constituency than the divided, largely poor citizenry. For the business community, getting desegregation and violence off the agenda, and the chance to exert some influence to improve the city's image and solve the entry-level job crisis, were equally important. And for local universities, the Compact meant getting more qualified graduates while extending their social commitment — at least on paper — to helping schools.

At the school, incentives were more concrete. Although the central office offered three different programs as part of its mandate, headmaster Mark Cohen decided to put his improvement eggs into a single basket: that of the Boston Compact. The Compact was really an umbrella under which Agassiz could assemble all sorts of improvement activities: the improvement program components and activities would gradually grow, and fit together in a loose but relatively integrated way. The precise shape of the initial plan was thus relatively unimportant.

Cohen guessed that the program was flexible enough to encompass a rough "game plan" he already had in mind, and it would give him some of the resources he needed to begin. Another person recalled,

> When he first started, I'd talk to him about curriculum issues and he'd say, "No, I've got to get discipline under control first," or, "I've got to get the building renovated first." . . . Naturally I didn't believe him. . . . But this was because I really didn't know him (yet). . . .

Probably no one at Agassiz knew *precisely* what they hoped for from the Compact in the summer of 1983, although Cohen felt it could raise the image of the school, rebuild morale, and help achievement. It was a start.

The Story of Implementation

When Cohen was appointed in the fall of 1982, he realized that if the Compact was to succeed he would need "to deliver to the skeptics" — the teachers who resented Spillane's implications that they were second-rate and indifferent to students.

Chronology

Cohen's first moves, even before the Compact relationship developed, were characteristically sensitive to the politics and culture of his setting. Aiming at safety and climate improvement, he successfully battled with Court Street to use a million dollars of desegregation funds for visible, cosmetic repairs: windows, lockers, repainting, auditorium renovation, and glass backboards for the gym. He said, "I knew that if the boiler failed later they would have to repair it anyway."

Cohen's first year also saw a lot of attention given to new systems for monitoring attendance, including procedures for calling parents whose children were absent. Cohen also reorganized administrative positions to focus virtually all of the three assistant headmasters' time on discipline — but using his philosophy of combining discipline and guidance, with attention to follow-up, parent contact, student referrals, and feedback to teachers. These efforts paid off: Faculty felt that order and safety, already on the upswing, were improving; students felt their disciplinary treatment was more fair.

Cohen also started laying the groundwork for his second year: improving programs and resources. He mobilized energy for a magnet program on health services professions, based in the Science department. The chair, Mindy Materos, proceeded with active planning for a multi-year program of courses and internships that looked good enough for the central office to fund a full-time nurse and a coordinator. And he got the Junior ROTC program in place by the fall, feeling that it was well structured, offered job potential, had rewards (uniforms), and could lead into college ROTC. Finally, an Adolescent Parenting program for pregnant students began.

In the second year, these programs moved forward, and were amplified by Agassiz's participation in a "Human Services Collaborative": The idea of a Student Support Team was to help coordinate social services to students; Dee Guild, a "seize every opportunity person" with good connections to local agencies, was appointed head and the team began meeting. And the Compact-associated Private Industry Council (PIC) developed a significant number of summer jobs, providing much-needed and visible evidence to teachers that the Compact was serious. Cohen and Murphy also managed to link up the school with two UMass programs: "Urban Scholars" and "Challenge," which provided weekend campus experiences, with guaranteed college admission for successful students. These too were meaningful to teachers, who had often felt frustrated in their attempts to encourage the small nucleus of able students who went on to attend college.

Meanwhile the school system's plans for work with the Boston Compact were developing. A Court Street office was set up, and school liaisons were appointed. Though participation was mandated, each school would design its own plan. In the summer of 1983, Agassiz administrators and some teachers drew up a plan for their Boston Compact work. It was distributed to about 40 people, many of whom were still skeptics. The planning group expanded and remained rather active in subsequent years.

Cohen saw the 1983–84 program thrust as an effort to rebuild the internal and external image of the school, and to improve community and parent involvement. With the help of Ginny Fiske (the liaison from Agassiz's business partner, New England Telephone), Cohen planned a variety of activities intended to attract positive publicity for Agassiz: The Junior ROTC marched in an annual East End parade; a *Boston Globe* article appeared; a business-sponsored pancake breakfast attracted over 100 parents, much to the faculty's amazement; follow-up and publicity efforts got over 300 parents to back-to-school night; many assemblies and awards programs touted student achievement; school spirit was promoted through buttons and banners, and through a successful year for several sports teams.

During 1983–84, Cohen and Murphy also wrote a $135,000 proposal with the PIC to fund a cluster program for ninth grade at-risk students. Kent Jansen, a dynamic ex-social studies teacher who had "dropped out" to run for city council, was recruited for the position, and this program was designed in the summer of '84.

Faculty members' skepticism diminished, but they were still not energized or participating actively in planning in the way Cohen and other administrators had hoped. Cohen's longer-range goal was to reach more deeply into the classroom to affect curriculum and teaching, and he thought involvement in planning would be a way in. Over the year he, Murphy, June Ferrara (from UMass/Boston), and Ginny Fiske worked on the problem. New England Telephone sponsored a one-day retreat for administrators and department heads, on planning strategies and skills for the coming year. Fiske and Cohen realized that additional training and support were needed for administrators, and she located a program used for NE Tel management training, "Investment in Excellence." The workshops emphasized enhanced self-esteem, motivation, and personal goal setting; administrators who attended were so enthusiastic that another workshop was done for more staff (including Cohen). It led to high enthusiasm and reports of dramatic personal changes (weight loss, stopping smoking, and so on).

Kent Jansen was trained in the first group. After a successful first year organizing the ninth grade cluster program, he was looking for a new activity for the Compact Ventures component of the school's effort. Fiske located a junior version of the "Investment" program, called "Keys to Excellence." It occupied three weeks of class time, and was piloted in Social Studies; by the following year nearly half the student body had participated, and stories about student interest and achievement gains circulated widely through the school.

In the meantime, during the spring Fiske and Cohen had worked out the details for a bottom-up planning process for the third year of the Compact. Cohen and Ferrara worked with department heads to improve their curriculum planning and their supervision skills, so individual faculty could in turn improve their own planning and self-evaluation strategies. Departmental planning was the watchword for the year; department-developed goals for which departments could be held accountable became part of the basis for the third-year Compact plan. Much effort was focused on the English department, which was traditionally the fulcrum of curriculum activities; the head had been openly supportive of Cohen since the beginning. The English department had begun having daily brief meetings as early as the fall of 1983.

1985–86 looked like a year of consolidation for the efforts at Agassiz. Keys to Excellence was the only new program venture. Most energy was going into making existing efforts work well; into monitoring and enhancing the departmental plans; into teacher training in goal setting; and into institutionalizing "soft money" programs. But one suspects that Mark Cohen and Bob Murphy were still looking for new programs and funding that would enhance their efforts, and fit more or less with the goals of the Compact program.

Throughout implementation, Agassiz has received steady, vigorous assistance — externally from Fiske and Ferrara, each spending well over half their time. Fiske, in her late thirties, radiates energy, intensity, and enthusiasm: She's an "idea-a-minute" person with an almost missionary fervor about Agassiz. She has helped on planning strategies and skills, and the Keys to Excellence program. Ferrera, with a background in curriculum and instruction, is flexible and patient, and firmly committed to the idea that teachers can make a difference with disadvantaged students. She has helped with content, mostly curriculum planning, implementation, and supervisory skills, In effect both were roving planning assistants and a trusted source of advice, part of Cohen's kitchen cabinet.

There have also been strong internal assistance resources: a full-time job development coordinator, Kent Jansen's full-time position on Compact Ventures, and Dee Guild's on social services. These are "soft money" positions heading for permanence. Furthermore, Bob Murphy as development officer spends at least 25 percent of his time on program coordination. It appears that at least 4.5 full-time equivalents go to managing and supporting the change effort, along with a large amount of energy from other administrators and staff.

Problems and How They Were Coped with

The evolutionary planning approach at Agassiz has, like any improvement effort, run into many problems. During early and later planning these included low staff morale, skepticism and reluctance to invest energy, lack of planning skills, and scheduling constraints. During implementation, there were problems of "fit" between new programs and the schedule and district regulations, and tension between the goals of raising attendance and improving retention; uncertainty about the future of "soft money" programs; conflicts with other mandated programs (such as new system-wide curriculum changes); new time-consuming tests; key staff losses due to system cutbacks; lack of staff understanding of all the pieces of the complex, wide-ranging improvement effort; great variability among department heads in their willingness and ability to be instructional leaders; and teacher needs for close-up training and support as they learned new teaching styles and strategies for working with students.

Many of these problems were dealt with through technical coping — analyzing the problems, redesigning programs, applying resources. The style has been to try and ensure that each identified problem has a solution in progress or on the drawing board. Examples include the Investments in Excellence program as a way to deal with staff burnout and cynicism; training in planning skills; the active use of NE Tel and UMass assisters; additions of full-time coordination positions to strengthen the management of change; Cohen's careful interviewing of faculty candidates from the district's "excess pool" to informally discourage people who did not fit his expectations and the school's developing character; and his laying off teachers who were eligible for recall.

Other coping methods were more political, aimed at image building and getting influence and resources. Cohen has backed his staff and challenged Court Street at a number of points: going for cosmetic, morale-boosting plant improvements; fighting off program elimination efforts; insisting that the right key staff member for the bilingual program be hired. He also publicizes school successes internally and in local media (a notebook with press clippings is lovingly maintained for inspection by visitors).

Finally, some coping efforts were culturally oriented, aiming at changing shared values: staff parties and a Christmas dance, the pancake breakfast, back-to-school nights, attendance and honors plaques, color photographs of honor roll students, wall charts summarizing "effective schools" principles, and even the fact that the school's goals are emblazoned on a big poster just over the photocopy machine that most faculty use every day. Moving more and more toward a participatory planning emphasis (the kitchen cabinet, a school site council, and department-level planning) is a major style of problem coping, along with a commitment to what can only be called *patience*: knowing when next steps are timely, staying with the slow process of helping teachers change, living with poorly fitting curriculum and testing because the long-term goals are right.

Preliminary Results

The improvement effort at Agassiz can be seen at two levels: that of specific student-oriented program components (ROTC, Keys to Excellence, etc.) and the more general effort to engage the faculty and staff in a sustained participatory planning and change process.

As of late 1986, specific components were quite well implemented. Coordinated social services was in its first year; weekly staff meetings to discuss at-risk students were well carried out; and external agencies were beginning to deliver services within the school. The Junior ROTC was popular, and carried out without setbacks; the instructors were seen as excellent resources. The ninth grade cluster program staff had high esprit as a team in creating a personalized environment for students. Keys to Excellence was a real "upper"; faculty saw it as effective, with real student impact. Furthermore, it was fair to say that all students were involved in one or more of the various program components, both in and out of the classroom (social services, peer counseling, activities program).

At the more general process level, all administrators were involved, and were getting a great deal of support and training in goal setting, planning, and supervisory skill. In at least three departments — English, Math, and Bilingual Education — serious efforts at curriculum development were under way, and planning was widespread among departments.

Implementation at the teacher level was more uneven. Responses ranged from the highly committed teachers who were excited with their new autonomy, the emphasis on teamwork, and the new resources Cohen had brought in, to the apathetic and the angry.

> Teachers are in a no-win situation. We're working harder but getting very little to show for it. The system is trying to improve standards but these [kids] just don't have it.

However, there was little evidence of a split between "inside" implementers and "outside" kibitzers and opponents among the teachers: "There's no real division regarding who's involved and who's not." And it seemed that most staff felt energized.

Parents were actively involved in school social functions, and home–school relations were said to have improved substantially. As yet they had not been involved in governance and planning.

What have been the short-term impacts of the work at Agassiz? Adults at Agassiz said, to a person, that the school felt better. Even the most skeptical observers pointed to concrete changes in climate (teacher energy and enthusiasm especially) and morale. Leadership style had changed: Many people referred to vision, a challenge to excellence, and a concern with the educational process. Collaboration and collegiality were improving, but unevenly.

Though ownership of the vision, common goals, and a diagnosis for change were still not widely shared, and the school site council was not seen as a mechanism for participatory planning, the culture of the school was so strong that many of the sentiments and goals were implicitly shared.

Short-term outcomes for students were very clear. Very simply, Agassiz was a much better place to be in 1986 than it had been five years before. Relationships with adults were friendly and caring; students thought school was fair and improving. A representative 1986 anecdote from a researcher:

> I saw a teacher take off down the hall to chase a student, obviously in a bad mood, who was wearing a baseball hat against school rules. He was gentle but firm: No hats allowed, and by the way, what was the matter. . . ? The visibility of staff in the halls is immediately apparent, as is their clear concern with maintaining student behavior.

What longer-term changes were evident? Agassiz's reform program focused on improving the structure of the school and the abilities of its members to implement short- and long-range planning for the education of students. There were already changes in communication, collaboration, and planning/problem-solving capacity at the administrator and departmental level. Administrative staff tended to feel empowered; some, but not all, teachers sensed the changes in the school's climate. Good community feeling had been restored among the staff, and a sense of accomplishment was added, along with increased emphasis on quality and accountability.

Student-oriented outcomes were impressive. There was a marked improvement in the sense of order in the school; discipline problems had reduced substantially. Climate changes were repeatedly mentioned. A youth worker who attended the school before Cohen began said,

> Things are really different here now . . . before you could smell the pot in the halls, and kids didn't care if they did any work. Now the kids are a lot more serious about what they're doing here. . . .

There was increased responsiveness to student needs, supported by new counseling/guidance structures and procedures. New internal testing and monitoring programs were being introduced through department-level planning, especially in Math and English. There was great success in improving home–school relationships and parent involvement, and movement on improving the school's image in the community.

Less effort had gone into changing teaching methods, use of classroom time (except in the Math department, where classroom observations were now firmly entrenched), or increasing individualized attention to students in non-class time. Even so, student outcomes were already visible. Student attendance went from 73 percent in 1981–82 to over 83 percent in 1984–85; tardiness has also improved. Student achievement in standardized testing programs improved: In the same years Metropolitan math scores went from the 18th percentile to between the 34th and 28th percentile (more improvement in ninth and tenth than in the eleventh grade). Metropolitan reading scores were up for ninth graders (from the 20th to the 35th percentile), but did not show as much improvement among tenth and eleventh graders. On these scores, Agassiz had moved up from the depths to about the average in the system. However, after extensive coaching, all but 5 seniors passed the district minimum skills reading test in the spring of 1986, when more than 60 had failed the preceding fall.

The proportion of seniors saying they would go on to further education hovered around 45 to 50 percent. Job placement for graduates had, however, improved greatly. There was consensus that dropout rates (except in the ninth grade cluster program) had not improved much, although accurate dropout figures were unavailable. On "softer" measures, school spirit, participation in school events, and general attitude to learning had all improved, according to teachers.

As of 1986, the prospects at Agassiz appeared bright: The strategy was in place, a cohesive management team was emerging, staff skepticism and resistance were diminishing among most groups, and there was plenty of help to design support and assistance strategies. The trajectory was toward real improvement. Several program aspects seemed well routinized (central administrative planning, job development, and work on discipline and climate), but others less so (the departmental planning, curriculum development, and supervision aspects).

The main sources of instability came from the outside. Many of the programs were still running on "soft money." As could be expected with any new superintendent, Laval Wilson's emphasis and direction were still in the formulation stage. There was uncertainty even about the Compact itself (Could it, or would it, become institutionalized in the face of low enthusiasm at Court Street?). Central office staffing cuts, new programs, or erosion of resources could easily disturb the heightened — but fragile — morale and sense of efficacy in the building. Furthermore, Fiske and Ferrara would be reducing their time over the next year, and the improvement effort probably remained dependent on the continued presence of Mark Cohen, whose vision and planning stimulated the present program. So there was some uncertainty.

Epilogue

We returned to Agassiz two years later, wanting to learn what had happened subsequently, how the improvement program stood, and what its outcomes were.

Subsequent Events and Changes

Between 1986 and 1988, several staff left. Headmaster Mark Cohen moved to administering other programs in the district, and then returned as headmaster in the fall of 1988; two assistant headmasters have been reassigned or promoted; the Math chair Frank Levesque is at another school; the Bilingual chair is gone; and Dee Guild, who headed the Student Support Team, has moved on to graduate school at Harvard. The PIC representative and Ginny Fiske of NE Tel have been replaced by new people. Bob Murphy remains, but is now Student Support Coordinator rather than Development Officer. Given these changes, one might expect disarray, or at least sluggishness in the improvement effort. But that does not seem to be the case.

How the Program Stands Now

As of 1988, Compact Ventures, the ninth grade cluster program for dropout prevention, has expanded to the tenth and eleventh grades. People at the school were very tenacious in obtaining funding. Rather than wait for district action, they went directly to the state and got money through a new state program, "Commonwealth Futures."

The Student Support Team, beginning implementation two years ago, now meets once a week. A team including the coordinator, a guidance counselor, assistant headmaster, Compact Ventures teacher, and school nurse has conducted case conferences on 182 students this year — about a quarter of the student body. Using a quasi-case management approach, the team has offered interventions ranging from obtaining added within-school adult support to outside services. The team has succeeded in spite of the demise of the Boston Human Services Collaborative — the district effort that originally fueled the Student Support Team concept.

The ROTC program is still going strong with over 100 students. In June one group was at Fort Devens for two weeks of training that included rafting and rappelling — a sort of Outward Bound with uniforms.

The self-esteem enhancement program, Keys to Excellence, is still being used, mainly in the Compact Ventures program. "Choices," a NE Tel self-development program that brings middle managers into the school to speak about careers and decision making, has been added for all ninth graders.

The partnership with NE Tel and the association with PIC remain quite strong. Both still provide career awareness and job preparation courses, and more important, jobs. Two hundred Agassiz students had summer jobs in 1988, forty of them with the telephone company. The NE Tel partnership was recently recognized by the Massachusetts Manufacturers' Association as one of 6 exemplary partnerships (out of over 500) in the state.

The connection with UMass Boston, also established through the Compact, continues to be strong. June Ferrara has stimulated much curriculum development work, this year focusing on revamping of the business section of the Career Education cluster. She coordinated a team of teachers (some from other departments), administrators, and the PIC and NE Tel representatives that examined the existing business curriculum, streamlined it to meet city and state requirements, and added new courses for key job-market skills. The business program will be a special cluster in the school for up to 100 students. Future plans include developing specialized business English and business math courses.

Mayor Flynn, bypassing superintendent Wilson, has appointed a panel and consultants to consider restructuring governance in the system; more decentralization is likely, and parents would be able to choose among twenty or so schools within one of three zones. If these changes materialize, they will probably support the improvements that have occurred at Agassiz.

Outcomes

Dropout rates within the Compact Ventures program are 11 percent, compared with the city-wide 22 percent rate; the rate for other students has not changed much. ROTC has been praised as "having turned around some of the biggest losers in the school." Attendance has gone slightly higher, to 85 percent. Achievement scores have increased slightly over their previous levels.

The climate remains positive, and people still talk about the school as a "refuge" for students who encounter so many problems outside. As before, there is a strong sense that teachers and others care deeply about students and will go out of their way to get involved.

Progress is not uniform. Work on instructional improvement hasn't gained much ground. Cohen's hopes for training department heads in observation skills have progressed little. But a telling illustration of progress is that Agassiz applied for and was selected as one of 10 finalists for a new state "Carnegie School" grant. If it is awarded, they will start a multi-year effort on reorganizing structure and management, and improving instruction. The project, which involved months of faculty planning in work groups, will examine length of the school day and year, regroup students, and put teachers in leadership and decision-making positions. The faculty pulled together very well on the proposal.

Bob Murphy speaks of how programs are being "institutionalized." The transition between Mark Cohen and Dick Cronin, the new headmaster, went smoothly; he did not act to shelve existing programs, and supported the team approach and bottom-up planning approach. Ferrara says that Cronin, like Cohen, has vision and an "eye for the bigger picture." Cohen's return to the school was equally smooth.

Why Did This Happen? A Reflective Review

As we have described events and processes at Agassiz, the reader has undoubtedly begun to think of reasons *why* they occurred. We too have our explanations, drawn from both the original visits and the follow-up contact. Our explanations are aimed at why program implementation occurred as it did, and at why the program's outcomes took place.

Why This Implementation?

Why did things go as they did at Agassiz? Some features of the early context seemed important, particularly the new superintendent and his pressure for improvement, shared by Cohen as the new (but knowledge-able) headmaster. Because Cohen chose the Compact out of the programs Spillane was mandating, it could be an umbrella for many different new programs, and an evolutionary approach could be used. That approach was especially useful in a school with little recent innovative history, and a demoralized, skeptical faculty.

The Compact partnership was especially useful in providing added resources — not only funds to support new programs, but strong technical, training, and consultative support from NE Tel representative Fiske. The same was true of the UMass relationship and the help of June Ferrara. Between them they ensured a thoughtful approach both to change processes and school content. The addition of "assisters" from within the staff — Jansen, Guild, Murphy — increased the amount of helping substantially.

It's also important to remember that Agassiz has only 750 students and now 90 support staff and faculty. So training interventions (such as the striking Investment in Excellence program) and new student programs can have a stronger effect than in a school four times that size, like our cases Bartholdi and Chester.

It seems clear that while Cohen was a strong headmaster with a vision of where he wanted the school to go, and of how it might get there, the internal network dubbed the "class of '69" was equally important. Cohen could mobilize much energy internally with less difficulty than in a school with more distant relationships. Furthermore, he and his network were patient, accepting the gradualness of the process rather than pressing hard. "The slower you go, the faster you get there" was a sort of tacit motto.

Cohen was far from being the charismatic "mover and shaker" figure that is often lauded in media accounts of school turnarounds. Rather, using an evolutionary strategy, he exhibited tenacity, flexibility, supportiveness, good problem-analysis and problem-solving skills, and a constant pressure on staff to take small steps, along with a tolerance for setbacks. His style is not that of the stereotyped masculine decision-maker, but that of a nurturing — and demanding — parent.

There were also some important strategic sequencing choices. Cohen's choice to go for "early wins" by improving the dilapidated plant in mainly cosmetic, visible terms, and the new jobs that came as part of

Compact activities, along with the early work on discipline and attendance, provided a sense of success and reduced skepticism. The training
programs, such as those for planning and Investment in Excellence, a
more direct attack on morale and energy problems, did not come until
later; they increased both skill and sense of efficacy, along with
strengthening social bonds among teachers and administrators. The actual bottom-up planning effort, and the work on classroom teaching
methods, came even later.

The problems were not minor: orchestrating a complex, multi-part
improvement effort, developing the required planning skills, fitting the
program components to existing regulations. But Cohen and his kitch-
en cabinet were adroit at supplying needed training, at buffering the
work from central office interference, and at garnering new resources —
including staff that would be sympathetic to the directions being taken.
They were able to cope with difficult problems through deep, structure-
changing methods, and rarely procrastinated or denied that problems
existed.

Finally, we can note that in spite of fairly substantial turnover —
including Cohen himself for a while and a number of key internal and
external supporters — the improvement effort has continued for two additional years, and appears to have sustained momentum. We might
speculate that the increasingly strong collaboration, the empowerment
of administrators and staff, and the reaffirmation of a clear, compelling
culture that emphasized "demanding caring" kept the improvement effort going — even when resources were threatened and new people entered the improvement effort at Agassiz.

Why the Outcomes?

The Agassiz program components, as they evolved, were relatively
well implemented. Because they had been chosen to be congruent with
a general vision of where the school should be going, were generally of
good quality (well planned internally, as in the case of the ninth grade
cluster and the health careers program, or externally, as in the case of
Investment in Excellence), *and* were led by committed and well-trained
people, they tended to work. They improved morale and energy for
staff, and did the same for students.

The personal effects of the Investment in Excellence program clearly played a part in mobilizing student (and faculty) energy. The strong
investment of the English and Math departments in curriculum development and planning also seems to have paid off in the increased
achievement results. But those would have been less likely without the

early attention to order, and the individualized attention evident in the attendance, social services, and ninth grade cluster efforts.

So the efforts at Agassiz worked, and we know something of why. Next we turn to Alameda, a school that was also on the move.

ALAMEDA HIGH SCHOOL: THE BIG FIX

[THEN]: Nobody talked about curriculum; they only told me war stories, but they liked those kids.
[NOW]: There is peer pressure to teach.

High school is not only school for students; it is a university for teachers.

Alameda High School,[3] with 2,000 students, 59 percent of them minority, is located in the semi-urban sprawl of southeastern Los Angeles County. Though it is a campus high school on 40 acres in a mixed low/middle-class area, its problems are genuinely urban. Before the improvement effort started, the school had gang activity, graffiti and vandalism, poor attendance, and low achievement. Alameda was known by district parents and staff as "the high school to avoid."

As diagnosed by the principal, Çara Mosely, who led the school from 1980 to 1985, the major problem was low expectations of students' ability to achieve and learn. The staff had positive feelings about students and each other — but "they cared more than they taught."

The improvement effort at Alameda included a state-funded, school-based planning program with a participatory emphasis (School Improvement Program, or SIP); strong, visionary leadership that emphasized higher expectations for students and staff; and an active staff development program led by a well-structured team of teachers. Much effort has gone into clinical supervision, peer coaching, and specific subject-matter projects.

Alameda High School has changed: As a veteran teacher said, "It has become a school again." Students are back in the classroom and increasingly in academic classes. There's excitement about teaching and learning, and freedom from worry about social control. Vandalism and gangs are no longer major issues; absenteeism is sharply down, and achievement scores are strikingly up (reading scores, for example, went from the 16th percentile to a high 62nd percentile in 1983, with a slight drop in subsequent years).

The implementation process and outcomes at Alameda were similar in some respects to those at Agassiz, and interestingly different in others. A careful comparison will, we think, help the reader see more clearly "what works" in urban high school reform.

A Picture of the School in 1985

Alameda High School was opened in 1954. Like many Southern California high schools, it's a campus with eleven one-story buildings interspersed with walkways and courtyards, spread out over forty acres. The construction is simple, "no frills." Though there's a gym and pool, there's no auditorium; the library is small; and students eat their lunches in an outside courtyard. The spaciousness makes it hard to believe there are 2,000 students and 100 staff. The campus is officially "closed," but looks (and is) open enough that class cutting is a recurring problem. Only the walkie-talkies carried by the handful of young, informally dressed security staff are a reminder of tougher settings. The rules of no fighting, no weapons, no drugs, no drinking, and no smoking seem to have been successfully internalized by students.

The minority population breaks down into 35% Hispanic, 18% Asian, and 6% black. Eighty percent of Alameda's students come from poorer families than those at other district schools; over 15 percent have free lunch, and half of the ninth graders receive Chapter 1 compensatory services. There's a lot of mobility — 1,000 students transfer in or out during the school year. The annual dropout rate is said to be 7 percent, but attrition from ninth to twelfth grade is actually 36 percent.

There are 92 professionals, including 88 teachers organized into 13 departments; most department chairs teach a full five-period day (though English, Math, and Social Studies have an extra planning period). They have a day a month to work on curriculum and supervision.

The principal is Carl Jones, a soft-spoken, popular black man who had been assistant principal for discipline for six years under his mentor and predecessor, Cara Mosely. Mosely, often called the "white tornado" for her energetic forcefulness, recommended him for the principalship when she was reassigned in the summer of 1985. Jones, who sees himself as an instructional leader, has continued Mosely's initiatives in a more subdued style, and has worked mainly as a problem solver and operations manager.

There are three assistant principals (A.P.'s), for curriculum/counseling/guidance, discipline, and special services/budget. Each of the A.P.'s also has a counseling case load of 100 to 150 students, keeping them in close touch. They form a "cabinet" along with Jones and four teachers (directors of activities, athletics, and the SIP program). It meets regularly for decision making, and the members see each other daily.

Three guidance counselors also serve as administrators (for example, of attendance, financial aid, and college and military recruitment). They share responsibilities for teacher observation and evaluation with the assistant principals. Overall, the administrative staff is lean.

The curriculum, given California's policy emphasis on post-secondary education, stresses college preparation and meeting state requirements. But it also includes business, industrial arts, vocational education, and special education components. Alameda houses a range of programs for diverse language groups, and offers many limited-English proficiency and bilingual classes. Many advanced placement, honors, and gifted classes have been added in the last few years, along with a few for special education. The range of student activities is typical: athletics, plays, dances, trips, clubs, a leadership/Student Council class, student employment as aides in the school, and a popular rock climbing/wilderness program. Opportunities for student involvement in the school and its operations are widespread, although the participation rate is not out of the ordinary. What *is* unusual is the level of harmony and integration of the diverse student body, despite some occasional conflict between black and Hispanic/Filipino groups. When conflict incidents occur, they are rarely on campus.

The staff climate is collegial, and has been for years; everyone is on a first-name basis. But there is also a strong substantive emphasis, and a good deal of cross-department contact, normally rare in high schools. There is a cadre of staff who work either as state-funded Mentor Teachers or as district-funded Instructional Resource Teachers, together known as the MIRT team. It leads a wide range of staff development activities, and the core of "true believers" in staff development is substantial.

The Context

As usual, we need to look at the community, district, and state environment Alameda exists in — and to get a feeling for the historical context as well.

The Community and School District

Alameda High School, as part of a unified school district since 1965, draws from five city jurisdictions, including a barrio with 80 percent of its population on welfare, another area with a mostly working-class population, and another with middle-class parents. The area was formerly Dutch dairy farms, but housing and commercial development have burgeoned, and the municipalities sending students are simply part of the continuous semi-urban sprawl that surrounds Los Angeles.

The school district has 22,000 students K–12, plus 6,800 in adult school. Of the 30 schools, five are senior highs. Financially, the district is neither poor nor rich, though staffing levels are relatively thin compared with other schools in our study. Rather than having subject-matter specialists, curriculum development is managed through district-wide committees composed of teachers and department heads.

The superintendent, Thomas Evans, has been in the job for nine years. He is considered dynamic and innovative, with a strong interest in instructional improvement, staff development, and teacher empowerment. He assigned Cara Mosely to Alameda, and also supported Alameda as the first high school in the district to apply for sip funds. Evans notes: "Change very seldom begins at the teacher level without leadership," but also says, "Teachers are usually underutilized." He sees change efforts as needing to be deliberate, purposeful, school-based, and school-wide, with active use of teacher competence.

Generally, the district supports innovation and improvement efforts. A representative policy is that principals rotate jobs about every five years ("Change creates enthusiasm."). Also, use of an alternative "continuation school" to absorb students with substantial difficulty in their regular high schools, temporary cross-transfers of disruptive students, and district-wide truant services free each school to concentrate on its primary mission: education and serving students.

The State

California has a tradition of being on the cutting edge of innovation. The State Education Agency (sea) is considered a strong support for school improvement. A recent law, SB 813, provides funds for the School Improvement Program and the Mentor Teacher Program, both of which compensated for reduced funding under Proposition 13. But state funding goes hand in hand with a tradition of strong local control over implementation and monitoring. As we shall see, sip is essentially a method of distributing funds for school improvement through plans made locally. An evaluation of sip (Berman & Gjelten, 1984) was critical of the program's impact in high schools, and there is a movement to cut funds for secondary schools—recently warded off by the lobbying of a high school network led by the Alameda High School sip coordinator.

Other state initiatives have included increased graduation requirements, curriculum guidelines, and state proficiency tests. In general, the SEA provides little direct assistance, but much is available on request from county, district, university, and former SEA personnel.

Innovation History

Alameda High School was opened in 1954. In 1965 it became part of the present unified school district, which urbanized rapidly. There was an influx of poorer, Hispanic, and other minority students. These changes were accompanied by an increase in problems. Gangs, high absenteeism (28%), low scores on the California Achievement Test, declining enrollment (from 2,500), weak parental participation because of fear of attending night meetings — all added up to "a school in trouble."

One improvement effort that began in the '70s was a rock climbing/wilderness experience aimed at reducing student violence, integrating the student body, and motivating weaker students. (It was successful enough to be expanded and continued in later years.) The district also participated with John Goodlad of UCLA in the League of Cooperating Schools. Goodlad's approach to school change and the involvement of school staff had a strong influence on many in the district, including the superintendent. In the early and mid-'70s Alameda High School was also affected by the hiring of many young staff members — '60s-trained, collegially oriented, idealistic — who consolidated a school culture of caring, both among staff and with students. Even today people say, "We grew up together."

But progress in alleviating school problems was slow. The 1978 math scores were at the 21st percentile, spelling was 14th, written expression 17th, and reading 16th. Discipline was lax. In the spring of 1979, Alameda was still functioning poorly. Superintendent Evans encouraged the then principal of Alameda to be the first to apply for a SIP grant to a district high school. Though the principal was not a categorical grant enthusiast, he agreed to work with his staff to determine whether they should apply for funding and start a program. That launched the improvement effort; it was strongly reinforced when Evans shifted Cara Mosely into the principalship in the summer of 1980.

The Improvement Program

The Alameda improvement effort has two main strands: SIP, and the later-emerging Staff Development Program, led by the MIRT team (Mentor and Instructional Resource Teachers).

The School Improvement Program (SIP) has four basic elements. First, funding: about $117,000 to $125,000 each year, based on $70 per student, for support of a coordinator, administrative assistance, consultants, and staff-proposed projects. Second, the coordinator (currently Paul Hernandez), who manages the budget and keeps SIP activities coherently connected. Third, a Site Council, with elected representatives of administrators, teachers, other staff, parents, and students that makes policy, allocates the funds, reviews projects, and sets priorities. Fourth, a required written plan developed by the Council and coordinator, which is needs-based; includes goals, priorities, and strategies; and is updated every few years based on ongoing evaluation.

SIP is thus a "process," which the local school fills with content. As such it has no intrinsic program coherence — something that must be achieved through a local vision. However, it's more than the sum of its parts when one considers the way decisions are made and power is shared. Though SIP is sometimes looked on as a slush fund for materials, aides, and so on, the Site Council as a multi-constituent team has been vigilant in protecting priorities, and has on occasion rejected proposals from administrators, including the principal.

The Staff Development Program emerged only when Cara Mosely came to the school in the second year of the SIP process. Her plan for school renewal was primarily staff renewal, aiming at increasing teaching skills and upgrading the level of instruction. The core of the state-funded program is the MIRT team, which plans and implements the program with the help and advice of the principal and the assistant principal for curriculum and guidance. The team includes four *Mentor Teachers* (local master teachers, in effect), who receive an extra state stipend of $4,000 plus $1,700 for substitutes and materials, and after special training provide in-service training and consultation. It also includes five *Instructional Resource Teachers*, who receive a $1,200 stipend and are trained to do peer coaching (a variant of clinical supervision) on teaching methods with up to ten other teachers, and conduct needs-based in-service sessions on such topics as cooperative learning and use of computers. The MIRT team, which is larger than those at other schools in the district, meets formally at dinner once a month, and much more frequently informally.

This strong in-service emphasis is supported by a schedule that permits extensive all-staff in-service: biweekly one-hour sessions on Fridays, three to four all-day meetings, and several retreats each year. In addition, the department chair role has been shifted toward instructional leadership: Chairs have an extra conference period a day, plus a day a month to do clinical supervision with their teachers.

Why These Programs?

SIP and MIRT were both state-funded programs, which could fill in some of the gaps resulting from the state-wide budget cuts after Proposition 13. Both fit well with the prior culture of the school, which was informal, supportive and collaborative, and built on the norm of positive feelings toward students. They also fit well with superintendent Evans' commitment to school-based instructional improvement and teacher empowerment. And the programs themselves were right: SIP had the flexibility, resources, and collaborative emphasis needed for a serious effort, and MIRT had the teacher renewal emphasis implied in Cara Mosely's vision: "a school for students and a university for teachers." She believed that school improvement was essentially staff improvement.

The Story of Implementation

Though SIP and the Staff Development Program are intertwined, it may be useful to look at them one at a time: how they developed, what problems each encountered, and how these were dealt with.

Chronology for SIP

SIP was born in California in 1977; in 1979, as we mentioned previously, superintendent Evans encouraged the Alameda principal to apply. He believed SIP could improve climate, performance, and school image, bringing school and community closer together.

The first coordinator, Anne Cooper, created an ad hoc site council, whose first task was to decide whether to go through with the process and apply for SIP funding. Cooper recalls the initial meeting as a milestone event: It was the first time anyone had seen a school-level committee including parents and students that was empowered to make a major policy decision.

The ad hoc council agreed to go ahead, and was successful in getting a planning grant. In the spring of 1979, Cooper coordinated elections for the official Site Council, and worked with it: "We began to put together a plan to produce a plan." That procedural plan was to involve the entire faculty. At a faculty meeting in the fall of 1979, the site council described SIP and its promise for moving the school forward and to "do whatever was needed to bring the school and its curriculum to the highest standard in the field." Task groups on subject-matter areas, school climate, career/vocational education, and audiovisual resources were set up and began work; in parallel the Site Council conducted surveys of students, faculty, and parents. With SIP funds for released time, groups visited other schools, canvassed the county office, and developed materials. This sort of support for innovative activity "was unheard of in the district, and was a major boon to the staff." In this process a good deal of faculty ownership and energy developed.

The planning process ended with 30 proposals. They included releasing teachers for curriculum writing and visits, which would lead to new courses in basic science, health science, careers, and geography; new teacher aides (aimed at freeing teachers from clerical duties so they could focus on curriculum and instructional improvement); and continuation of the rock climbing/wilderness program (aimed at school climate improvement through bringing hostile gangs together with other students and faculty). The Site Council prioritized them systematically — but were able to fund all by asking for bare-bones budgets from the task groups.

These proposals did lead to the new courses envisioned, and since its initiation, SIP has continued along the same general lines. The Site Council meets monthly for several purposes: to review programs, budgets, and allocations; to revise the school plan; to assess component implementation; and to review new proposals as well as the annual application to the state, which also includes funds for Chapter 1 (disadvantaged) and LEP (bilingual) programs. Yearly elections for new student, parent, and teacher members are held.

SIP has some external assistance: an orientation workshop for new site council members given by the district office, and occasional external consultants. But most assistance is provided by the coordinator and administrative assistant. Many Site Council members have also been MIRT members, and have brought group process and other skills to help SIP work go well.

Cooper moved to another school in 1982; her successor, a teacher, became SIP coordinator for the district in 1984; Paul Hernandez, the present coordinator, also coordinates standardized testing for the school and can quickly detect curriculum or instructional weaknesses. Hernandez is an adjunct member of the school's cabinet, and has had a close working relationship with Cara Mosely (and now Carl Jones).

As of 1985, about 50 percent of SIP funds go to core staff (coordinator and administrative assistant) and operating expenses, 25 percent for aides, and 25 percent for special projects (such as the rock climbing program; curriculum development in such areas as computer learning, study skills, and reading/writing across the curriculum; and campus beautification).

Problems in SIP and How They Were Coped with

Initially, trust in the planning and decision-making process had to be developed; it turned out that the process was open and participatory enough to overcome this barrier. Later there were problems of funding uncertainty (resolved at the state level), insufficient funds to meet all the requests for support, the risk that SIP would become a piecemeal set of projects and aide positions, and the low involvement of the Industrial and Vocational Education departments ("our needs are too big to be funded by SIP"). Most of these, except for the latter, were coped with by careful, periodic reassessment of priorities and program monitoring by the coordinator and Site Council. However, the non-academic departments at the "back of the campus" (except for Home Economics) remained at a distance; there were "two schools," not one.

Chronology for Staff Development

Now let's turn to the chronology of the parallel Staff Development Program. Cara Mosely arrived at Alameda in the summer of 1980. She was a former nun and Mother Superior, who had run a parochial school. A maverick, she left the order during the '70s. But she retained some important values: a strong sense of authority, passion and commitment, and belief in the dignity and potential of each individual. Her style was a combination of "no nonsense" and humaneness.

She felt the faculty was caring and qualified, but were not *teaching*; many had accepted the idea that poor minority students could not be expected to learn. She said:

> Nobody talked about curriculum; they only told me war stories, but they liked those kids. . . . they spent a lot of time rapping, but not much time on task.

Her vision of staff development as a central thrust in school improvement had been influenced by work with John Goodlad of the University of California at Los Angeles earlier in her training and career. It entailed creating a true partnership with staff, empowering teachers, and expanding their own vision of what is possible.

Mosely also had a process vision of how to get there: first try to work on school climate (both the physical plant and discipline), then move to staff climate — which included creating high expectations for students and improved classroom management and teaching strategies, along with increased excitement about teaching.

Her vision was strongly in keeping with the effective schools literature. Key concepts were embodied in a poster visible in many places
around the school, called "A Changing School." It listed four "very
observable climates in a school that is moving toward excellence": physical climate (cleanliness, good maintenance, etc.); academic climate (for
example, "expectations are high but reasonable, and failure is tolerat-
ed"); organizational climate ("students know how to influence school
policy and believe that they can"); and social-emotional climate ("effective schools anticipate student needs and fill them with fanfare"). It
concludes with a key statement.

> The creation of a school culture is more dependent upon the behavior
> of adults in the school than on characteristics of students or economic
> climates of the community in which the school is located.

Her first step was to work on campus climate and restore pride.
Graffiti were removed (and subsequently re-removed at 6 AM when they
re-appeared), and the school was repainted from its institutional green.
Rules were tightened, and discipline was enforced, firmly but humane-
ly, with backup assistance from the district (temporary out-transfer of
rule violators, and redrawing of attendance areas to exclude a rival
gang), and internal changes as well (elimination of in-school suspension,
and addition of Saturday work days for those who accumulated detention points). A closed campus was established, and free or study periods
eliminated.

Once rules were in place and the fact that the school meant business was clear, the students were back in class. It was easier than teachers and administrators had thought it would be. Now it was quiet, and
teachers could teach. The need was to reinforce teaching as a priority,
and get teachers the required assistance.

There was resistance: Teachers complained that "you're too hard on
them; you don't know our kids; they're poor, they need job skills." But
Mosely said, "'Poor' and 'dumb' are not spelled the same." She was
convinced that the teachers had low expectations for students, but
didn't know it.

In the second year, 1981–82, staff development work began in ear-
nest. Superintendent Evans had obtained funding for Instructional Resource Teachers, and three IRT's worked closely with Mosely from the
beginning to create a staff development plan.

A critical event was a spring retreat attended by 24 volunteers, both
teachers and administrators. It focused on goal setting: desired student
outcomes, and qualities of students, teachers, and administrators that

were needed to achieve them. The retreat also worked on strategies, including more time-on-task, diversified teaching methods, assertive discipline, and workshops on both generalized strategies (critical thinking, cooperative learning) and subject areas (teaching writing, special math programs).

During the 1982–83 school year, staff development became an integral part of the school, and a cadre of core "believers" began to grow. Teachers began talking with each other more about teaching. As one person noted: "Teachers are lonely: When doors are open, curriculum change really happens." In February and May of that year, there were department leaders' retreats to identify and develop the skills they needed, including group dynamics and managing meetings. Further retreats in the summer and fall of 1983 led to the creation of a partnership with UCLA (five schools in the district), which support a project called IMPACT (Improving methods, programs, and classroom techniques) that focused on critical thinking in math, reading, and language arts; the partnership also worked on special education issues.

During 1983–84, retreats worked on learning and teaching modalities, reviewed the UCLA partnership, and identified ways to continue supporting and empowering the staff and expand school renewal. Mentor Teachers were funded. There was a great deal of in-house staff training and development, carried out in quarterly all-day sessions and bimonthly one-hour sessions. Groupings deliberately included a mix of highly motivated with less-involved teachers. There was an immense range of topics, including special education/mainstream relationships, computer use, guidance counseling, outcome-based education, critical thinking, a new math program, phonology and writing, composition, learning styles, inquiry skills, ESL resources, coaching methods, business education, test taking, substance abuse, physical fitness, self-esteem, and world cultures. Advanced placement courses were added to the curriculum, and workshops conducted for teaching them. These initiatives and others continued during 1984–85.

The MIRT team grew from three to nine. They continued to meet monthly to plan. They brainstormed on ways to improve the environment of teaching and decided which strategies to promote. They developed areas of expertise for delivering in-service (cooperative learning, use of communications, computers, etc.). Though some outside assistance was received from the UCLA partnership, consultants for other research-based innovations, and the district and county office, most of the expertise required was developed and delivered within the school.

Teacher empowerment began to pervade the school as teachers took on more and more responsibility for school improvement through SIP

and the staff development efforts. The process was forcefully led by
Mosely, but she was a strong and confident enough leader to share
power and "let go"; like the superintendent, she believed in staff ownership of change.

All MIRT members were also trained in clinical supervision (Made-
line Hunter's Professional Development Process), and used PDP techniques to observe and coach other teachers. In the following year vice-
principals and department chairs not on the MIRT team were also
trained in PDP. The underlying approach was labeled "modeling": District office personnel served as models for changes, the principal "modeled" enthusiasm for learning, and teachers modeled changes for other
teachers and students. As a result student involvement has pervaded the
school as well, not only through their empowerment as decision makers
on the SIP Site Council, but in more informal ways, abetted by a school
culture that supports communication and sharing. Students relate to
staff with ease, informing teachers and administrators of their views.

Problems in Staff Development and How They Were Coped with

Concern for time demands ("overcircuiting") was a problem (to the
point that four or five teachers, by mutual consent, left the school). But
the attitudinal issue was deeper: A core of teachers (variously estimated
at 10 to 30%) resisted, feeling threatened by the changes (as Mosely said,
they felt MIRT members were saying, "unless it was a new way it was not
a good way"). Some felt they were "unloved" and unappreciated, or that
the approaches were irrelevant. As might be expected, the Mentor
Teachers' special status was resented ("too big for their britches . . . too
ambitious"), and there were difficulties with the clinical supervision
roles of department chairs. In 1985 Mosely fired a coach, and a crisis
rose, fueled by some English department members who felt her leadership was heavy-handed, and that the staff had been "pushed too far."

These problems were often coped with structurally: schedule
changes to allow for more staff development and meeting time while
student rallies were being held; use of budgets for substitutes for MIRT
members and department chairs; and special deployment of staff. Mosely was good at getting the district to let her reallocate budget lines for
retreats. Her message to staff was, "Do whatever you can to make things
better; don't worry about the money. I'll take care of it." The resistant
staff problem was the hardest. Some staff were encouraged to leave; the
SIP coordinator or others served as "buffers" between Mosely and some
staff. But mostly the coping strategy was to target attention to those
already active, and those at the margin, ready to buy into the process.

Resistant teachers were not overtly pressured to change, and some who were considered less effective with low-income students were assigned primarily to college preparation or advanced placement courses.

In general, Mosely did not capitalize on the existing staff collegiality (she never had a "TGIF party," as she once mused) to defuse the tension and fatigue that was building up in the frenetic pace of activity. And the "crisis" was never quite resolved while she was principal: Mosely was reassigned to another school in the summer of 1985. But she felt the changes would continue, saying, "Leadership is no longer in the office, it is in the [staff] ranks." But she also felt that unless the crisis were resolved "by those who made the crisis, there will not be institutional change."

Preliminary Results

Looking first at implementation, it appeared that sip had reached a steady state and was a smoothly functioning, accepted, integral part of the school. It seemed likely to continue as long as funding remained available, but vigilance would be required to avoid the "potpourri" scenario.

As of 1986, staff development and instructional revitalization were well implemented at Alameda. Teacher-planned and delivered in-service was a fact of life at the school. All staff were affected, since they had to attend—even though not all had bought in to the process. The extent of the new techniques and information was broad and deep. Most staff had internalized new techniques and information. There was strong impact in Social Studies and Home Economics, moderate in Math and Science, mixed in English, and low in Industrial Arts and Business. All administrators had been trained in clinical supervision.

But the program had in some ways developed a life of its own. The MIRT team members were "always brainstorming . . . always talking about the pyramid of heightened awareness," one administrator said with some frustration at the abstractness implied. Some MIRT teachers were away from their own classes so much (though a cap was placed on days out of class) that they could have been losing sight of the program's concrete objectives: improved teaching by themselves and others, and student academic excitement and achievement. And the percentage of marginal or non-involved teachers was no smaller, and could have been growing. There was some feeling of an ebb after the flow of energy in 1983 and 1984.

Despite these potential problems, the norm of focus on instruction and staff development seemed well established at Alameda. The future was promising, though a bit uncertain. The new principal, Carl Jones, was well liked; he was a calm and skillful problem solver with strong instructional priorities—but was less forceful than the "white tornado." His style was to facilitate; he tended to rely on the MIRT team and department chairs to continue the patterns of staff development and instructional leadership that were set in preceding years. A new superintendent with unknown priorities was coming, and it was not clear whether the well-launched improvement effort would withstand a substantial change in priorities or leadership.

What can we say about the results achieved, as of 1986? There was a clearly improved school climate: Alameda was functioning in an orderly, effective way. Teachers communicated with each other and the administration freely, with little "we–they" feeling. Teachers, both individually and through the MIRT team, SIP site council and coordinator, and department chairships, had a lot of influence on school operations. The school's problem-solving, planning, and innovative capacity had all strengthened considerably. There was more interdepartmental cooperation. Most important, teachers felt revitalized. A teacher who returned from a leave of absence said, "I couldn't believe it: This is what I went into teaching to do." Another teacher who joined in 1985 said he found "peer pressure to teach." Being a "ditto" teacher who hands out work sheets and gives instructions was looked down on. Expectations for students were higher, especially in advanced placement and college preparatory courses.

Basically, there was a strong focus on teaching, and on academic subjects, where enrollment had increased. Not surprisingly, test scores had risen substantially, as had attendance, which rose from 75% to 92%. Students going on to post-secondary education went from about 50% to 75%.

As early as 1983, math achievement was at the 78th percentile, and reading 63rd. (Recall that equivalent scores in 1979 were under the 20th percentile). That year, Alameda was one of four high schools recognized by the Department of Education as a model school for its improvement and excellence. We should note that these outcomes were less strong for low achievers and less academically oriented students, however.

And we should also note a "peaking" effect. As of 1986, attendance was slightly down to 89 percent, and achievement was lower, though not to the 50th percentile.

But we can say that Alameda High School had become a school again. Its faculty were engaged and delivering; its students were learning more. There may not have been strong institutional change, but as

Ms. Mosely put it, it was a "good fix." Could its excitement and results continue? That remained to be seen.

Epilogue

What did things look like two years later at Alameda? We returned to look at what had happened, the status of the change effort, and what its results turned out to be like. And we wanted to understand something of why all this had happened.

Subsequent Events and Changes

Several important events occurred between 1986 and 1988. Carl Jones was transferred to the central office as Director of Personnel in the fall of 1987, and an outsider to the district, George Latif, was appointed. A self-study of the school was conducted to meet the requirements for a Program Quality Review as stipulated for schools receiving sip, Chapter 1, and compensatory education funds.

There were also changes in the central office, which had enjoyed a long period of stability until 1986. The new superintendent, who arrived in the fall of 1986 supporting Evans' policies, resigned in 1987 after a controversy with the board over the selective University Prep School in the district. His successor also stayed only a year, during which the district suffered severe state and local financial cutbacks that cut seriously into the district support for curriculum development activities. A new superintendent arrived in the summer of 1988, and Alameda staff are uncertain what his priorities will be. Cara Mosely, who came to the central office as a special assistant to the superintendent in 1987, became Director of Elementary and Secondary Education.

During 1986–87, as anticipated, the momentum of staff development and the staff sense of professionalism and participation continued, but at a somewhat reduced level. Carl Jones, who was seen as a "maintenance principal," was rotated out of the school faster than the typical five-year cycle. Latif, who had been recommended by people close to Cara Mosely, seemed more in keeping with her tradition of strong principal leadership and staff empowerment. He has reset the momentum: The sip coordinator notes that "the teachers have grown tremendously . . . [he has] tapped into the professionalism of the staff." Most are involved in peer coaching, teaming, and working together as a unit. Curriculum emphasis is increasing. Latif has also instituted some structural changes, including decentralization of decisions and budgets to departments. He says, "You can't have empowerment without the tools."

How the Program Stands Now

Staff development decisions have been moved from the MIRT team to the departments (at the team's suggestion). The MIRT members may act as facilitators or assisters to departments, however, and there are frequent cross-department efforts in areas such as Writing Across the Curriculum and use of computers. More recently, Career Infusion across departments has been initiated.

The principal has also established a leadership group more broadly based than the cabinet: a steering committee of 30 Key Planners, "thinking people working together." It includes administrators, coordinators, all department chairs (who are teachers), MIRT team members, guidance staff, coordinators, and the president of the SIP Site Council. The Key Planners group makes policy decisions and steers their implementation. For example, when the California Assessment of Progress scores went down, they mounted an intensive campaign the next year to motivate the senior class through "adoptions," slogans, a breakfast, and test score improvement advice.

The SIP committee is no longer a decision-making body that directs curriculum change through the power to distribute funds, but is an advisory group recommending programs; curriculum leadership is now in the hands of the principal and departments. SIP funds now flow differently. One-half are allocated on an enrollment basis to all departments, to enable them to implement activities according to the SIP plan. The other half goes as before to specific proposals, which are reviewed by the Site Council, which makes recommendations to Latif. The final decision on awards is made by the Key Planners and principal.

Outcomes

The self-study for the Program Quality Review had the effect of consolidating the staff by providing a focus of joint activity, mostly on curriculum issues. The major strengths found in the study included a strong and cohesive staff, peer-oriented leadership, open lines of communication among teachers and between teachers and administrators, and the use of varied instructional techniques (more small-group work, less lecturing) in many departments. In general, the school has a strong, committed, and satisfied staff.

But the study also located weaknesses: The school is often inconsistent in how it implements curriculum, and more coordination and articulation are needed. Further, despite the high level of staff engagement, the school is not moving further toward consistent and desired results with students. Attendance and dropout rates continue at 1986 levels, and achievement levels are sometimes disappointing. These worrisome trends are particularly evident for the middle/average and below-average students, who are typically from the Hispanic population at Alameda. The school, after its earlier meteoric rise, has experienced decline in scores on the twelfth grade California Assessment of Progress — even allowing for the fact that some of the school's percentile ranking drop was affected by a change in technical rating procedures.

A major thrust of the coming year is to tackle these issues and to foster a link between teacher engagement and student engagement, focusing especially on the "neglected" part of the student population. Plans for increased parent support and community involvement are under way.

Why Did This Happen? A Reflective Review

We turn from the descriptive account to the question of explanation. Why did Alameda achieve as much success with implementation as it did? And what led to the outcomes achieved?

Why This Implementation?

The implementation process seems to have gone as it did at Alameda for many reasons. State funding, augmented by some university resources, was doubtless important as a foundation. But many California districts have used SIP and IRT funds with little impact, and weak school–university linkages are quite typical. Furthermore, the funding was not especially munificent — only a fraction of what was spent at our sites Chester and Bartholdi, where far less was accomplished.

Most of the credit probably should go to the leadership and management strategies within the school, and the ways in which they carried district policies the extra mile. In particular, we might mention the local synergism of a fairly willing and ready staff, the visionary leadership of the principal, and the use of outside resources.

The congruent, active support of the superintendent, and the atmosphere where practical negotiation could occur and disagreements be aired suggested the importance of a good mix of top-down and school-based power. Furthermore, the district provided buffers and safety valves (for example, removing disruptive students, providing an alternative school).

Mosely's leadership was extremely strong, but empowering; she was unafraid to share authority, power, and influence. That was another point of congruence with superintendent Evans' leadership, and it led to a system where teachers were both empowered and well utilized. (Perhaps it is no coincidence that both district and school administrative staffs are rather lean and non-bureaucratic.) The basic idea was an expansion of the leadership pie, rather than the struggle of a zero-sum game where the assumption is that giving others power means losing it yourself.

Coupled with this style were certain cultural expectations on Mosely's part: a willingness to take risks, apply pressure, and even be unpopular; a combination of confident demands and humaneness; and the sense that the only barriers are "no expected outcomes" and "low expectations." In effect, her style, like that of the superintendent, combined vision, support, and pressure.

Both SIP and MIRT fit well with the school's prior culture. SIP was "democratic," and brought together the full range of constituencies, including students. And they fit with the principal's vision of outcomes and processes to get there. She was faced with a warmed-up audience from the first mobilizing year of SIP, and both SIP and MIRT empowered people further, and moved quickly to generate early rewards — SIP benefits included materials, aides, and even campus beautification, very early on — and heightened enthusiasm, commitment, and willingness to go further. Broad-based ownership was the goal, and though it was not wholly achieved, the critical mass was large enough for real movement to occur.

We should also note the importance of managing diverse strands of improvement. The SIP Site Council and the MIRT team, which had overlapping membership, both served as centers of coordination and orchestration. The SIP office was a hub of the renewal effort; its coordinator did a great deal to tie together curriculum, testing, and teaching strategies. And principal Mosely was actively involved in both groups. (We can speculate that Jones' leaving more initiative to SIP and MIRT during his year was associated with weaker implementation and outcomes — but it may also be that the improvement effort simply needed a resting plateau, as we suggest below.)

Why the Outcomes?

We could argue that Alameda's population was reasonably "manageable," because there was a mix of less- and more-advantaged students, and a range of ethnic groups. Perhaps — but many such schools are not doing well.

More centrally, the fact that SIP was well implemented ensured a flow of resources, and teacher empowerment was enhanced. The MIRT implementation extended empowerment, and brought both concrete curriculum ideas and new instructional strategies into the hands of teachers. Given the reasonable stabilization of school climate that supported more teaching emphasis, the teachers could — and did — deliver.

It also seems likely that the enthusiasm and energy that peaked in 1984 and 1985 played an important part in sustaining momentum — the momentum that began with the moves on rules and discipline to bring more order to the school, and was picked up and boosted by the big staff retreat and the intensive staff development thrust. But peaks also imply valleys. Perhaps the reduced, plateau-like level of outcome after 1985 was an organizational response to the "overcircuiting," and the tensions between "true believers" and "resisters" among the faculty. School improvement needs resting phases between those of high energy.

Alameda, like Agassiz, is a success story, with some notable similarities to Agassiz (the sustained work over several years, visionary leadership, a collegial cadre with shared humanistic values, willingness to make structural changes when needed, assertive garnering of resources, for example). But there were also some interesting differences: Mosely was more of a charismatic pusher than Mark Cohen; teacher empowerment and instructional improvement went faster through SIP and the MIRT team than through the special projects and department work at Agassiz; the flow of outside funds was more predictable at Alameda; direct attention to classroom issues at Alameda paid off faster in terms of teacher mobilization and change. But we do not know if the less-flamboyant, slower-going process at Agassiz will get further over the long haul than the high-energy, somewhat principal-dependent work at Alameda. We'll need another epilogue to see.

Next we turn to two schools with somewhat less success, Bartholdi and Burroughs. They worked hard and began to achieve hoped-for outcomes, but neither got as far as our "A" sites. Once again, we invite the reader to reflect on *why*.

NOTES

1. Anthony Cipollone was co-author of the original case on which this version is based (Louis & Cipollone, 1986). Quotations in this report are drawn directly from the case.

2. For a fuller description of the Boston Compact experience, see Farrar & Cipollone (1988) and Farrar (1988).

3. This report is adapted with additions from the original case study (Rosenblum, 1986). Quotations in this report are drawn directly from the case.

5

Struggling and Improving

MATTHEW B. MILES   ELEANOR FARRAR

We continue our case accounts with a look at two schools, Bartholdi and Burroughs, where the improvement efforts, while moderately effective, were not quite as successful as at Agassiz and Alameda. People put serious energy into changing these high schools, and they began to see improvements in morale, classroom teaching, and student outcomes. But more was needed. We think a careful description of what happened will help clarify what is important about school improvement efforts. What's the difference between a clear and a partial success? And what explains that difference?

BARTHOLDI HIGH SCHOOL: REACHING AT–RISK STUDENTS

These kids need warmth, love, stroking . . . they're sweet kids who won't cuss you out in English.

When I sat in on the cabinet, I felt like a flounder in a shark tank.

Coming together is a beginning.
Staying together is an accomplishment.
Working together is a success.   [motto in principal's office]

This is a story of a high school beginning to move. New York's Auguste Bartholdi High School,[1] named for the creator of the Statue of Liberty, has 2,360 students, of whom 70 percent are Hispanic (mainly Latin American and Puerto Rican), and 29 percent are black.

Bartholdi has not been performing well; student achievement has been weak, attendance marginal, and dropout rates high. Many faculty are discouraged by the size of the remedial task they face. But there has been movement, and staff say the school is "coming back," doing better, "has a lot of life"; only a few say it's going downhill. Even so, dramatic change is still to come.

The improvement effort at Bartholdi centers around a well-funded dropout reduction program called CASA (Caring Action for Student Aid) that delivers extra services to an at-risk population of about 300 students (long-term absentees, and those seriously underperforming), with the hope that curricular and procedural changes will ramify outward to the school as a whole.

This case study begins with the story of how CASA was implemented during its startup year in 1985–86. Two years later, there is evidence of well-carried-out sub-programs ranging from a Job Corps to tutoring, attendance enhancement, new remedial courses, and intensive case-work services — all managed by a cohesive group of administrators and teachers. Security is better, dropouts are down somewhat, and school climate is more upbeat. As one administrator said, "It's better than cautious optimism." But improvement in academic achievement is still to come.

How did the work at Bartholdi come this far, and why hasn't it been even more successful? The rest of this case looks at these questions.

A Picture of the School in 1985

Bartholdi High School is a six-story brick building put up in 1912 that looms over a neighborhood of two- and three-family tenements, sprinkled with vacant lots. After extensive blockbusting real estate activity in the '60s, and insurance redlining, many buildings were burned in the '70s. The population is now mostly Hispanic and West Indian black.

Street crime is high. When David Martinez, the present principal, came to the school on his first day in 1981, he walked out to find his car's battery stolen. There's a wry saying at the school that new teachers in New York are allowed to refuse only two assignments: to Riker's Island (a prison) and Bartholdi.

The school is a warren of cramped departmental offices and class-rooms, showing their age. There is an occasional kicked-out door panel, missing floor tile, or vandalized bulletin board, but the rooms are reasonably well kept.

As of November 1985 there are 2,360 students officially enrolled. But only 1,700 or so students actually attend on a given day — and the register dwindles over the year (by June it was 1,911). Even so, they and the over 170 staff strain the facilities (to 138% of capacity). A former annex closed in 1984, flooding the school with at-risk students. Unused rooms are rare (though home economics and many shops often lie empty when they could be valuable for Bartholdi students).

The Bartholdi staff characterize the kids as "good," with only a few disruptive ones. They're "horribly deprived" (91% on public assistance, much unemployment), "upwardly mobile but not hostile," "sweet kids who won't cuss you out in English." They "have low self-expectations." Many people mentioned their "need for warmth, love . . . stroking," and their willingness to do service work in school or community—but not, someone noted, anything academic. Most come in with severe academic weaknesses from poor feeder schools; many have unstable home situations with parents who "don't stay on the kids' butts." Parent involvement is weak in spite of the school's efforts. The principal, returning this year from a neighborhood walk, was appalled, saying, "This [the school] is heaven, a kingdom, by comparison. You wouldn't believe how our kids live."

There is a range of teachers, from those inexperienced and new to the school (31% because of recent turnover) to those with moderate to substantial experience (a third have been at Bartholdi more than a decade). As is usual in New York, teacher and student ethnicity do not match: 70% of teachers are white, 18% black, and 11% Hispanic. Several teachers and some students mentioned the cultural distance between them.

People in the school say that "it's a staff you can't beat for dedication," and that "we have a special sense of community." Many do care about students' welfare. But the teaching is said to range from boring to superb, and "morale is not great," given the frustrations of working with low-performing kids and the reluctance of many faculty to do remediation. Though some teachers watch for hallway incidents and intervene constructively, more than a few ignore them.

It's also said that the same handful of people are always tapped for change projects, then "run ragged." The attitude of many others is said to be, "It's a job. Why should I cooperate?" There is a long history of lack of follow-through on proposed changes, and the typical attitude is "wait and see."

Some of the Bartholdi culture can be inferred from a look at the faculty handbook, where 51 pages cover bureaucratic rules, and only 9 cover "instructional suggestions"—which are defined as departmental matters. In spite of all the rules, one person commented that the school is "very disorganized," with many problems of coordination. Another called it "a Rube Goldberg machine."

As in most New York City high schools, there is an assistant principal (A.P.) for administration and one for guidance; there are 8 A.P.'s who supervise the 12 subject-matter departments. The well-experienced A.P.'s, who vary from "entrenched" to able and energetic, are charged with observing and supporting teachers, developing curriculum, and completing assorted paperwork. Their offices are typically crowded with students and teachers, chaotic and noisy, with paper piled on most available surfaces.

They and principal Martinez meet regularly as a cabinet, but with a meeting style that varies from "complaining" to "plodding" to "crisis management." There are some competitive overtones; one CASA team member visiting a cabinet meeting reported feeling "like a flounder in a shark tank." Still, cabinet meetings are said to be getting better.

David Martinez had a difficult entry to the school four years ago (the faculty had hoped for an internal promotion). But he stayed and has strengthened his position. He is seen by some as energetic, "working his heart out," forthright and honest, willing to reach out for help, child-oriented, caring, and supportive. He is also described as inexperienced, being too cautious, "forgetting things," not following through on decisions, and not seeing the forest for the trees. But during the three years covered by this case study, he actively supported improvement efforts and provided constructive school leadership.

Bartholdi is a comprehensive, non-specialized high school; the courses range from remedial-level to "regular," with a smattering of honors courses. Students are sorted into a range of levels: college-bound (13%); business, "mainstream" (37%); the remaining 50% are in bilingual, remedial, co-op, and special education.

There are few extra-curricular activities and no supporting structure for clubs. The athletic program is seen as mediocre by many staff, and student attendance at sports events, especially basketball, is forbidden city-wide because of a history of fights between competing teams; thus the knitting function of sports, like that of clubs, is absent.

There is much evidence that the school has not been performing well. Student achievement is weak; failure rates on math competency tests in 1984–85 ranged from 67% for ninth graders down to 33% for eleventh graders. Reading competency failure for eleventh graders was 44%, and writing 53%.

Between 43 and 59 percent of regular students have failing course grades, many of them because of absences and cuts. Figures for special needs students are higher. Over half of students at all grade levels taking Regents' course exams failed them in both the first and second terms of 1985–86.

Attendance percentages have been running in the high 60s to low 70s for the past five years. The figures often drop to the 50s and 60s in January, when students go "back to the islands" with their families.

Considering student behavior, staff say there is a hard core of 25 to 50 bad, disruptive kids. There were about 250 principal (5-day) suspensions in 1984–85, mostly for fighting, and 35 superintendent (indefinite) suspensions, often for weapons. About 2,000 "pink cards" for severe infractions are written yearly, which averages out to about a dozen a day. There's agreement among teachers and administrators that there should be better hall control of students and improved security.

Student–faculty relations, however, are reported as fairly positive, with occasional instances of disrespect on both sides. Still, a researcher noted:

> When I asked a group of tenth grade "mainstream" students what they liked about the school, the first response was "When it's time to leave," followed by "free periods," "friends," "talent show," and "softball teams." Though they acknowledged that some teachers "were nice, helped," there were many complaints: "teachers too slow or too fast," "bad attitude to students," and "boring old books," "counselor mistakes," "no activities," "student troublemaking," "same lunch every day," and "students have no say-so."

The actual dropout rate is 17 to 18 percent *annually* (the official figure last year was 13.6%).[2] Of 1,000 ninth graders, perhaps 500 to 600 drop out by twelfth year (the city-wide rate is 42%). Last year there were only 189 graduating seniors, in a school of over 2,000 students. Of those seniors, 31 percent went on to college (nearly half of them to two-year colleges), and only 10 percent were known by the school to be employed. For over half of the seniors, no post-graduation data were available.

The Context

We need to look at Bartholdi's context — the city, school system, and state — and at its historical context as well, if we are to understand current events.

The City and School District

New York City is . . . well, New York City. It's a place where eight million people live their daily lives, and which countless other millions find "a nice place to visit, but. . . . " Immense wealth, aesthetic energy, and cosmopolitanism are juxtaposed with homelessness, racism, AIDS, drug-related violence, a decaying infrastructure, and almost all other known social problems. New Yorkers, including the educators who work there, are fond of believing that there is no place on earth just like New York, and that recipes from anywhere else don't apply there.

New York City has the largest school system in the country, including 609 elementary schools under decentralized control in 32 districts, 179 intermediate schools, and a central office staff of about 4,500. The 111 high schools are sorted into the jurisdictions of five borough high school superintendents. An executive director of high schools in the central office is directly accountable to the chancellor.

Chancellor Macchiarola (1980–83), in a strong effort to improve high schools, moved out over half of the high school principals; his director of high schools, Nathan Quinones, instituted a renewal program based on organization development (OD) principles, and later a "management by objectives" program that stressed accountability. In 1984 Quinones succeeded Macchiarola's successor, Anthony Alvarado, who was forced from office on charges of improper financial practices. There has been a good deal of turnover in upper administrative positions as well, since each chancellor tends to bring in a new team. The central office (known as "The Board," or "110 Livingston Street") is seen as responsive, but as "immensely slow."

A newly appointed special superintendent, Nelson Walters, manages a new program for dropout reduction in 10 high schools (including Bartholdi). He is accountable to the chancellor through a deputy, bypassing the executive director of high schools. A charismatic man, he was principal of the notoriously difficult Goldman High School and had turned it around dramatically. Walters has been vigorous in creating and promoting the program, mobilizing private-sector support, and keeping the program visible in the media.

It's important to remember that severe budget cuts occurred during the city's fiscal crisis of 1975. Since then staffing and student activities have stayed minimal. Schools are said to be "skeletons" of what they should be. However, mayor Ed Koch's 1985 campaign for re-election stressed transit and schools, and he added $10 million to the state's $1 million devoted to intensive dropout reduction.

High schools in the city are considerably restricted by central office regulations. For example, neither the principal nor department chairs at Bartholdi have official authority over teacher hiring; they are expected to accept whoever appears from the central office, even if, as one person complained, they seem like "bag ladies." (To some extent, an aggressive A.P. can succeed in refusing a new teacher, or in disposing of one with temporary per diem [TPD] status.) Teacher prep periods, new-teacher orientation, and many other matters are centrally controlled and governed by union contract.

The borough superintendent's office does not specify curriculum — the state does — but the superintendent visits Bartholdi and monitors the performance of A.P.'s. He has pressed for improved attendance and achievement, and gives positive feedback about the school's tone and its efforts to be less of a "problem school." However, the principal sometimes feels caught between two bosses: the borough superintendent, who has authority, and dropout superintendent Walters, who provides funds. They are not always in close communication.

The State

New York State schools are not doing as well as they should. The dropout rate (37.8% from ninth grade to graduation) is the fifth highest of the 50 states, and SAT scores have slipped to mid-level, in spite of the fact that per-pupil expenditures are the second highest in the country. The poor results may stem from high immigration, transiency, poverty, and unemployment rates in New York City — which has one-third of the schools in the state — but whatever the causes, improvement action is needed.

The state has always emphasized school quality through its Board of Regents, which specifies curricula and grants diplomas based on state examinations. The five-year Regents' Action Plan went into operation in 1985. It includes increased course requirements and competency testing. School districts must also develop discipline policies, do annual staff performance evaluations, do an annual competency assessment report, and develop a Comprehensive School Improvement Plan (CSIP) if they show up in the bottom 10 percent across the state on reading, math, writing, dropouts, and attendance. The plan must focus on effective schools factors such as academic goals, student monitoring, order and discipline, and positive school climate. But state funds cover only 18 percent of the estimated costs of the plan, and little assistance is provided.

As it turned out in November 1985, 72 New York high schools fell in the bottom 10 percent category. Bartholdi was among the 30 seen as needing most attention.

Teacher and administrator unions are historically powerful in New York, so improvement efforts must typically be contract-congruent. At Bartholdi, such problems have been rare; the principal and the chapter chair work well together.

Innovation History

There's been a long history of special programs at Bartholdi: work experience (1962); co-op (1967); a mini-school (late '60s); special drop-out projects and an after-school peer tutoring program (1970).

Starting in 1970, when the school still had 3,500 students, Bartholdi had a working relationship with Irving Trust through the New York City Partnership of the Economic Development Council (EDC). Executives were supplied on loan, and helped develop special programs such as peer-mediated math, and a "World of Work" program. In 1974 EDC and the Division of High Schools co-sponsored an organization development program called School Renewal. Bartholdi teachers and administrators worked in task forces to develop and implement solutions to the school's problems. Over several years, morale and communication seemed to improve, along with a sense that "teachers could do something." But enrollment and performance continued to drop.

In the fall of 1983, the chancellor chose four poorly performing schools for the first implementation of the High School Improvement Program (HISIP), an offshoot of the original elementary-level effective schools program developed by deputy chancellor Ron Edmonds. The principal and cabinet worried that they were being "set up" for a school (or annex) closing. But with reassurances, they agreed to proceed.

Two program facilitators helped a group of 33 staff, students, and parents carry out a general needs assessment. By June 1984, three task forces (administrative style, instructional emphasis/ongoing assessment, and school climate/teacher expectations) had created many plans, including redesign of truancy programs, hallway sweeps, a course failure diagnostic form, a student questionnaire, a school discipline code, an orientation for new teachers, and a mid-year pep talk assembly. In addition, a plan was proposed for block programming (several shared periods) of ninth and tenth grade chronic truants and at-risk students with courses called "Survival for the '80s" and "Social Learning," and a support team for counseling. Participants felt the work had addressed real problems (for example, the conflicts between departments), and "wasn't bullshit." Task forces regularly reported to department meetings. The principal sat in as a working member.

By the time the plan was completed, however, the Board decided to close the annex, leading to serious overcrowding in the main building and use of a staggered 10-period schedule, and, most crucially, to loss of hope in many of those who had worked on improvement plans.

Some of the plan's features were carried out during the 1984–85 school year: the discipline code, a short-lived student newsletter, a new procedure for cafeteria duty and cleanup, orientation for new teachers, allocation of a police officer to the school, an orientation program and recognition dinner for freshmen. The curriculum proposals fared less well because they were "under the domain of the A.P.'s," but one participant noted that most of the plan's emphasis had in any case been on school *order*, not on students' needs, the curriculum, or teaching methods. The hall patrols idea was dropped because it ran into union objections.

The HISIP program lost its funding and helpful facilitators in 1985. The borough superintendent never showed much interest. Task force and implementation work was hard because of rigid scheduling. Many key people in the program went on sabbatical, and attendance dwindled. "The work was like pulling teeth," one person said. The principal, who had been attending only "as a member," came less frequently. Since few A.P.'s had been involved, implementation was difficult. Other problems, like 40 job vacancies, got higher priority from the school. In effect, no one really owned the program, and there were no reprimands for not following through.

There may have been some useful residues: some sense of progress, "a start," a chance to "ventilate"; a sense of involvement in a change process; a better "tone" in the halls; increased awareness of the student failure problem; a reduction in barriers between departments as people *talked* to each other; and perhaps more attention from the central department of high schools.

The flow of prior *school-wide* change efforts (EDC, School Renewal, HISIP) often seems to have been marked by lack of successful action and follow-through. Cynicism is not intense—perhaps because expectations were modest—but optimism is not high either. Many externally supported specific programs focused on *special populations*, such as STEP (work experience), peer tutoring, SPARK (drug abuse), PREP (remedial), and College Bound, have survived, however. A recent addition involves cooperation with NYU in a tutoring program for bilingual students.

The Bartholdi Commercial Academy (BCA), a magnet program designed by the A.P. for Business Education to draw students from all over the borough, began in the fall of 1984. It now covers about 150 ninth and tenth grade students. Their attendance is high and academic performance good. The BCA experience was a programmatic change strategy that worked.

In October 1984, the director of high schools asked a retired administrator, Emanuel Samson, to come to Bartholdi two to three days a week to support and advise principal Martinez. Samson built a trusting relationship, and offered advice on such matters as scheduling, programming procedures, data needed for monitoring school performance, style of running cabinet meetings, classroom observation, and selection of A.P.'s. His primary objective was to help the principal expand his technical administrative skills, and his influence; progress appears to have been made on both counts. Some administrators believed that Samson represented the school's needs successfully to the central office. His role has continued.

As we'll see in a minute, the main improvement effort described in this report is CASA, a dropout program begun in 1985. But even after that, yet another change effort, begun late during our field work, was the Comprehensive School Improvement Plan required by the state and district. Beginning in February 1986, a planning group of two A.P.'s, eleven teachers, a counselor, a dean, the program chair, three students, and a parent met to assess the school's current functioning and prepare an improvement plan covering six areas: dropouts; reading; writing; math performance; school climate; and parent and community involvement. The plan, hastily developed under pressure, was firmed up in mid-April; participants gave it a modest to fighting chance of succeeding, depending on the commitment of A.P.'s and the principal, extra funds, and the will to follow through.

The Improvement Program

In the context we have just described, we are focusing mainly on a major improvement effort that was part of superintendent Nelson Walters' ambitious Dropout Reduction Program (DRP). It was launched in the summer of 1985. Ten low-performing high schools were invited to join, and to develop three-year proposals that would involve school-based planning teams, linkage to the private sector, employment programs, and the use of community-based organizations to provide additional support services.

A Bartholdi planning group met during the summer, and with some enthusiasm developed a proposal for a program they called CASA (Caring Action for Student Aid), which included new attendance staff and an attendance "robot," a mentoring program, a Job Corps, and intensive outreach and counseling services supplied by staff drawn from the South Street Settlement House. No private-sector linkage could be managed, but Bartholdi developed a linkage with the public-sector City Planning Department. A rewards/incentives component would provide T-shirts and calculators to students who performed well. The first year's budget totaled $539,000, covering the time of about 16.8 people, 8 of them from South Street Settlement House.

As one person said, "CASA is attendance." The program is essentially a heightened delivery of add-on services to an at-risk population of about 300 students (long-term absentees and those seriously underperforming), with the hope that curricular and procedural changes will ramify outward to the school as a whole by providing a model of what can be done to keep at-risk students in school and performing better. The program does not emphasize in-service training, and does not attempt to mobilize the whole faculty for organizational improvement; it is essentially a collection of programmatic innovations. The sequence of work is not pre-planned but evolving.

Why This Program?

The Dropout Reduction Program (DRP) designers believed that the connection to a community service organization (such as South Street) would "free the school to do what it can do best," and that a private-sector connection would attack the employment problem. The strongly programmatic emphasis was natural. Legislators and politicians, and their constituencies, usually don't think of general school organizational improvement or even skill development, but of "concrete" programs that will reach kids. Furthermore, dropout programs are easier to sell than school restructuring programs designed to improve curricula, reduce student alienation, and stop causing "pushouts." The "dropout" label focuses attention on the student, rather than on the properties of the system. (However, Superintendent Walters was also concerned with how systemic issues cause schools to lose students.)

The resources were attractive. As Martinez said, "Who would say no? If I'm drowning and a toothpick goes by, I'll grab it." People at Bartholdi were used to targeted change efforts like CASA, run by part-time or specially assigned people. Many such programs had come, and some had stayed. Perhaps this one would too. And there was a core of dedicated, still uncynical staff who wanted better things at Bartholdi.

The Story of Implementation

What happened as CASA was planned and implemented? What problems were encountered, and how were they dealt with?

Chronology

In February 1985, Bartholdi got a small-scale planning grant from DRP, and a month later Arthur Golden was appointed coordinator.

Golden, a friendly, energetic teacher, had been centrally involved in the annex's Holding Power program, and generated a memo for the DRP program using many of its ideas. Edward Ornstein, from the borough superintendent's office, was assigned as supervisor.

The summer planning team of eleven included two A.P.'s, a dean, guidance people, and several teachers, with some participation by the principal. They met for three weeks, and produced a substantial proposal with the features just described. They invented the name CASA, and ended the summer with some enthusiasm.

In the late summer, Ornstein, who was seen as a "man without a country" by Bartholdi staff, suffered a heart attack and stroke. Though Ornstein kept coming to work, Martinez asked the respected Social Studies A.P., Carole Fisher, to begin taking on his role. By February, Ornstein had been reassigned to the superintendent's office, and Fisher continued doing supervision and general coordination. Fisher is a calm, matter-of-fact, supportive person with strong abilities of coordination and orchestration.

The planning team continued periodic meetings during the year. By November, eight South Street Settlement staff members were in the school (though it had been extremely difficult to find places for them to work). Curriculum proposals were made to the cabinet. A faculty dinner was held to explain CASA (though it did not clarify the program much), and the committee developed a teacher screening form to refer at-risk students to CASA.

Walters and the Board's Curriculum and Instruction division approached the New York City Planning Department (CPD) to develop a new type of public-sector partnership. CPD responded well, proposing jobs and use of a "House Sense" curriculum they had developed. In May the formal linkage with CPD was celebrated.

By December a first awards/incentives assembly was held. In January daily attendance had been computerized, although the "robot" and ID cards were not in place until June. Thirty-four students had been placed in jobs, and students served by the various other program components increased to about 275 (the original target group had been 389). Bartholdi was treated to a visit from a CBS *60 Minutes* camera crew.

Meanwhile the state's CSIP effort had started up, with the first meeting in February and a plan produced by April. A number of the CSIP activities were in fact CASA activities, folded into the plan. A rough plan for DRP's second year was ready by June, and the planning team looked forward to the next summer institute.

The planning and change work at Bartholdi was carried out without much outside assistance. South Street and CPD were essentially delivering programs, but gave little help in the overall implementation of

CASA. During planning, help from Walters was narrowly technical (program planning and budgeting); he did not seem to have a vision of, or help with, issues in the organizational change process. During implementation, Walters or one of his staff members provided occasional advice, but initiative rested largely with the school. The coordinators from all ten schools met twice a month for information, and also had three days of training during the spring in planning, team management, and resource use. But beyond that, people were just doing the best they could, on their own. The assumption seemed to be that resources should go into *programs*, not external assistance—that appointing good *people* should somehow obviate the need for support. Yet Bartholdi people said they would have liked more help. Carole Fisher's integrative work, and coordinator Arthur Golden's troubleshooting, "firefighting," and external representation of the school were the main internal assistance sources.

A few people from the Board, and from CPD, did help with curriculum development efforts. And we should not forget the support provided to the principal by Manny Samson, though it predated CASA.

Problems and How They Were Coped With

CASA work was problem-rich. Many problems came from the *context*: lack of space; conflicting agendas (with vocational and special education, and other programs); lack of legitimate power for change in the CASA group, along with uneven support from the powerful A.P.'s (there was real CASA hesitancy to "reorganize the school" or get into curriculum, scheduling, or the issue of the unused shops); lack of the process skills of effective group and organizational functioning (poor meetings, unresolved conflicts, weak planning). Some of these continued right through later implementation.

Other problems came from the design and operation of the CASA *program* as such: the Catch-22 problem and the hard-to-reach kids that CASA was aiming at, coordination weakness, and overload. Many of these were present throughout the year as well.

The Catch-22 problem was a bundle of dilemmas. If long-term absent (LTA) students were discharged, attendance figures would improve, but dropout rates would get worse. If LTA students were kept on the rolls in an effort to reach them through CASA, attendance would look worse though dropout rates would look better—though they might not in fact *be* any better. Thus a "game" was typically played with attendance figures. Both the district superintendent and the attendance secretary tended to want to discharge LTA students, but the CASA staff tended to want to keep the students. So, "we yell at each other a lot," people said. And—another irony—as one person said, "Suppose we get a lot of them back in. What is there here for them?"

The second problem was an irony too: Since CASA dealt with hard-to-reach kids, they were hard to reach, and thus didn't receive program services. Only 5 of 51 incentive awards went to CASA kids. Attendance was poorest in CASA—it has run from 41 to 53 percent in various months this year. (The school-wide average is 73 to 80%.)

The problem of coordination had at least three aspects. First, CASA had entered a school with many existing programs for the same general population (SPARK, PREP, STEP, co-op, support services, and so on). The summer proposal said these functions "needed to be redefined and a management structure developed," but that did not happen. Second, CASA had internal relations to deal with (which kids would get what services, and how these would be tracked). And third, CASA strained the existing school functions (attendance, programming, guidance, cutting, discipline), and constantly had to be aligned with the routine work of those functions, but there was much isolation and poor communication. One administrator said, "We need someone who understands the whole thing, the big picture, and has power." Paradoxically, as CASA succeeded in delivering more and more services, the problems of overload, conflict, and coordination became more pronounced.

Many of the problems were embedded in the school's organization. The CASA program bumped into the existing school procedures for guidance, attendance, cutting, and programming—which even before CASA were said to be inefficient, conflicting, and uncoordinated. As CASA put added stress on these procedures, it pointed up their problems, making people feel defensive. Furthermore, the more successful CASA was in reducing dropouts, the more stress increased, because there were more at-risk students to deal with.

Overload was occasionally severe: Key people felt overwhelmed with problems, resources to manage, paperwork, meetings. Carole Fisher had only a period a day for CASA work, and often took work home. People said, "It would have gone down the tubes without her." Arthur Golden's desk usually had a blizzard of paper obscuring it. Most people except for the South Street staff were also teaching or supervising, and did CASA work in extra periods or "per-session" time.

How did people cope with these problems? Most coping efforts were focused on *technical* program issues. Space was juggled; a screening form was designed to reduce coordination problems; a new system was created to record class cuts. Emphasis was on day-to-day survival, putting fires out, improvising. Some coping was *political*, aimed at negotiating bargains and agreements: regular reporting of CASA events

to the cabinet, with efforts to get their approval; blocking the attendance office's discharge efforts and getting the right of final approval
over discharges for CASA; South Street's pressuring of the principal to get
space. Most rarely, there was *cultural* coping, addressing symbolic issues
and the life of the school. The faculty dinner was such an event, as were
regular printed updates supplied to the faculty by Carole Fisher, which
created a sense of progress, movement, and involvement.

But the coping efforts often seemed brief, scattered, and infrequent. There was a lot of "on-the-spot" improvisation, solving specific
problems day by day, one to one, and disorganization as well. For
example, student awardees were called at home the night before the
ceremony, although it had been known for weeks that awards would be
made.

Though many of the problems were organizational, there seemed
to be no one skilled in *organizing* (as contrasted with improvisational
coping), which made overload even worse. And there seemed to be no
legitimated way to deal with problems. There was much uncertainty as
to whether the problems could in fact be resolved — or by whom.[3]

As the year went on, coping became deeper and more active (creation of the screening committee, attendance books, and a new cutting
scheme, along with more frequent meetings of the steering committee,
and so on). Many underlying problems were not resolved, however, and
too much seemed to depend on Carole Fisher.

The CASA program contained little built-in motivation to do things
better. Irrespective of the substantial dedication and energy of the people implementing it, CASA was often viewed as little more than a source
of extra resources, or as just a way for Bartholdi to look a little better to
the world.

Preliminary Results

How good was CASA implementation? As one observer said, "Considering what they were up against, it's pretty good." The CASA program
put into place most of its key components, and didn't trivialize them.
Across all services, a total of 227 students were involved. The South
Street case management work covered 110 students, and was strong
("Six people seemed like 16."); the Job Corps placements were well
carried out for 110 students, and basic procedures for referring students
to CASA were in place — though ambiguity and uncertainty about attendance and programming were only gradually reducing. There were 25
CASA classes involving 14 teachers in 10 subjects. Thus the program did
not have a very wide impact on the school, except through its atten-

dance component. But CASA was accepted, and was said to have increased its foothold, with key people more willing to work together on it. The original proposal was quite ambitious, aiming to ripple through the whole school; implementing that hope is just beginning.

The likelihood of program continuation after the money would run out was weak to moderate. Though the classes, attendance machine, and block programming might stay, most of the other components were add-on services that most people thought would go when the money stopped ("The Board discontinues programs that work."). And there was a sense that too much depends on the continued efforts of Fisher and Golden.

Key Bartholdi planners believed that in comparison with the other nine DRP high schools, Bartholdi did a better job with its community-based organization (started faster, got excellent services), made a better connection with the principal and at least some A.P.'s, got block programming in place, and got its attendance machine working. Those judgments may reflect local pride — but that itself says something about accomplishments.

What outcomes did CASA get? As one person remarked, "Not becoming worse is good," and very few people said that Bartholdi had gotten worse this year. The CASA people said that things had gone far better this school year than last. At the same time, one key CASA person had doubts about the real impact of the program: Services had been delivered, but what was the result? "There's a bottomless pit, and we had high expectations."

In general, there appear to have been weak to moderate, sometimes uncertain, changes on most of the hoped-for outcomes, given the earliness in implementation. For example, program ownership and cross-department communication and collaboration had improved only slightly. It's not clear whether the general climate had improved. Some shifts in structure and procedures had occurred (the guidance screening, attendance, and programming methods). Curriculum fit to student needs and teacher responsiveness were said to be up for the 14 CASA teachers. The linkage to external agencies (employers and CPD) was stronger. Recognition of student success was uneven; many incentive awards were ungiven.

Student behavior was somewhat improved (154 rather than 250 principal suspensions). And attendance was up: 73–75% monthly, versus 64–75% last year. For February through April, the figures were 5–6% over last year (the "back to the islands" phenomenon was reduced). But CASA students' attendance was only 42–53%. Dropouts were "projected" at 10% (vs. the previous year's official 13.6%). Students who got outreach and counseling were said to have more hope and self-esteem. There was no evidence available on achievement changes, even course failure rates.

Of the 185 students classified as "CASA" at year-end, 72 (39%) were retained for work next year. Another 44 percent were referred elsewhere: 62 to the General Equivalency Degree program (GED), and 19 to the STEP work experience program. Those were productive actions, helping to coordinate student services. But CASA could be said to have succeeded directly with only the 17 percent of its students (32) who were referred into the mainstream.

We should remember that the summer planning group had ambitions to affect Bartholdi as a whole, not just the at-risk target population (which turned out to include only about 10 to 15% of the students). Of course an urban high school can't be turned around in a year, but there was not much evidence of school-wide progress at the end of 1986.

Yet the feeling at Bartholdi as the school year ended was one of modest optimism. The cabinet had "mellowed some"; the principal was said to have become more decisive and to follow up better, and to have a network of people he could rely on for improvement effort; the feeling was that the programs started through CASA were working. Some job changes were occurring: Both attendance and programming would have new heads, the next year. The first issue of a faculty newsletter came out.

In early June, the final version of the CSIP plan was sent to the state department. It included a number of CASA activities, such as various attendance functions (the attendance machine, family assistants, the Telsol phoning machine), South Street, Job Corps, and the re-entry tutoring. The CSIP coordinator attended the summer CASA planning institute, and the CSIP plan, which covered a range of other activities from improvement of discipline to student activities and instructional improvement, was seen as having a "fighting chance," in spite of some cabinet reservations.

In summary, the picture was of a programmatic, relatively narrow improvement effort that began to founder through lack of overall planning, assistance, and coordination as its technical demands bombarded a school that was not functioning very well to begin with. Through heroic coordination and communication efforts, and capable service delivery from a partner organization, the program began to achieve moderate successes and to stabilize. But much remained to be done if the hopes of the CASA program's planners were to be achieved.

Epilogue

As with our other schools, we returned to Bartholdi after two years. In 1986 the researchers had given the school a "C" pseudonym, "Caruso," believing that it had achieved few of its hopes. But by 1988 it was clear that it deserved a "B" rating, and "Bartholdi" it became. What had happened over those two years? And what explanations were there?

Subsequent Events and Changes

No major job changes occurred in 1986–87, but there were new incumbents in attendance, programming, and security — all functions that had been shaky.

During the summer of 1986, the CASA planning team was quite productive. They reviewed present and incoming CASA students, and the work of the guidance screening committee, and got approval of positions for job development and testing. They generated new projects: cafeteria safety and food improvement; a revised cutting program; a partial "house plan" that would support students and coordinate guidance and services not only in existing programs (CASA, College Bound, bilingual, STEP, etc.) but for newly defined subgroups called "Discovery" (incoming mainstream ninth and tenth graders) and "Renewal" (tenth graders who had failed ninth grade work); a "safe room" for students violating disciplinary rules; a continued incentives program; and a student services office labeled the "lost document" room.

Most important, they committed themselves to regular monthly meetings during the year, with each project managed by a specific team member. They also planned coordination with other existing programs, and better communication with the faculty.

Most of the projects were implemented during the year. The most remarked-on was the "safe room," which grew out of a security task force stimulated by the CASA proposals.

During the 1987 summer institute, the team, feeling it had a strong license to plan, produced a still more comprehensive and very detailed set of projects, reported like the 1986 ones in a thick "book." The proposals included: a new HOPE program for long-term absent students; an "AM–PM" school (suggested by the principal) that helped students make up credit needed because of course failure or prescribed remediation; better linkage between CASA and the special education program; an expanded Job Corps that was an umbrella over not only CASA students, but those in co-op, another dropout prevention program, a senior pro-

gram, and a new guaranteed jobs program organized by a church association; procedures for class cutting records; clearly specified lines of
coordination among the nine different offices and roles involved with
attendance; and a parent letter on the more than 20 different special
programs available for students.

As before, implementation progressed fairly well. The change most
noted by administrators and teachers was the increased coordination
("It's all interconnected."). There was a regular meeting of the casa
team, which included 14 people (deans, three A.P.'s, coordinator, attendance director, and others); one casa team member said, "This same
group is really running the school." There were also regular meetings of
a group that covered the relationship with cpd, new courses, curriculum, and jobs; a council of the "house" coordinators; and reports from
the "safe room" to house coordinators. Some summer team members
worked on csip projects (which included work on awards/incentives and
attendance, which were officially part of the casa effort). Coordination
could sometimes be sketchy, and projects sometimes needed better follow-through, as one A.P. noted, but the structures for better communication were in place.

There was some turnover in South Street staff, and some slowing of
momentum. A new, "fairly supportive" director of high schools was
appointed. Superintendent Walters himself moved to a principalship in
another borough, while supposedly continuing his dropout program
management responsibilities. Chancellor Green succeeded Quinones.[4]

A new initiative from the Corazon Foundation gave training in
leadership and "how to get things done" to 12 "Fellows" — teachers from
special education and social studies. When they returned they took
initiative to make an intensive community survey, leading to recommendations on improved vocational education and other matters. The
sports and activities programs took a turn for the better: new teams,
a dozen new clubs — and audiences were finally allowed for basketball
games.

How the Program Stands Now

As the 1987–88 school year ended, the program components had
"gone well in a lot of respects" (this said with occasional skepticism,
with allowance for naturally optimistic claims). Total casa students,
still a *really* hard-to-reach group, have fallen from 330 to 250. The Job
Corps covers 204 students, and has been praised as being "at the fore-
front" of city school efforts. Work with the City Planning Department,
covering 19 students, seems to be proceeding well, including the "House

Sense" course and a vegetable garden. The hope is to get an actual building to be used for construction trade and GED teaching. A block program in English, and new courses in global history, life skills, and world of work are in place or planned. A mentoring/peer tutoring program continues, but was cut back in the spring. The attendance machine with photo IDs had some bugs, but it and the telephone robot with pre-recorded messages for absent students' families are working reasonably well. South Street continues to supply family assistance outreach and supportive casework services, after some difficulties because of personnel turnover. An add-on "big brother" tutoring program that began in 1986 with a local university continues. Incentive awards have continued: Bartholdi dog tags and watches, and trips to Yankee Stadium.

Outcomes

Bartholdi High School is beginning to move. As one administrator said, "It's better than [a] cautious optimism." Most people agree that security is better, the halls are quieter, with fewer discipline problems, at least for girls. Dropout data are not available for the current year yet, but the figures are said to have gone from "18 percent in 1984" to 9 and 8 percent in the following two years. Attendance has improved from 68 to 74 percent; this is not much different from 1985–86, but the end-of-year slump of earlier years was still absent. Staff turnover is down, it is claimed.

Several people noted climate changes: a tone that meant more understanding of students' needs, more feeling that "people know where they want the school to go." Students now "see the school as a place to get jobs"; those touched by CASA services are "more involved, have someone to speak to."

More positive publicity is appearing; articles on the Job Corps and the CPD linkage have appeared in city newspapers and a national magazine, and on network television. Still, one person noted, "the programs work, but we have a terrible image."

And person after person on the staff, given closer contact with students and the Corazon community survey data, worries about the serious home, family, health, and achievement problems of students. There are improved articulation efforts with sending junior high schools, but much concern remains about the adjustment and achievement levels of incoming and current students ("We're getting fifth grade reading."). Has academic achievement improved? Most people interviewed in 1988 do not know, and some express doubt. Bartholdi feels like a better place for students and faculty, but its productivity as a learning environment has not shown striking change.

Why Did This Happen? A Reflective Review

The implementation and outcomes at Bartholdi were not as strong as those at Agassiz or Alameda. Still, they were a marked improvement over the past. What can we say about possible reasons?

Why This Implementation?

During the first year, 1985–86, implementation began slowly, because the narrow technical emphasis avoided issues that CASA pointed up in the creaking Bartholdi organization, where the history and prospects for real change were not bright. Though a "program" vision was clear, few people had any clear vision of how the change *process* could or should proceed, and clear implementation plans were not made during the summer. The CASA effort was complex, weakly assisted, and poorly coordinated at first, and that created much overload.

Some key events were the appointment of a respected A.P. with a talent for active monitoring, follow-through, and coordination (Carole Fisher) as CASA supervisor; the decision to involve a competent, active, community-based organization; and the decision to hire several active, competent, job developers for the Job Corps work. In one sense, just having extra resources (remember the 16.8 FTE's) was a strong force for getting things done. Schools like Bartholdi have very few slack resources for improvement. However, the issue of resource *quality* is important too. Carole Fisher, South Street, and the job developers were people who delivered. Given a clear program vision, technically good improvements (such as the attendance machine and computerized reporting) could ensue.

Better coordination and South Street competence also led to the creation of new structures and procedures that went beyond "business as usual" (such as the referral form, the screening committee, the cutting cards system), and to increased interaction, particularly among guidance, CASA, and South Street. In effect, Bartholdi moved toward tighter coupling among its parts.

It also appears that the periodic printed updates given to the cabinet and CASA staff were important — especially in a setting like Bartholdi, where most right hands did not know what left hands were doing. These reports reduced the sense of chaos and increased coherence; they aided coordination; they pointed to needed next-step actions; and they heightened program credibility by producing an image — both internally and externally — of successful implementation.

It seems that implementation was hampered by certain factors: the narrow definitions of the target population and the Catch-22 regulations hemming it in; the technical nature of the program, along with internal organizational conflicts among departments and functions; lack of group and organizational process skills; and, ironically, the substantial three-year funding assurance, which made the idea of getting CASA into the regular budget an impossible dream.

When asked why program implementation had gone well during 1986–88, many people mentioned the initiative and empowerment of the cross-role CASA team, and their networking and improved coordination with others. (Even so, it was said by several that much more involvement of the faculty at large was needed.) The Job Corps success was laid partly to school system and business commitment, but the energy and competence of the coordinator seem to have been important as well.

The principal has also increasingly supported the change effort. David Martinez seems to have become crisper and stronger — clearer on what needs to be done, welcoming initiative from others and working in partnership with them, and continuing to attract external resources. His monitoring is much stronger: He has begun to tour the building regularly, and demands more *evidence* that improvement work has been carried out. He has continued to receive regular assistance from his consultant.

The teachers' union has been supportive; the chapter chair was actively involved in CASA summer planning, and led a CASA-inspired project on long-term absent students.

Why the Outcomes?

The specific interventions of the CASA program were not terribly effective with the target students as such, who proved both hard to reach and disruptive when they *were* reached. But CASA brought new resources to the school, and led not only to improved services but to the summer planning and initiative taking of CASA-related staff, and their de facto empowerment ("they are a group of committed people who are on everything"). So CASA efforts did ramify outward in ways that were not evident in 1986, when the emphasis was on "programs" with little attention to school-wide organizational issues. The legitimized influence of the CASA group, and their strong emphasis on coordination and linkage, have begun to make broader organizational changes possible.

While there are occasional complaints about lack of follow-through, that weakness is much less frequent than three years ago. Success experiences with second-year projects seem to have fed further effort ("Hey, we did that. Let's try *this*.").

Positive outcomes were also attributed to stability in key roles (few major players moved), as well as getting the right people into jobs where school functioning had been poor (programming, guidance, attendance, security).

What will happen next at Bartholdi? Remember the motto on the wall in the principal's office.

> Coming together is a beginning.
> Staying together is an accomplishment.
> Working together is a success.

That message is not altogether trite, and is a good summary of what has happened. New projects are anticipated: a health center, a task force on long-term absence, more integration of CASA into the school at large, a bilingual business education program, a training videotape for new teachers, a revised teachers' manual. Some people worry about what will happen when the dropout prevention funds stop next year. And the major worry remains: Can we reach our students academically better than we have? Despite these uncertainties, which are decidedly realistic in a school setting as turbulent as this one, Bartholdi does feel like a school that's moving in the right direction.

BURROUGHS JUNIOR HIGH SCHOOL: PUSHING REFORM TO THE LIMITS

She has remarkable judgment. She listens to what we suggest, but kind of knows right away when the idea is faulty or unfinished. She sends us back to the drawing board. In a way, she's teaching us all a lot about good administration.

They didn't want to do reading, partly because they thought it wasn't their job and partly because they thought it would interfere with teaching their science or social studies or math. . . . They were not child-centered; they were content people. They didn't want to change.

We're not exactly setting policy for the school, but . . . how to put it. If you come up with a good idea and present it to the committee, before you know it, the school is doing it. . . . Miss Storm would make a policy statement and we would work out the actual plan and schedule for doing it.

These quotes—about the principal's role, about resistance, and about teacher empowerment—are drawn from our story of how the faculty and administrators of John Burroughs Junior High School[5] moved to create a better work and learning environment for themselves and their 610 seventh, eighth, and ninth grade students. It's a story of gradual progress on a wide range of social and academic objectives— progress won through persistence and volunteerism, and in spite of obstacles that originated largely outside the school, in the district office, the union contract, and court orders.

The improvement program at Burroughs, developed with local foundation support, was called E2 (Educating for Excellence). Its components gradually evolved over three years of implementation. They included a range of "effective schools" interventions, student "advisories" (a type of counseling group), and transformation of Burroughs into a middle school. The change projects were steered by a small but highly involved group of teachers, working closely with the principal.

It is not a story of dramatic success. Rather, it's an account of how an urban junior high school, already functioning well in its milieu, took school reform seriously, and pushed it as far as possible, working within the constraints of a difficult, often chaotic district setting. As with our account of Bartholdi, much remains to be done. But Burroughs, too, is moving. Let's see how, and why.

A Picture of the School in 1985

The 30-minute freeway drive to Burroughs from the center city offers an eerie view of America's industrial past, with factories lying idle and abandoned. Smokestacks spew grey clouds over the acres of manufacturing facilities called "The Flats." Off the freeway, the car heads through miles of urban decay. Disintegrating Victorian frame houses stand next to brick commercial property, mixed with smaller frame houses, equally neglected. The potholed roads are as forgotten as the neighborhoods.

The small houses around Burroughs need paint; there are well-worn cars in the driveways. The neighborhood is black and largely working class, but many receive some public assistance. Most students are from the neighborhood, but a quarter of Burroughs' students are bused in as a consequence of the city's court-ordered desegregation plan.

John Burroughs Junior High School's low-slung and rambling building opened in 1950. There's a large auditorium, a gym, generous cafeteria facilities, and a sizable, attractive library/media center built when the old library burned in 1980. It's not crowded: A new wing built in the '70s permits a student population of up to 1,000. The actual enrollment of the school — 610 students — may help to explain a sense of calm, a lack of tension in the building. Even during change of classes, corridors are not crowded and the noise of young teens does not ricochet off the walls.

The Burroughs staff includes a principal, one vice-principal (a second V.P. slot was vacant most of the year), two guidance counselors, thirty-six classroom teachers, ten special teachers, and two security guards. Maintenance, cafeteria, and office personnel bring the total of adults in the school to 60. The staff is evenly split by race.

Margaret Storm, the principal, is black. As our first epigraph suggests, close colleagues praise her judgment and willingness to involve staff in the development of ideas.

But Miss Storm has little patience with staff whose standards fall short of her ideals. Consequently, staff opinions about her vary: Her style is described as "dictatorial" and "heavy-handed" by some, and "collaborative," "demanding," and "fair" by others.

"Collaborative" is a key word. The E2 committee of nine teachers essentially steers the main improvement program. There is also a site administrative council of department chairs, some faculty, and parents. And there's a staff-led team required by a court desegregation order to develop in-service programs and faculty meeting agendas.

Department chairs also serve as a communication link between administration and faculty. "It's important for teachers to know that other teachers are involved with the administration in running the school," said a department chair. Front office policies are announced and clarified, and complaints about faculty skipping hall duty and the like go to department chairs. Chairs must also ensure that teachers follow the district curriculum guides. They share responsibility for evaluating teachers with the vice-principal and Miss Storm, who, unlike many principals, observes and evaluates teachers on a regular basis.

About two-thirds of Burroughs' students are black. Sixty-three percent of their families are below the poverty level (the city's average is 74%). About 23 percent of students are developmentally handicapped and learning disabled. But the large number of special education students does not seem to be an issue. More than one teacher says, "These kids are less trouble than the regular kids."

Burroughs does well for its students. In 1985, the school was the highest-achieving secondary school (based on reading scores) of 41 in the district, excluding 3 magnet and exam schools. But a decade ago it ranked much lower, and as recently as 1981 was in the bottom two-thirds of the city's schools.

The Context

To understand Burroughs, we need to look at its community and especially its district context, which has exerted strong, and not always positive, influence over the school's improvement efforts. The state's role and Burroughs' own innovation history play a lesser role.

The Community

For years, the Cleveland schools have had a large black enrollment. Well before World War II, the city's thriving industrial economy had drawn Southern blacks to work in its steel mills. A sizable black middle class developed to provide leadership and stability, but residential patterns remained quite segregated. Eastern European ethnics, who worked next to blacks in the factories, lived on the West Side, and blacks on the east. As in-migration continued, the black population moved further eastward into elegant nineteenth-century white neighborhoods and suburban enclaves, pushing middle-class whites into adjacent suburbs.

For many decades, few whites of substance had lived in the city proper. The ferment of the late '60s riots led to even more white flight from the east side of Cleveland. The district enrolls few middle-class white students; the city's white leadership is minimally involved in education. In 1985 no school board member had a child in the schools. The current (black) superintendent's four children attend suburban schools.

Today there is simmering animosity between Cleveland's ethnic working-class and black communities, often sharp in the formerly black East Side schools to which white West Side youngsters are now bused. Racial and class issues are rarely confronted by the district, which leaves them to schools to handle if they wish. Most don't.

The School District

The district is the eighteenth largest in the country. As with other urban districts, enrollment has dwindled from a high of 155,000 in 1970 to under 74,000 in 1985, while racial composition changed from majority white to 62% black, 28% white, and 10% mostly Hispanic and Asian populations. The city also has a Catholic school system (80% white students), enrolling about a quarter of all students eligible to attend Cleveland public schools. There are 140 schools, 41 of them secondary.

These numbers say little about the underlying reality: In the battles of the late '60s and '70s, the school district was one of the major casualties. The recent history of the Cleveland public schools may rival the histories of Boston and New York for its nasty politics, overt racism, and disregard for educational quality.

By most accounts, the school system is still in disrepair. The movement of the black middle class to the suburbs has left the most poor in the schools; white leadership threw up its hands and black leadership developed its political muscle rather than working to restore order and civility in the schools.

The district has had serious financial and leadership problems. Twice in the past seven years it has filed for bankruptcy, getting $44 million in state loans. The federal court's 1976 desegregation opinion found the district segregated by race, and not trusting the district to correct imbalances, established a dual administration. A court-appointed superintendent and staff were to oversee those already in place—which simply doubled the opportunities for fighting. The arrangement was disbanded in 1982.

Through that twelve-year financial and administrative maelstrom, the district had eight superintendents. Of the four since 1982, one committed suicide, blaming board infighting and partisan politics. His acting successor filed a multi-million dollar suit against the board when it sought to break his contract. The next superintendent was besieged by charges of incompetence from the start; the board bought out his contract after a year. His successor is the ex-acting superintendent, who upon appointment to a five-year contract agreed to terminate his lawsuit.

The 1976 desegregation opinion stipulated an agenda of issues from administration and budget management to student testing and the development of magnet programs. Managing and improving the curriculum were central. The district's progress on this agenda has been littered with false starts, contempt of court charges, the dual superintendency, and wheel reinvention by successive superintendents. But as of January 1986, several changes had been introduced.

First, a new curriculum in reading, writing, and mathematics was developed and mandated; tests were developed and used; compensatory reading programs were added. Second, a state-designed, school-based management plan began in January 1986. Schools were given much control over budget, some freedom to tailor district policies to building requirements, and limited principal participation in new staff hiring decisions. Schools were to convene a team of parents, teachers, and administrators to make policy and budgetary decisions.

There were personnel and school changes as well. The interim superintendent negotiated a master contract with an early retirement buyout for teachers and administrators in 1985 and 1987. In 1985 there were 260 retirements, including 85 administrators. He also won agreement for a "facilities use plan" that would reorganize some schools and close others.

Most of the pieces of the district's reform program are now in place. But are the city's schools getting any better? An administrator gave a mixed review.

> We're paying lip service to improvement, but people are still blaming each other. But there are some schools trying to push ahead despite problems in the district, despite parents' lack of commitment to their child's education, in spite of kids' low self-esteem, in spite of the teachers.

And though Comprehensive Test of Basic Skills (CTBS) scores have risen over the past few years, as they have in many districts, many attribute those increases to curriculum–test alignment, coaching, and test-wiseness.

An education writer for the Cleveland *Plain Dealer* says, "Some schools are improving, but things are getting worse in the district office." She believes the schools' governing principle is to mind their own business and call on the district office only when absolutely necessary — for building maintenance, for example. Public education operates at two different levels: The schools try to carry out the task of educating youngsters, and the district office struggles with the unions, the school board, the court, and the taxpayer coalition.

It has not helped that after a flurry of in-service courses tied to salary increments in the '60s, the district all but eliminated its in-service division as fiscal problems mounted. Monthly one-hour faculty meetings are the main vehicle for teacher assistance, if the principal wishes to use them that way. The recent reform initiatives — curriculum, testing, school accountability — were not accompanied by training for teachers.

The State

The Ohio State Department of Education has been involved in the city's education from necessity: The federal court in the desegregation case had nowhere else to turn for help in developing implementation plans. Although Ohio is considered a "local control" state, the department was required to intervene with loans and fiscal oversight when the district filed for bankruptcy.

The district, like others in Ohio, has been only modestly affected by state-wide reform efforts that sprang up like mushrooms since the "Nation at Risk" report in 1983. Though Ohio was the second state in the nation to claim the right to intervene in districts it found "academically bankrupt," that has rarely happened. Districts are only required to implement minimum competency testing for grade-level promotions. However, a few Cleveland schools have participated in the state's effective schools program, and in the desegregation-oriented effective schools programs the state jointly sponsors with Kent State University.

Innovation History

The stable black families that began moving in to the white working-class Burroughs neighborhood in the late 1950s gave education a top priority. The first wave of redistricting under the 1976 court order brought poorer black students to the school, along with much conflict between the newcomers and the neighborhood kids. When mandatory busing was introduced a few years later, some Burroughs students traded schools with West Side youngsters. But the social class mix was maintained, along with the conflict. One teacher candidly admitted,

> When I came here 11 years ago, this school was the worst junior high in the city. There were graffiti all over the walls, trash ankle deep in the halls. The faculty was very alienated and angry, and we had poor leadership in the front office. I felt very inadequate, like I was starting all over.

None of the school's veteran teachers could recall attempts at curricular or organizational innovation of the sort popular in the '70s.

> This was a very traditional school. A lot of problems; gang activity. The district didn't offer programs that dealt with behavior, etc. You were to just keep the lid on. . . . We had all we could do to get through each day. Classes were huge; 42 or 45 students in a class was not uncommon.

Even so, the school's statistical profile for 1981–82, the year before Educating for Excellence got underway, was by no means terrible. Only 7.5% of the students were not promoted at the end of the school year.

Annual student mobility stood at 19%, though faculty mobility was 45%. Average daily attendance for students measured 85%; the faculty's absentee rate was 15%. Discipline problems had not gone away: there were 241 suspensions and 223 incidents of corporal punishment, about 1 a day of each. By most measures, however, Burroughs was not doing badly.

But the principal, who was in her second year on the job after 15 years in other Cleveland junior highs, felt that student achievement, discipline, attendance, and parent involvement needed to be improved. She wanted to make other changes as well: team teaching, and movement toward a "middle school" concept, more child-centered. When E2 came along, she saw an opportunity.

The Improvement Program

Educating for Excellence (E2) was conceived by James T. Carr, of the Henry Harman Foundation, which supports civic and education affairs in Cleveland. The E2 program began in 1981, during the ill-fated dual administration. Carr did not have a clear idea of what to do to help the schools, and so began by inviting outside experts to speak. One was Ron Edmonds, deputy to schools chancellor Macchiarola of New York City.

Edmonds, then becoming the acknowledged spiritual leader of the fledgling effective schools movement, presented a compelling case for the relationship between high student achievement in urban elementary schools and factors he and others had found in these schools: a shared sense of purpose; high expectations for students; increased time on task; monitoring of student progress; and the principal as instructional leader. Edmonds argued eloquently that any urban school could raise student achievement greatly by creating the key conditions he had identified. Jim Carr was sold.

To the school board, the Foundation proposed $65,000 for starters, plus an additional $5,000 for board planning. The board decided to invite the principals of the 80 poorest-achieving elementary and junior high schools to hear about the new project, and to apply for $2,000 planning grants for proposal writing.

According to Dr. Elizabeth Callaway, who oversaw the project for the district,

> The idea was to build a staff planning group in the schools. Schools already had experience with planning as a result of desegregation, and the decision to use Edmonds' ideas as the basis for planning was

easy. But the first group of schools to get involved were hearty souls. The irony is that the Foundation wanted it to be a simple process, but then it required proposals.

Twenty-four schools subsequently applied, but only four of the initial proposals were acceptable: two from elementary schools and two from junior highs, including Burroughs. Carr says that unacceptable proposals "put the blame for their problems out there. They didn't see the problems [such as poverty, student apathy, and parent lack of interest] as things they had much control over." With some coaching, proposals from 20 rejectees were funded.[6]

In each subsequent year schools were asked to describe upcoming plans in areas of school climate, curriculum, instruction, parent involvement, and program evaluation, and to submit a budget and timeline.

Over six years beginning in 1981, the Harman Foundation committed nearly $600,000 to Educating for Excellence. In 1983, two years after the program began, the district began to contribute to the program's support as well; its $444,000 brought the total E2 budget to a bit over $1 million, less than $50,000 per school over the six years.

The Foundation designed an E2 management system to give it control over the project. The district assigned two administrators to act as liaison with the central office: Elizabeth Callaway, a veteran of many positions in the district, and Michael Lee, assistant superintendent and a staff development expert, spent eight or nine days of each month in the schools, watching how things were going, providing in-service sessions when invited, and trying to win the schools over to use them as serious consultants. Lee remains with the project as its district coordinator. Callaway retired after the 1985 school year.

The Harman Foundation also negotiated district-level flexibility for its schools. It insisted on giving money directly to the schools, a practice most districts prohibit. According to Carr,

> In part we wanted to by-pass the chaos in the district office, and we also wanted to reinforce the decentralization of authority being pushed by the court.

A "gentlemen's agreement" was reached in 1981 that during the program's life, the principals in E2 schools would not be moved. The district agreed to leave the schools alone to work on school improvement under the aegis of the Foundation and with help from Callaway and Lee. These may seem small concessions from the district. But the union was still bruised from its latest strike and contract negotiations, and the glow was fading fast from the new superintendent's crown. Preferential treatment for a few schools could have been cause for accusations of inequity, if not for world-class grandstanding from the board. Jim Carr was grateful for small favors.

Why This Program?

For the Foundation, according to Carr, "The idea behind Educating for Excellence was to end run the district, to try to do something that would wag the dog." For the district, Harman money was a resource that couldn't hurt, and might help.

For Burroughs, E2 came along at the right time, Margaret Storm noted.

> We had started to work on some ideas to improve student attendance and tardies. . . . When they announced Educating for Excellence, I said, "Here's some money; maybe we should give it a shot."

Storm's experience had convinced her that grades seven and eight were the "make or break" point for success in high school. There the shift from "child-centered" to "subject-centered" school experience took place, while parents were separating from their growing children and leaving more to the school. She wanted more emphasis on skills and attitude development to correct elementary-school deficits. And she wanted a "middle school" concept — a transitional organization that kept students together for core academic courses, taught by teams who also attended to student problems.

When E2 was announced in early 1982, Storm already knew she could adapt Ron Edmonds' strategies and techniques for elementary school improvement for use in junior highs. "Our kids may be older, but they still like praise, like having people respond to their needs, like having school spirit." And the Foundation was offering funds when there was "hardly any in-service in Cleveland. I said, 'Here's a chance to get some consultants to work with us on reading.'" The prospect of E2 funds was thus critical for mobilizing faculty interest in trying to change the school.

The Story of Implementation

The years from 1982 through 1986 were, as in all improvement efforts, beset with problems and successes. In the beginning, enthusiasm propelled the school forward.

Chronology

In the spring of 1982, Storm told her faculty about E2, and "eight people stepped forward who were really willing to put forth for it. I felt that was enough support to go ahead." Over the next few weeks, after school and over dinner, the group of teachers and department chairs drafted a planning proposal for a program that emphasized reading. When the $2,000 planning grant was awarded, the school's E2 Committee did more planning in the summer and early fall: They read about effective schools and middle schools, found reading consultants, and visited campsites with the thought of holding a reading camp the following summer. Storm attended a workshop on effective schools run by the Ohio State Department of Education, and she and the E2 Committee went to a proposal-writing workshop.

In the fall of 1982, Miss Storm and the E2 Committee began to implement some of their ideas. They did a faculty-wide needs assessment keyed to the characteristics of effective schools. They used some E2 planning grant money for Dr. Janet Bailey, of Cleveland State University, to conduct seven workshops during the year on reading in the content areas. And Miss Storm organized a seventh grade team of English, math, science, and social studies teachers, arranging their schedules so they could coordinate their curricular units and discuss problem students. Weekly meetings began with a guidance counselor and Miss Storm participating.

The E2 Committee also spent weekends and many evenings working with the principal on the full E2 proposal, which was submitted on November 9, 1982.

1983–1984. Rather than waiting for the Harman announcement, the school pushed ahead, assuming it would be selected. In January 1983 Burroughs was awarded $15,000 for the next 18 months of work.

The project's official focus was reading in the content areas ("Let's Celebrate Reading"), but Storm's unofficial intent was to change to a middle school structure. The two themes had a common objective — to improve the faculty's ability to work with early adolescents — but they were handled separately. Reading was approached as a school-wide objective, while Storm planned to introduce the more difficult, controversial structural and role changes gradually, starting with half of the seventh grade.

Dr. Bailey's monthly sessions during the 1982–83 school year were aimed at showing teachers how they could teach reading in their classes. "About two-thirds of the faculty had secondary level credentials and didn't know anything about reading," an English teacher noted. Twice-weekly "reading alerts" were introduced — 10-minute sessions randomly announced on the PA system, when all work would stop for a recreational reading break. The E2 Committee also held four evening meetings, when parents worked with their children on reading and study skills to prepare them for the district's spring competency test. The first summer reading camp was set up for 1984; student participation was offered as a reward for doing 10 book reports.

The E2 Committee, now nine members, also began to recruit other faculty to work on tasks including building a professional library, increasing parent involvement, starting an "Educating for Excellence Newsletter" for parents, providing refreshments for the many small-group meetings now held in the school, and getting computers for the school. Teachers and students planted spring bulbs; special education students built picnic benches for the schoolyard.

Early in the year, the Middle Grades Assessment Program (MGAP) was carried out. MGAP is a tool for determining how well a school is responding to the academic and social needs of young teenagers; it also suggests improvement strategies. Miss Storm had long wanted to do an MGAP assessment, so when gratis training was offered, she raised expense money to send five teachers and two parents to North Carolina for training.

The assessment results, based on interviews with 15 teachers, 15 students, and 10 parents, were given to everyone. They showed that the school needed more structure and clearer limits for students; increased parent participation; closer personal relationships between staff and students; a wider variety of instructional methods; better coordination within and across departments; and greater effort to promote student competence and achievement.

The assessment mostly confirmed what the principal and the E2 Committee already knew, but the advice that came along with MGAP provided the E2 Committee with a clear agenda of proven activities. It didn't just tell them *what* they needed to do; it told them *how* to do it. The E2 Committee subsequently built a number of MGAP's suggestions into the school's future plans: assertive discipline training for faculty; monthly reports to parents; a high expectations seminar for teachers; team planning; individual counseling; reading alerts; regular assemblies; and student awards.

Staff training, mostly in the monthly one-hour faculty meetings, focused on testing, as the court and the district had made much of the need to improve student achievement on standardized tests, and district competency testing was coming shortly. Both Elizabeth Callaway and the district supervisor of reading spoke to the faculty.

Harman money was used to contract with Dr. Bailey for a second year, to work weekly with the seventh grade teaching team to develop test items geared to the district's seventh grade reading objectives. But the results of much teacher time and hard work were in effect thrown away when the district revised the reading curriculum and objectives. People justifiably felt as if the rug had been pulled out from under them.

EARLY PROBLEMS AND HOW THEY WERE COPED WITH.   The E2 planning and implementation dropped an avalanche of new ideas and activities on the school. It was the biggest event to hit Burroughs since the school library burned down. "There was a great deal of resistance in the faculty," one E2 Committee member said. "They just wouldn't get involved." The Harman Foundation awards at that time forbade compensating teachers for in-service or project time. At the start, the union position was, "If you don't get paid, don't go." In the first year, over 900 hours of contributed service went into E2, mostly from the nine-member E2 Committee. But few faculty came to meetings scheduled after school hours.

There was also resistance to the reading program. Only 12 of the faculty had reading credentials.

> They didn't want to do reading, partly because they thought it wasn't their job and partly because they thought it would interfere with teaching their science or social studies or math. . . . They were not child-centered; they were content people. They didn't want to change.

Dr. Bailey's in-service work gradually allayed some of the fears, but faculty still grumbled. Their resistance prompted the abandonment of another hope in the E2 proposal: work on mastery learning, which would have required heavy voluntary attendance at in-service training.

A third big issue centered on Miss Storm's middle school philosophy and her management style. Both were controversial and began to polarize the faculty. Storm was not shy about expressing her belief that the faculty should become more child-centered. Teachers from secondary schools disagreed with this tenet. As one teacher viewed it,

> It's more of a mothering type attitude, versus letting kids be independent and responsible for what they do. The kids pay a price in terms of developing independence. It isn't very good preparation for high school.

Miss Storm moved slowly, starting with the one seventh grade team, which met regularly, and successfully, to discuss student academic and discipline problems.

Storm's management style was both collaborative and demanding. Her closest advisors shared her objectives and gave a great deal of time to E2. One of the group of nine who participated in many decisions about E2's direction reflected,

> We're not exactly setting policy for the school, but . . . how to put it. If you come up with a good idea and present it to the committee, before you know it, the school is doing it. Miss Storm would make a policy statement and we would work out the actual plan and schedule for doing it.

But Storm did not hesitate to make demands, nor, when faced with layoff demands from the district, to transfer out as many staff as she could who resisted E2. She brought in new teachers with elementary school credentials — teachers who were more child-centered and suited to middle schools. And she was a risk taker.

> You can't worry about getting in trouble with the district office or doing something parents don't like. If an idea has sound educational reasoning, you just have to step out and do it.

On one occasion she scheduled needed in-service during school hours, while she, her V.P., and a few parents supervised the entire student body through a two-hour film.

> If something had happened to students, I could have been cited for insufficient supervision. But I needed more than the one hour a month the contract allows. There will always be limitations put on you. You have to push ahead.

Some faculty felt threatened by her demands and excluded from the E2 inner circle, which was becoming known to less-involved teachers as a "clique." The E2 people seemed like "big shots," moving around the school with a new sense of authority and better access to administration, and participating in key decisions. Most faculty fell between these extremes, liking some aspects of E2, objecting to others, and taking a "wait and see" position.

At the end of 1983–84, Burroughs' report to the Foundation reviewed the first 18 months' accomplishments, from a tripling of library circulation to new attendance policies, the MGAP assessment, and advanced reading classes. It also showed that CTBS scores had gone up slightly.

1984–85. During the second full year of E2, the project's focus shifted to math in the content areas: "It All Adds Up" was the Harman proposal title. The plan was to continue work on reading, and to improve school climate by "decorating our halls and rooms with student papers and projects." The proposal also planned for activities to "allow faculty to voice concerns and to make accomplishments known," to improve communication.

The $5,000 grant was used for the E2 newsletter, another summer reading camp, field trips, library acquisitions, and materials for the faculty. The school did not contract outside for consulting services; monthly staff training and in-service were provided by faculty members and the district office, including work on math teaching skills and assertive discipline training.

As the faculty worked on math, and plugged away at getting parents more involved, Miss Storm slowly expanded her structural innovations. She organized an eighth grade teaching team, and began planning to expand teaming to the ninth grade. But joint teaching was rare, since the district's curriculum revisions had torpedoed the team-oriented curriculum development Bailey had done with the seventh grade team.

All the teams began focusing on students' academic and behavior problems. They discussed consistency in dealing with individual students, and devised strategies for specific skills problems. They also met with parents or with parent and child. And in group meetings with students, they made it clear to youngsters that they could not play off one teacher against another or flirt with failure unnoticed.

Many other specific activities were planned using teacher released time: celebrations for high-performing students, development of student profiles and a study skills course, plans for student advisory groups, fund raising for summer camp, and student field trips.

During this year, more faculty began to climb aboard the E2 bandwagon. One of the E2 chairs noted,

> There was an open invitation to people to attend the E2 meetings. After the first year, when [test] scores went up and parent involvement went up, teachers began to get enthusiastic.

The year-end report to Harman mentioned sizable increases in parent participation, and cited the fact that 35 of the 43 faculty had stayed after school for 4 hours to plan next year's proposal. Even so, some said that resistance had only gone underground and simmered. As in the previous year, reading scores went up slightly, and Burroughs retained its district standing as third best in attendance.

Most activities this year had focused on student motivation. As one team member said, "Our focus now is more on student behavior and socialization than academics." And there were more whole-grade activities — assemblies, field trips, and group projects to replace the labor-intensive work on relatively few problem students and their parents.

PROBLEMS AND HOW THEY WERE COPED WITH. The "in-ness" of the E2 group was still a concern. The E2 Committee continued to do the lion's share of work, but other staff began to make modest contributions, through special events or hall displays: "We keep a mission for the year in everyone's mind and try to find a niche for everyone."

The school experienced a 25 percent turnover in staff, and the E2 Committee was also concerned with bringing new people "up to speed." Thus they decided to postpone work on writing in the content areas, which had been originally contemplated for the next year.

1985–86. Burroughs' third full year of E2 began in an atmosphere of uncertainty. The new superintendent was considering junior high grade reorganization to 6-7-8 or 7-8, with ninth grades going to the high schools. But it was not clear which plan the district would adopt, or when.

At the same time, Miss Storm and the E2 Committee had decided to replace homeroom periods with "advisory groups," a type of counseling session. Storm saw them as a way to increase personal contact between teachers and students. She had previously decided to phase them in once more basic changes, such as teaming, had been introduced, and staff knew more about middle school theory.

So beginning in September, all students were randomly assigned to meet with a teacher and fifteen schoolmates for ten minutes four days a week, and for a full period on the fifth day. Activities for these sessions were developed by a creative E2 Committee member — the very union representative who had avoided the program three years earlier. They included, for example, discussing the meaning of New Year's resolutions or considering the contributions of Martin Luther King, Jr. Staff were introduced to advisories during an all-day, in-service in the summer (funded by E2) and two follow-ups during the year.

> We worked on how to be non-judgmental, accepting, being a good listener, the role of body language in relating to kids . . . listening skills . . . how to do good counseling.

As Storm said,

> Almost anything goes on in the advisory meetings. It depends on the
> kids' needs. The idea is to give them added support, for the teacher to
> be a sort of confidante for the child, one they see as a friend.

For many teachers, this was an uncomfortable and unwanted role.
Even faculty who supported E2 and liked the middle school concept
were struggling to find ways to "promote a sense of family" in the
groups.

Activities planned for the advisories reflected the 1985–86 proposal
to the Harman Foundation, which explained that "academic achievement cannot be realized by students if they have negative self-concepts
and are not strongly motivated to do school work." Only one new academic program was initiated—a study skills curriculum taught the first
two weeks of school. The E2 Committee felt that the faculty should
continue past activities, such as the reading alerts, advanced reading
classes, math in the content areas, and the teaching teams, infusing
them with activities that would enhance self-esteem.

The school also proposed "Pride Alerts"—school color days, dress-
up days—to break up the daily routine of school and improve attendance, and to expand its "motivational awards" program: displaying
photographs of students and student papers, rewarding achievement
and good attendance with field trips, and running a fourth reading
camp the next summer.

A new faculty lounge was proposed to help with "interpersonal
communication" among staff, and the number of faculty retreats was
increased from one to three, while library acquisitions and the newsletter were continued. The Foundation awarded $6,000 to Burroughs,
with the understanding that the school could expect one more year of
modest support.

PROBLEMS AND HOW THEY WERE COPED WITH. Several persistent
issues dogged the school and E2 throughout the year, some a result of
anxiety about the future, some related to uneasiness within the faculty
about the advisory groups, and some provoked by the usual vicissitudes
of life in big-city school districts.

Halfway through the year the district decided to move the ninth
grades and leave grades seven and eight in newly organized intermediate schools. Burroughs' enrollment would drop to about 350 students,
and about 10 faculty members would have to go. Storm, who was co-
chairing the district middle school committee, was worried about union
seniority issues, and about losing some of her devoted E2 participants.

I'll try to keep them by moving them into other subject areas they're qualified to teach. I definitely feel that whatever I need to do and can do to keep them, I will.

The advisory groups were still a problem. Though many of the teachers liked the idea in theory, they disliked the schedule or student assignments, or didn't know how to manage meetings.

Kids won't do the exercises; they won't open up. Mixing grades seven to nine in the same group is intimidating to the younger students, and the older students sometimes set a bad example for them . . . students are bored . . . students don't get a grade and know they don't have to take advisories seriously.

About a quarter of the teachers interviewed disliked the innovation, saying,

We play silly games and probe into what students feel and why. I think that's inappropriate for a classroom teacher . . . I don't think learning about responsibility and interacting with others are things schools should teach. Besides, if they haven't learned it by now, it is probably too late.

A few teachers enjoyed the challenge and purpose of the advisories and encountered few problems, though they were in a clear minority.

The advisories' format and schedule were revised by winter. The content was more optional; faculty could choose to use them for help with academic work. The weekly full-period session was rescheduled to alternate with a period for teacher-led clubs and activities.

Some staff continued to feel like outsiders. The E2 Committee had gotten used to doing most of the work, and while participation of others increased, few new members worked at that pitch. Resentment grew, especially as the district's school-based management program enabled the E2 group to participate in budget, personnel, and program decisions that had formerly been made downtown.

There *were* real rewards. Miss Storm provided E2 members with opportunities for special training during school time, and visits to middle schools in other cities. And when Burroughs' program was selected as the district-wide model, the E2 Committee began to visit other faculties, giving talks and sharing the Burroughs experience. They were becoming stars in a world outside of Burroughs, and this did not sit well with many colleagues. Some staff complained of not knowing how decision were made, how foundation funding was used, or where other staff were that week.

Some of this was reluctance to invest in the program. Those who made an investment devoted endless hours to the school; it's noteworthy that E2's most active members did not have spouses. And some younger faculty with little seniority were openly reluctant to get involved, since their chances of being transferred out within a year or two were high.

Furthermore, E2 Committee members were beginning to burn out. An E2 participant acknowledged that sub-committees and regular meetings were less frequent because of the external presentations. Another committee member said,

> A tremendous amount of time and energy is required to keep this going. Sometimes we've been able to get subs, but that's infrequent. It really zaps your energy.

And E2-related activities were done less frequently. The assertive discipline procedures were seen as

> a very draining thing. You grade them all [papers] then go back and put stickers on. . . . as the year goes on you get like the kids. You get tired of it.

One of the grade-level teaching teams was meeting only every four or six weeks, instead of weekly. They were doing more grade assemblies and pizza parties, and little coordination of teaching units or vocabulary across courses. The pressures of the district-mandated curriculum and preparation for competency tests ("It takes 93% of the time," one teacher said) did not help.

> To fit in different activities was a lot easier a few years ago. We can't do reading alerts, reading in the content areas, and other things as easily.

There were efforts to deal with the energy problem through incentives—for example, extra supplies, and faculty-wide meals and retreats—and these may have gotten some otherwise abstaining teachers involved.

Preliminary Results

Even so, the faculty's engagement in substantive issues was remarkable. For example, a faculty meeting in late 1986 was essentially managed by E2 group members, who successively reported on achievement gains; plans for the coming year (climate and achievement thrusts, and "The Home–School Advantage," with a new logo); incentives for improving faculty attendance; rewards for students (for math projects, and for students who could produce a book they were reading when randomly stopped in the hall); and instructional plans for next year (expanding teaching teams, work on study skills). In effect, teachers were evaluating the initiatives of the principal, proposing changes, and defining next year's program agenda. At the end of the meeting 29 of 32 teachers, rather than exiting hurriedly, stayed to watch a videotape of a student art exhibit, and to chat and laugh together about the day's and week's events and trade plans for the coming summer.

It's fair to say that the middle school concept had been fairly well implemented in two eighth grade sections, and in one seventh grade section. All faculty were assigned to an advisory, though relatively few actually carried out its intent. However, in spite of resistance to involvement by some teachers, it appeared that nearly all favored E2 efforts, valued the energy put in by others, and respected Storm.

Even those who disagreed with the middle school initiative and avoided participating in E2 beyond the minimum believed that Burroughs was a fine place to work. Several faculty told of substitutes' comments that Burroughs was the best junior high in the city, with the friendliest faculty. A guidance counselor new to Burroughs said,

> Even if people don't like each other, it's in the way you don't like family. There is still a loyalty to the larger unit.

Faculty also believed that Burroughs really had improved, and they credited E2 and Miss Storm with the changes. A teacher who had arrived eight years earlier said,

> It's like two different schools now. It's entirely different in terms of attitude and commitment that wasn't here when I first came.

Perhaps the most frequently cited improvement was the high level of teacher interaction.

> We work together much more, on projects or meetings. We used to be far more isolated. . . . The faculty is more likely to confront problems with each other because we know each other better since E2 began.

People felt unanimously that Burroughs had a friendly faculty free of cliques and groupings along racial lines.

> About 80 percent of the faculty will extend themselves one way or another for the school over the course of the year. There are very few who do only the minimum. And even they are pretty friendly.

What about student outcomes? The general picture is one of continuous gradual improvement in a school that was doing well for an urban junior high school. In 1981–82, the year before the project began, 27.3% of the seventh graders performed below the national norms on the reading section of the Comprehensive Test of Basic Skills, according to the district. By 1984–85, that figure had dropped to 13.4%. Similar changes occurred in grades eight and nine. All CTBS scores were slightly above the district average.

On the Cleveland reading competency test, which measures the percentage of students who master three-quarters of the objectives, Burroughs seventh graders scored at 47%, eighth graders at 54%, and ninth graders at 43%.[7]

Average student attendance for the 1985–86 year was 84% (better for blacks than whites), as compared with 82% for junior highs district wide. However, this figure was no improvement over the 1981–82 figures. Teacher absences averaged 9.6 days, or about 5%, an improvement over the 1981–82 15% figure, even though there had been a district-wide decline (incentive bonuses for perfect attendance had ceased).

There were only 8 reported instances of corporal punishment, down from 77 the year before, reflecting the assistant principal's conviction (with which many Burroughs staff disagreed) that physical punishment rarely solved the problem. But 810 in- and out-of-school suspensions were recorded during 1985–86, compared with 597 the year before, the results of a new "get tough" policy with disciplinary problems.

So, in general, despite staff resistance and district- and contract-created obstacles, the school maintained its quality and made progress with students. If faculty satisfaction is any measure, Burroughs had much to be proud of.

In addition, E2 and Miss Storm had provided an unusual opportunity for willing teachers to have an exceptional professional experience. Those who took advantage of that opportunity acquired experience, sometimes expertise, in areas that are seldom available to teachers.

Educating for Excellence set out to encourage public schools to be effective. Though commitment, skill, and aspirations for the program varied, Burroughs had now become a more effective school for its faculty.

What remained to be done in 1986 was making the school even more effective for its students. Many teachers had done that, some who did not participate in E2 as well as some who did. But the challenge facing the program as it entered its next phase was to really improve the educational prospects of its urban teenagers. That would require moving beyond the psychological prerequisites to academic work, beyond the parties and rewards to providing sound teaching and learning experiences in every classroom.

Epilogue

Two years later, in 1988, Burroughs has continued to revise and develop the E2 program, but under much-changed conditions.

Subsequent Events and Changes

First, the expected district restructuring has taken place. Burroughs Junior High became Burroughs Middle School, with 350 students in grades seven and eight. The smaller size and genuine middle school structure made it easier for Miss Storm and her staff to pursue their middle school objectives. Storm explained,

> [Before restructuring] we were a junior high attempting to do a middle grades school in philosophy, thinking, structure, and organization. Now that we're fully a middle school, these concepts work more naturally.

Second, as a result of the enrollment cut from 600 to 350, the school lost many faculty members, including a key E2 member, the English chair. But Storm, through her knowledge of the transfer process, got back another E2 veteran who'd been transferred out earlier. The professional staff now numbers 35, down from the 43 when the ninth grade was still at Burroughs.

How the Program Stands Now

Though support from the Harman Foundation ended in June 1988, the district superintendent intends to take over the E2 program and extend it to 48 elementary and middle schools—double the original number supported by Harman. Miss Storm expects $6,000 in discretionary money from the district to continue E2 activities.

Faculty resistance to E2 has virtually disappeared—not without intervention, as Storm noted.

> Some people still object, but those people don't have the opportunity to get on a soapbox; I took away the opportunity.

Staff turnover during restructuring also helped.

> I was very, very selective in who went and who stayed. I made decisions on the basis of teacher quality, not on what subjects they taught.

Other changes in school structure and program have helped Burroughs move toward its middle school objectives. The advisory groups, a major bone of contention two years ago, have been redesigned to everyone's satisfaction: A student activities period alternates with an advisory period daily throughout the week.

After an in-house study finding that students working—with the same teachers—in afternoon reading classes were less productive than in morning English classes, the school rescheduled academic classes in the energetic morning and electives in the quieter afternoon.

The seventh grade language offerings have been replaced by a "cultural awareness" course that covers French, Spanish, and German to help students make better eighth grade language choices. A new "creative expression" course emphasizing speech and drama helps students learn how to express themselves orally before groups. A new computer literacy course for all seventh graders gives them nine weeks of daily computer work, followed by an eighth grade programming course.

Changes in non-curricular areas also express the "child-centered" objective of the middle school. The old internal suspension room in the basement has been replaced by an intervention program in the cheerful, comfortable, flower-filled counseling center, staffed by a non-certified tutor. A local community center counselor does group counseling for students with attendance or discipline problems. The summer reading camp has been changed to "Project Adventure," a five-day camping expedition that covers all seventh graders over the course of the year. School staff serve as voluntary camp counselors, helping students learn about outdoor life while working on trust building and leadership development; staff say they see real differences in the behavior of "problem" students after camp.

The E2 program continues to develop and evolve, sometimes circling back on itself. Miss Storm noted,

> We will do refresher in-services this year on reading in the content areas. We'll also do some staff relations training. And I want to shore up the teaching teams and do some reassignment. Teams working together too long begin to take on established roles . . . the leader begins to make all the decisions and ownership of the others isn't there.

Outcomes

Student performance at John Burroughs, for several years near the top of the roster of Cleveland secondary schools, continues fairly high. At the end of the 1986–87 year, attendance had risen to 90%. The number of suspensions was 341 (down from 810 the previous year). The dropout rate was only 2%. But the Comprehensive Test of Basic Skills found 79% of seventh graders and 66% of eighth graders reading at or above average—a significant drop from the preceding year.

As the 1987–88 year drew to a close, Burroughs was preparing for yet another change. Ironically enough, the district superintendent announced that Burroughs would be one of several schools to be closed at the end of the following year because of budget cuts and declining enrollment in the sending area. Tentative plans call for reopening Burroughs as a magnet school, to be called Cleveland Classical Intermediate School, emphasizing athletic competition as part of a pre-college preparatory curriculum.

Why Did This Happen? A Reflective Review

Like Bartholdi, Burroughs was a moderate success. What might be some of the reasons for implementation effectiveness, and the outcomes attained?

Why This Implementation?

Broadly speaking, it seems that E2 was carried out as it was for several reasons. Principal Storm had a clear vision of where she wanted the school to go. She was willing to make demands, and supplied the support that hard-working E2 volunteers needed, along with rewards and benefits—visits to other schools, speaking opportunities, external training for the MGAP program. And Storm did not hesitate to transfer out uncongenial staff and replace them with those sympathetic to the vision. She knew how to manipulate the district office to get both human and material resources.

But it would be a mistake to see the Burroughs story as Margaret Storm's achievement alone. It's clear that an empowered group of teachers and external resources provided the energy and drive needed for steady progress. An E2 Committee member explained results by

> the voice that people are allowed to have. You have an idea and then you can do it. The grant money gave us the means to do what we wanted to do. [Miss Storm and E2] have given teachers new power to do things I never thought I could do before.

And Storm acknowledged,

> The number one thing is to build a support base. You can't think you have a fantastic dream and expect people to accept it. You have to have gradual movement; you have to build support.

There were certainly many externally derived obstacles to implementation. Among them we can note staff turnover (even with Storm's ingenuity, she had little control over who left and who came), and the continuing re-education required for new people, reduced foundation support, uneasiness over the impending restructuring, lack of district funds for continuing in-service training and support (full-faculty training would cost $438 an hour), the pressures of district-mandated curriculum and competency tests, and limited incentives for teachers, such as released time for project work. It's a tribute to the energy of Burroughs people that they got as far as they did.

There is a paradox here as well. By the third year, most faculty were positive about E2, seeing it as a benefit to the school that introduced flexibility and opportunity. And they universally respected Storm, and found the school a wonderful place to teach. But only 13 of 28 teaching staff were moderately to heavily involved. Those actually involved in teaming narrowed its focus, both because of the coverage demands of the district curriculum, and because they didn't know how to team teach. The resistance of the less-involved teachers to the advisories and teaming was serious at first, and resulted in revising the advisories, abandoning the idea of mastery learning, and turning the limited in-service work toward reinforcing what teachers were already doing (which on the positive side did help introduce newly arrived faculty to the program), rather than working on improving teaching skills and strategies.

It should be pointed out that some faculty resistance was rational: It made little sense to invest extra energy developing a program you might not be there to implement, or to work on team teaching when district policies might sweep it away abruptly. And in some ways it made little sense to invest limited funds in improving teaching skills if turnovers were going to continue to be high.

District policy also had the effect of reducing reading and math alerts by increasing the demands of the standard curriculum, and reducing effort on parent involvement by requiring that meetings be held at night. Lack of school control over faculty mobility (which came in large part from declining enrollments and union agreements about concurrently reducing faculty) and curriculum also led to reduced year-to-year continuity, and a gradual movement away from direct academic issues to "prerequisite" issues such as student self-esteem.

In one sense, the heavy involvement of E2 members did little to move resistant teachers from a general endorsement of E2 to specific personal engagement. Too few were doing too much. Though the E2 cadre learned a great deal about proposal writing, preparing activities for advisories, organizing reading contests and the summer camp, and something about training others, other teachers were not touched in the same way.

Why the Outcomes?

Generally, Burroughs inched upward on achievement and attendance from its already high status among Cleveland secondary schools, with some recent drops. We can only speculate about what caused the changes in Burroughs, but it may be that the "reading across content areas" work made a difference (even though teachers were mostly left on their own to continue it); the contest and the camp were also viewed as important. The direct work on student motivation through assertive discipline and rewards — and what seemed like increased cohesiveness among staff — may have helped student attendance and discipline issues. The slight achievement drops are perhaps not surprising, given the revisions of teaming and advisories, the turbulence about reorganization, and now the closing of the school.

And perhaps, as we saw in Alameda, Burroughs needed a resting place, a plateau or break from a demanding process before moving on. It's hard to predict where Burroughs, or its daughter magnet school, will head next. It's not clear whether the changes achieved would remain in the absence of Miss Storm. A lesson may be that vision, pressure, and empowerment of a few are not sufficient for maintaining movement, especially when the district environment, whether through disorganization, rigidity, or court-mandated changes, presents such serious obstacles. Burroughs took a structural-change approach (teaming, the advisories) — but, it seems, with insufficient resources available to support implementation. It seems likely that sustaining improvement would require more direct assistance from outside the school, and a real re-involvement of faculty. Progress toward cohesiveness is not enough. Faculty need support for reconceiving and reconstructing what they are actually doing in the classroom.

Burroughs, like Bartholdi, was a moderate success. There are a few similarities between them: the presence of an empowered group steering the effort, much overload, and good coordination. And in both schools it appeared that more effort needed to go into direct work on teaching behavior, and into ways of ensuring that the changes would remain after funding or key figures left.

But in many respects the schools are quite different, not only in size and grade level. Compared to Bartholdi's, the Burroughs effort was more school-wide, more educationally (rather than only remedially) focused, with a more central, visionary principal — and with somewhat more external turbulence and disruptive demands to deal with. Bartholdi had many more dollar resources, but used hardly any for assistance, which was sustained at Burroughs.

On balance, Burroughs looks more like a somewhat less-realized version of Alameda (the cadre and its associated faculty polarization, the sustained work, the structural emphasis, visionary leadership, and assertive resource getting). And Bartholdi looks something like an earlier, less-fully implemented version of Agassiz (programmatic emphasis, gradually evolving steering group, less direct attention to classroom issues, lower-key principal). These A-B similarities seem more nearly parallel than the experiences of the two B sites.

Next we turn to Chester, where the improvement effort had the least success among our five sites. Once again, we encourage comparative reflection.

NOTES

1. This report was adapted with additions from the original case study (Miles, 1986a). Quotations in this report are drawn directly from the case.
2. Official figures for a year are not ready until March of the following

year, and depend on arcane calculations (for example, a student going to the military has "dropped out," while one going to GED, an alternative school, or a job after age 16 has not). As one DRP official said, "It stinks."

3. A study of other dropout reduction programs in New York City (Public Education Association, 1986) showed that Bartholdi was not unique; orchestration and coordination were seen as critical needs by staff in most schools.

4. Chancellor Green died suddenly in the spring of 1989, and was succeeded by acting chancellor Bernard Macklowitz. Chancellor Fernandez was appointed in October of 1989.

5. This report is adapted with additions from the original case study (Farrar, 1987b) to focus more directly on implementation problems. The quotations in this report are drawn from the case.

6. The 20 rejectees received material on effective schools philosophy and aims developed by Colleen O'Brien, a nationally known consultant on school improvement, for use in revising their proposals.

7. The CTBS scores are unusually high for an urban district. The lower scores on the criterion-referenced Cleveland reading test may be a more realistic measure, and lend weight to the idea that CTBS scores are elevated because of "teaching to the test" and test-wiseness.

6

Limited Success

MATTHEW B. MILES

CHESTER CENTRAL HIGH SCHOOL:
WORKING AGAINST THE ODDS

So many people love this school. . . .

The newspaper reports crimes this way: "A graduate of Chester High School was arrested last night. . . . "

99 and 44/100% of efforts to change things here have conked out.

This is a story of an improvement effort that didn't work. Why did this happen? Though people approached the task with energy and good intentions, the odds against success were too high. There are important lessons to be learned from what happened in Chester; in later chapters we will repeatedly be comparing the Chester story to what happened at Burroughs and Bartholdi, schools struggling to improve and beginning to succeed, as well as to the most successful schools, Agassiz and Alameda.

Chester is a classic "rust belt" city of the Northeast. Once a prospering New Jersey city, its economic base declined badly in the last few decades, and has only recently started to recover.

Chester Central High School[1] has 2,300 students, 78 percent black, 12 percent Hispanic. There is a sense that Chester Central High School used to be a community centerpiece, and the current and previous principal have worked hard to restore this feeling. There has been a history of white flight, with many parents sending their children to private and parochial schools. Now there is a slight trend toward whites returning. But though Chester Central has been making progress, it still is not performing well in terms of student achievement, retention, college attendance—or the morale of teachers and administrators.

The story of the most recent effort to improve the school began in

March 1984 with the announcement of the state's Urban Improvement Program. Chester's proposal, written largely by the district office, was funded for $3.4 million dollars over three years. At the center of the proposal was a comprehensive planning approach (More Effective Schools, or MES), which was intended to improve school-based leadership and programming in a number of specific areas. This was coupled with an effective teaching program, Instructional Program Leadership, or IPL, developed by a regional laboratory, which emphasized curriculum alignment and supervision to increase classroom time-on-task. But neither MES or IPL seemed to have had much enduring impact by the end of the 1987–88 school year. In many respects, Chester Central High School staff were feeling less productive and more frustrated than when the improvement effort began, and there was little evidence of improved student learning.

How could a well-intentioned effort like this go astray? We need to examine the context, look carefully at the implementation work, consider the odds against success, and see if we can understand why the outcomes were disappointing.

A Picture of the School in 1985

Chester Central is in a solid and impressive building, built in 1932 with WPA assistance. The school covers a very large city block. It's well maintained, although furnishing and carpets are somewhat shabby. There are some beautiful features, such as an auditorium with Lenox chandeliers, and marble walls. The halls feature large posters (student travel club, upcoming SAT practice sessions, performance of *Godspell*, and so on) and student art work. Graffiti are seen in bathrooms and phone booths, and in some stairwells; elsewhere, the walls are clean. The immediate surrounding of the school is a working-class area, bordering on what was once a middle-class neighborhood, not far from the central city.

The school population (2,300 in grades 10–12) has changed from largely white (Italian city and Jewish suburban), 25 years ago, to its present balance of 78 percent black, 12 percent Hispanic, and the remainder mostly white. According to one staff member, "many students have poor self-esteem" and most parents lack a high school education. "There are some wonderful kids . . . but at the other end, many poor unfortunate kids not prepared for school work." One estimate was that only one-third are prepared for high school work. "They're not dumb. They just haven't been taught."

Furthermore, many have serious home problems: lack of money, abuse by parents, pregnancy, illiteracy. One estimate is that 20 to 30 percent of the students have children, and that 80 percent have at least part-time jobs; several staff members say students come to school for security, companionship, food, and heat, rather than education — "which won't pay off for them anyway," as one teacher noted.

Achievement tends to be low. For incoming tenth graders, though steady improvement has occurred since 1980, achievement test scores fall below the mean of all of the state's urban schools, and below the mean of districts with lower socio-economic status. And despite slow improvement since the late '70s, seniors' 1984 mean reading and math scores put them only at grade level 10.5. In 1985, 90 seniors (15%) had not yet passed the Minimum Basic Skills test, which measures performance at a ninth grade level, though with intensive work all but 20 eventually succeeded. Of 1984 seniors, only 29 percent of graduates went on to post-secondary institutions, over half of those being two-year colleges.

Along the way, course failure rates are high, ranging from 23 to 36 percent, depending on the marking period. The dropout rates are imprecise, but more startling: An administrator says that of 1,300 students at the end of junior high school, 900 actually show up at the high school (tenth grade) and 500 graduate — an attrition rate from the ninth grade of 61 percent.

Attendance is improving: 85.2 percent in 1984–85, up from 78.6 in 1979–80. But there were 4,121 out-of-school suspensions during 1983–84, over half of them tenth graders, and 223 in-school suspensions.

The subject departments are typical for a comprehensive high school, and the curriculum has levels ranging from honors and college-bound to business, remedial, and special education. But there is evidence of rigidity in curriculum and scheduling. For example, an impressive vocational education program provides up-to-date equipment in trades ranging from masonry to graphics — yet the program serves only 150 students in 1985–86. Many students did not pass the state tests and must take extra periods of remediation, which makes it "impossible" to schedule the "required" three periods a day in the vocational education program.

The school is well staffed, with an abundance of administrators and non-instructional personnel: the principal, 4 vice-principals, 12 department heads (supervisors) with no regular teaching responsibilities, 2 assistant principals, 13 guidance counselors, and 27 assorted support service personnel. The bulk of the 198 teachers and other staff are white.

The school's principal, Carol Hayes, is black; she went to Chester

Central High as a student, taught there, and worked as a guidance counselor. Mrs. Hayes is 53 and has been on the job for six years, since her predecessor, Curtis Bartlett, moved to the Chester superintendency. Respect for her is said to be "going up." She is liked by many staff as an insider who "knows the school inside and out." Though she has to be "political," she's seen as fair, and as student-oriented. However, she is also viewed by some staff as reluctant to intervene actively, to ruffle feathers or upset people ("she doesn't know that people are complaining"), and as unreceptive to suggestions. One has the impression that she does not feel wholly secure in her job, and is a low-key manager who aims at keeping things running smoothly. Unlike her predecessor, she is not much in evidence in the halls and rarely visits classrooms; her office is small and out-of-the-way. Students said, "We hardly see her."

The principal and V.P.'s work together fairly closely, meeting one on one almost daily. The supervisors (department heads) join them in a group meeting about every two weeks. Several department heads report to each V.P. But relationships are vague; department heads may go directly to the principal, and V.P.'s do not seem to observe or evaluate them.

Department heads, though most are well experienced and come from within the school, tend to feel they are not respected by the V.P.'s or the principal, and that their role — curriculum development, teacher evaluation, in-service, budgeting, ordering supplies and materials — is not understood by superiors. They are officially responsible for grades 7–12. But in fact almost all their work is in the high school, and they must ask permission from Carol Hayes to go to the junior highs, so they feel "caught between two masters."

Chester Central has a mostly veteran teaching staff. Few have had extended work experience elsewhere, and "most people retire from here." Like the principal, many staff attended the school as students; some tend to lament the "good old days." The staff are "good soldiers," but one has the sense that they share many of the motivation problems we observed in students. For example, many teachers say that they do not feel a sense of reward from their work with kids, and feel discouraged. For their part, some students report that they don't feel cared for. In a discussion with student leaders, one commented that though some faculty are "spirited," many are just "there for the paycheck . . . they knock down students to get out the front door." An administrator elaborated on this by saying, "Teachers are very mindful of the [union] contract . . . not much lingering after school." The time clock is crowded at 3:00 as people punch out; after-school meetings are difficult to arrange.

The school climate seems "okay," safe and relatively orderly, but rather lethargic. "Don't rock the boat" is repeatedly mentioned as a norm. But the boat is not a tight ship. Teachers say that people are not held accountable, and that rule violations are not followed up. "People don't get leaned on."

Current efforts to build faculty climate through parties, entertainment at faculty meetings, and student–faculty sports competitions do not seem to be having a strong impact. There is an undercurrent of tension, and the principal alludes vaguely to "polarization" and a desire to "avert problems." Conversations with people at the school often involve complaining and blaming, and suggest a sense of powerlessness. One teacher said, "We're treated the same way as the kids . . . allowed to be absent or late without punishment, get no rewards for doing things right, have no say in curriculum." Similar themes are raised by student leaders, who comment on inconsistency, lack of communication, and students being "treated like babies," with minimal consultation before decisions (like where to hold commencement) are made. Similarly, one vice-principal said that teachers "don't object to improvement efforts as such," and often have the feeling, "Why don't they [administrators] ask *us*?"

The Context

Much of what happens at Chester Central High cannot be understood unless one knows the community, district, and state context, and the school's innovation history.

The Community and School District

Chester has been struggling back from its decades-long decline, and unemployment is decreasing, though in 1986 it remained at 8.8 percent. Growing investment, new office buildings, an Urban Enterprise zone, and the growth of high tech in the sprawling suburbs create hope about Chester's future. The city's population is about 65 to 70 percent black; both blacks and whites are largely working- and lower-middle class.

Chester has 18 elementary schools and 6 junior highs, in addition to Chester Central High (the sole high school) for its 14,000 students.

Fiscally conservative whites have historically held most power on the board, but there has been recurring conflict with fiscally liberal blacks. A recent change to a mayor-appointed board was expected to create more interest in curriculum, but relations between the board and superintendent have not improved and their acrimonious meetings go on until the early hours, with conflict over budget cuts and the pace of change.

The Chester Education Association, the bargaining agent for teachers, is seen as powerful, and it has not been uniformly supportive of recent and current state-initiated improvement efforts (minimum basic skills lists and quarterly lesson plans, for example).

The central office reflects this long history of conflict and politics. It is characterized as having "a lot of superstructure." Historically dominated by Italian males, the central office has seen a steady infusion of black men and women since the early '70s. Politics is often mentioned as a reason for people's getting or holding jobs; one administrator said that the elementary principalship was "historically a dumping ground" for ambitious people with city hall connections.

The superintendent, Curtis Bartlett, is black. He was formerly Chester Central's principal, but he has still had to spend much energy in building a constituency throughout the district. He is variously described as active, overloaded, "too nice," "not knowing his own power," reluctant to crack down when people are not delivering.

The district is not resource-poor. The total 1985–86 budget comes to over $5,000 per student, which is considerably higher than the state average. However, the district has had a long history of "deep educational difficulty," culminating in its being taken over by the state during 1979–82 because of substandard performance. One central office person said, "The system was simply let go for 20 years . . . no one looked at achievement data or held teachers accountable."

But the district would not appear stagnant to an outsider. During 1984–85, according to its annual report, it carried out 59 improvement activities, including junior high school writing skills, Follow Through, summer basic skills programs, revision of curricula in grades 9–12, new promotion standards in grades 1–6, and cooperative in-service with nearby colleges and universities.

Seen from Chester Central High, there is much ambiguity about who is responsible for what. Carol Hayes, the principal, says, "I've had four different supervisors during my four years as principal . . . " and complains that she does not know to whom she should report.

High school staff and administrator attitudes toward the central office are not very positive. It is viewed as distant ("no one ever comes here"), entrenched, overstaffed, and not sensitive to the needs and concerns of a large secondary school. One administrator spoke, with some feeling, of wanting "good ambassadors, with integrity, not snoopervisors." A more charitable report from another administrator noted that central office people were cordial, but any action to work with them had to be taken through the principal.

From the district side, there is also frustration and blaming, with the high school seen as an enigmatic entity that is hard to influence. One central office staff member stated that their hopes for changes in the cluster program had been sabotaged by uncooperative high school people. But high school staff felt that the central office did not understand the scheduling problems the program created. From their perspective, the failure came because "the central office didn't follow through" to support the change.

In short, there is an uneasy balance: The high school feels dictated to by a distant, unsympathetic bureaucracy, while central office people feel the high school has unwarranted autonomy and is entrenched, with its staff not earning their salaries, unresponsive to system-wide needs, and not well organized.

The State

Recent state legislation and requirements have put the state of New Jersey among the most regulatory. There is a Compliance Intervention Plan for fiscal watchdogging. Minimum Basic Skills (MBS) testing began in 1977 for grades three, six, nine, and eleven. A High School Proficiency Test has been given to ninth graders since the spring of 1986, and graduation requirements have been increased. Students who fail the exams receive remediation, and may eventually be barred from graduating.

Other recent governor's initiatives include an improved starting salary for teachers, assorted teacher grants and awards programs, an "academy for teaching and management," and alternate certification routes, along with special programs in science, computing, and vocational education; new bilingual standards; and encouragement for districts to adopt "codes of conduct" for students. A new "effective schools" program is piloting in 12 sites. These programs, many mandated, must be responded to by the district and the school. And although the official intention is to accompany regulation with supportive assistance, such assistance is often thin or absent.

Innovation History

The historical context of efforts to improve Chester Central is crucial for understanding the current situation. For years improvement efforts have come, aroused energy and hopes, then gone. As one person said, "99 and 44/100% of efforts to change things here have conked out."

Many teachers speak of the '50s and early '60s as a kind of "golden age . . . a paradise . . . the gem of the East Coast . . . how could they *pay* you to teach here?" There were 4,500 students—75 percent of them Jewish: "Good kids . . . not a mark on the walls . . . they could get into any college they wanted." But gradually, cooperating suburban districts detached themselves. The last to leave pulled out in 1967.

By that time, the proportion of black students was approaching 50 percent. In December 1968 there were student riots, with racial overtones. Some faculty simply felt stunned; others were alarmed at the "revolution." There was a "revolving door" period: One principal retired; so did another; a third principal lasted only nine weeks. Staff absenteeism was up. By the summer of 1971, matters were severe: Not only black–white but inter-neighborhood black–black conflict was endemic. Police presence was strong enough to feel nearly like martial law. The school dwindled as white (and some black) flight continued, until it was 62 percent black and 5 percent Hispanic.

STABILIZATION AND IMPROVEMENT EFFORTS. Curtis Bartlett was appointed principal in November 1971. The school was chaotic—students were calling meetings over the PA system—and he spent his first year regaining control and stabilizing relationships among students and faculty.

In 1971–72, Bartlett initiated a large multi-year Title VIII program called Project Design, which involved a 22-member task force in a careful internally led diagnosis, along with visits to 17 exemplary high schools that involved "house plans," team teaching, modular scheduling, and other innovations. The project proved somewhat divisive, and the faculty opposed the basic house plan recommendation. There is disagreement about results. The program was said to have led, much later on, to use of block-scheduling procedures, and a cluster program in the tenth grade, but the fate of other proposals (team teaching, special needs classes, summer school) is unknown.

The school continued to dwindle, to 3,300 in 1973. During the rest of the '70s, many new programs were introduced: remedial courses, special education, bilingual programs, Right to Read, learning laboratories, in-service on teaching skills, accelerated (AP) courses, and organization development for the faculty. Bartlett was an active, visible figure throughout, stabilizing the administration and relying heavily on department heads.

In 1977, the first state Minimum Basic Skills test was given to students. In spite of Chester's improvement efforts, the state's review found the Chester schools so lacking that state monitors were appointed to run the district. During their two years in the central office, state officials devised many new programs and systems, bloating the administrative superstructure ("the flow chart just blew up"). But little of this activity reached the high school.

In the summer of 1980, Chester State College wrote a joint proposal with Chester Central High for a two-year, state-funded project ($100,000 annually) called Program Achieve. Bartlett recruited 60 motivated, innovative teachers to work in six task forces (reading, writing, math, administration, support services, and staff development). A college professor joined each group, and a change-oriented vice-principal (Jim Griffith) and a college person did full-time coordination. In retrospect, one teacher called the Achieve task forces "the first meaningful dialogue since the riots"; another commented on the unusual interaction and exchange of ideas; still another said it was the most effective improvement effort in 25 years.

The program led to a new cluster approach where teacher teams collaborated in a block-scheduled program for students who were "close to academic." The clusters produced visible improvement in achievement, attendance, and student attitude. Other projects included new grading and attendance policies, a well-developed and well-accepted "critical thinking" skills booklet for faculty, a writing style book, a discipline code, a new detention program, and new staff development activities.

A TRANSITION.   In the spring of 1982, Bartlett decided to accept the position of superintendent. The state's takeover of the district was over. The school was "moving, but had quite a distance to go." The various programs were working, and the school was reasonably quiet. He nominated his successor, Carol Hayes, began his new job in June, and turned to the question of district goals and plans for the next few years.

After Program Achieve funding ended in 1982, the district reduced its support. The program was criticized by some supervisors for its organization development emphasis and lack of focus on remedial students. Some unimplemented recommendations were neglected by the principal, or resisted by teachers. Time allotted for cluster planning meetings was cut, and a guidance job was dropped.

MORE INNOVATION.   But hope could still be aroused. A school climate improvement program developed by Phi Delta Kappa was mandated by Superintendent Bartlett and carried out in 1982–83. It was launched with some excitement and the strong support of principal Hayes. It was "well organized": Survey data were collected, and 10 task forces (pre-specified topics) were created, coordinated by a respected steering committee. The process brought a wide range of people together, reduced isolation, and generated enthusiasm for improvement — but then apparently lost momentum, without action on recommendations. As one person said, "We thought at long last this would work — but that was the last we heard."

In 1983, the superintendent requested plans for reorganizing the high school; the principal proposed seven different options, but says she received no feedback. In May 1984, Bartlett proposed that the high school be reorganized into four sub-houses, and gave the principal a year to study the idea. She and the V.P. for curriculum opposed it, and the idea was dropped.

But many other specific new programs were under way in 1984. Principal Hayes put an emphasis on improving the image of the school as well as the achievement and self-esteem of its students. "The school has declined, but the needs haven't." She responded positively to a range of innovations suggested by staff, administrators, and outside organizations, including an awards program; participation in a regional inter-school association, with student exchanges; a Junior ROTC program; a program to coach students who were 3-time failures on the MBS; a faculty suggestion box; after-school tutoring; the Peer Leadership program, which trains seniors to lead discussion groups of sophomores; a "Quest for Excellence" program including a summer trip to Europe; a requirement that students must attend 165 days for credit; and an incentives program (trips and concert tickets for 100% attenders).

Despite all of this energy and apparent action, there is in 1985 a good deal of skepticism about improvement; one person said, "We'll get there, but not in my time." Programs have come and gone, typically without follow-through on proposed actions. "We do things and drop them" is an often-repeated theme. "It's frustrating when things come to naught . . . I don't volunteer any more," one teacher said. In one meeting of administrators and supervisors, people repeatedly asked whether a new policy "would be in writing."

The Improvement Program

This lengthy history brings us to the most recent change effort, the subject of this case. The state's Urban Improvement Program had its roots in the arrival of a new state commissioner in January 1983, his recruitment of an assistant commissioner with a strong urban schools background, and Governor Kean's close-call election with less than adequate urban support. These factors led to the design of a substantial ($7–10 million) school improvement program that would include broad-based support to all urban areas, delivered through regional curriculum service units, along with more focused, intensive support for three districts. The three would receive funding for a More Effective Schools (MES) program, with direct assistance from a School Renewal Team located in the state department of education.

There were five main objectives specified by the state: improvement in pupil attendance, pupil performance, and principal effectiveness, and reduction of disruptive behavior and youth unemployment. Three supplementary objectives — improvement in educational technology, adult education, and special education — were added later, along with an additional $2 million from the governor. A request for proposals was sent to 56 eligible districts.

In the spring of 1984, the Chester district submitted a proposal for More Effective Schools, and was one of the three districts funded. Intensive district-wide planning began in the summer. As Bartlett had hoped, the MES program, which emphasized a long-range planning process, was supplemented by another program, Instructional Program Leadership (IPL), which he had learned about through a staff member at a regional educational laboratory. In IPL, central office staff are trained in the principles of effective teaching, and then go on to train principals, who then train teachers. The training deals primarily with curriculum alignment, and with monitoring of instructional processes to increase classroom time-on-task behavior. Bartlett's interest in IPL was so high that he volunteered himself as the trainer for Chester High School. Both MES and IPL were expected to run for three years.

Why This Program?

Bartlett was enthusiastic about the MES/IPL combination. It brought substantial add-on resources and free assistance, and it fit his goals and his preferred operating style. The state was also enthusiastic about the possibility of real change in Chester. But from Chester Central High's perspective, it was a "top-down program" whose goals and activities were chosen by outsiders. The goals of the MES program were set by the state, and were not clearly understood by faculty. The IPL component was originally rated low by principals during a district needs assessment that was part of the MES process. However, the decision to go ahead with IPL had already been made by the superintendent.

The Story of Implementation

What happened as MES and IPL were carried out at Chester High? Their ups and downs, and their relation to other events in the school and district need to be charted.

Chronology

MES AND IPL. Instructional Program Leadership began with laboratory-provided training for Bartlett and four central office staff in September 1984. In a "cascading" approach, they in turn trained the large group (40 plus) of all principals (Carol Hayes was accompanied by her V.P.'s and 4 supervisors) using pre-packaged training materials in meetings extending through April 1985.

Though the high school portions of the MES plan had been completed by December 1984, MES funds did not begin flowing until June 1985, and little was done except for some additional summer planning and training.

In the fall of 1985, IPL work at Central High began with curriculum alignment planning and the production of quarterly lesson plans (those for quarters 1 and 2 were largely complete by the spring). Some sections of the MES program began (for example, a career resource room). But the key assistant commissioner concerned with MES had already left, and the assistance expected from the School Renewal Team never materialized. The state department coordinator, who was too overloaded to be helpful, left her job in February. MES was very assistance-thin.

By midwinter, the principal, V.P.'s, and four supervisors had begun receiving IPL training in classroom "scanning," a way to observe students' time-on-task behavior. They in turn were expected to train high school faculty in these procedures, and began doing a little of it through department meetings in the spring. But superintendent Bartlett did not follow through on his hope to be the main training contact with the high school. And very little actual "scanning" was tried out.

School-level planning for 1986–87 MES work did not begin until May, though it had been asked for by the central office in March.

In brief, except for the curriculum alignment work, both MES and IPL work went slowly and somewhat diffusely.

NEW DISTRACTIONS. Conflicting priorities from other state programs helped make the MES/IPL implementation efforts diffuse. Much energy went into the Student Review Assessments, which involved detailed documentation, meetings, and plans for each of 76 students who failed the state's Minimum Basic Skills test three times, and into the Individualized Student Improvement Plans (ISIPs) for students who failed any course or the MBS.

And there was planning for the anticipated arrival of 800 students who were expected to fail the new High School Proficiency Test. Meetings among administrators, a few supervisors, and central office people led to some decisions: to tighten promotion policy so that a four-year student career would be typical; to offer double-period remedial work; to eliminate the cluster program (reversing the innovation started three years previously); to teach remedial basic skills within the vocational education program; and to permit tenth graders to take exploratory vocational education work, expanding student numbers there substantially. While some attribute the latter changes in part to the MES program's emphasis on vocational education, the proficiency test rather than the school improvement program was clearly the driving force.

THE REORGANIZATION, AGAIN. A few months later more confusion and uncertainty appeared. In March 1986, two board members, with the tacit support of the superintendent, revived the earlier proposal to reorganize the high school into four houses — academic, vocational, business, and general. A small committee (the two board members, principal Hayes, and three central office administrators) began to plan, and carried out staff and student surveys.

Staff responses ranged from strongly negative to moderately positive. Their main hopes included more individualization and faculty responsiveness to students; stronger, more autonomous academic and vocational education programs with decentralized administrative authority; student belongingness and sense of pride; better "cut-across" offerings (art, physical education, and so on); and "shaking up the existing situation."

The main concerns — downplayed in formal reports by the principal — were the large size (1,500) of the general house ("it will be a zoo . . . the colors will be black and blue") and staff reluctance to be assigned there; faculty fragmentation and morale problems; elitism, tracking, and possible resegregation; disruption of student relationships; battles over the place of special education in the school; scheduling; and increased difficulty in doing remedial work.

Student data were strongly negative, but similarly downplayed in formal meetings and reports. Though students expected possibly increased learning, they were concerned about divisiveness, "creaming" (pulling better students off into the academic house), losing friends, and competition between curricula, and were critical of the sudden, top-down introduction of the idea.

A September 1986 start was being pushed for, but most administrators agreed that the problems of scheduling, staffing, space reallocation, and painting and repairs would be "astronomical . . . a nightmare . . . impossible" in this time frame. In June 1986 the reorganization was postponed for one year.

In any case, the demands of responding to this initiative had taken center stage, and planning for the next year's MES work was done hastily and on a pro forma basis (a central office memo and meeting pushing it were on May 1, with a May 19 deadline). The IPL scanning work was tried out briefly in a couple of departments, but few expected it to go further during the 1986–87 school year.

As the 1985–86 school year ended, the more conservative V.P. for curriculum decided to retire. She was replaced by the more progressive V.P. Griffith, who had recovered from a heart attack and was ready to get back to work.

Problems and How They Were Coped With

Uncertainty seemed to surround the MES program. There was a school-level steering group, but it existed in name only: It did not meet. Some components of the program did not have a designated manager, and no vice-principal was in charge of the effort. The principal, nominally responsible for coordination, did not know the status of some major pieces when asked about them in 1986. The MES programs dealing with attendance, dropouts, and disruptive behavior tended to be technical in nature, and handled by one or two people. Thus for most teachers the program was largely invisible. The Vocational Education supervisor worked hard on his part of MES and found it helpful, but, as is typical of high schools, the Vocational Education department was relatively isolated from others in the school.

One administrator commented on the elusive quality of MES, saying that "whatever people perceive it to be, it is." Contributing to the vagueness was the fact that the planned technical assistance from the state, never strong, had largely disappeared during 1985–86. Overall, the MES program didn't seem to touch Chester Central as an organization; its components were inserted without changing anything very substantially.

If implementation of the MES part of the program was slow and uncertain, on IPL the central office "just dove in." IPL was *not* invisible. The curriculum alignment piece of IPL did stimulate active involvement on the part of core departments (although other departments, such as Fine Arts and Home Economics, were uncertain or resistant, and had no guidelines). The coordinating meetings of administrators and supervisors were viewed as productive. The pressure and support emanating from the central office were more consistent here than for MES.

However, IPL work did not proceed without problems. District support for the program was not always consistent. The schedule change that permitted the curriculum alignment work to go on had to be taken from school-level rather than district in-service time. As a consequence most school-wide faculty meetings and other in-service were eliminated for the year.

The proposed process of classroom scanning to determine time on task was almost universally viewed as inappropriate for high schools. Since all of the training materials showed elementary school classrooms, this skepticism was not surprising. In addition, teachers were not keen about the fact that the scanning would be carried out by administrators. There was little clarification of whether the classroom scanning would be connected to the district's and school's evaluation procedures, although it was not to be used in that way "this year." The main response to complaints about the controversial scanning program was to delay it until it could be better adapted to the secondary setting and the supervisory relationship could be clarified.

Confusion about classroom scanning was met with limited clarification. Bartlett's initial enthusiasm for acting as a trainer and facilitator for the high school's IPL program indicated his support, but in fact his responsibilities kept him from carrying the promise into practice. The principal had never been a strong advocate of IPL, although she was unwilling to oppose the district office's enthusiasm. In the absence of any strong advocate within the school, there was much muttering, "downtown is jamming IPL down our throats." Others saw it variously as something that "will tear the school apart," and as something that will "just go away."

By the end of the first year, many teachers seemed demoralized. The norms that made implementation hard ("here it comes again," "don't rock the boat," "we are not good finishers") were being substantially reinforced.

Administrators also said, "We have been directed to do it . . . we have to find something we can use [from this program]," and "I don't know if this can be our main thrust [next year]. Every year we get a new one." Thus, dealing with the complex demands of MES/IPL became a sort of weary acceptance of the inevitable. In one cabinet meeting where objections to scanning were raised, the principal's response was simply,

"It doesn't matter whether we are pro or con. What we're here for is making it work."

Preliminary Results

By the summer of 1986, after nearly two years of involvement with MES/IPL, it was fair to say that MES implementation had been scattered and incomplete, with the possible exception of a few portions: the computer lab, in-school suspension room, vocational education, career advisement, and the testing center. But most of this was not very visible to teachers. The IPL curriculum alignment work had proceeded moderately well: Lesson plans were ready in most departments for quarters 2 and 3, with work on 4 and 1 to come. However, little or no work had been done on classroom scanning.

It was probably still too early to draw any conclusions about the long-term impacts of the program on the school, students, or teachers. Some administrators were guardedly optimistic: "The first year is like a death. You just have to go through it. You stumble anyway. Next year maybe we'll fly." "Next year I hope you could come back to see how did it go." But most teachers and administrators believed that MES and IPL would "be forgotten after the summer, or when the MES money goes away." "Programs only last as long as the money's there; then they fall by the wayside."

Generally speaking, though the district office continued to push the MES/IPL program, a sense of excitement and ownership was lacking at the high school. The state-funded "mother program," MES, which was supposed to be an umbrella planning effort, was largely invisible in the school, as we've noted.

IPL was, at best, controversial, although it had generated some energy in core departments for curriculum alignment. Tying MES/IPL to actual instruction, where it would make a difference for students, seemed problematic to all involved. One other positive payoff was more time for collaborative work in departments, as a consequence of the curriculum alignment work. It was unclear whether this would continue, as the work had been largely completed.

Epilogue

As with our other sites, we returned to Chester Central two years later to see how the change effort had fared, what its results were, and what might explain implementation and outcome.

Subsequent Events and Changes

During 1986–87, people at Chester Central High School were deep-ly involved in preparing for the reorganization of the school. In addi-tion, a central office-mandated basic skills remediation program, which involved pulling students out of their regular classes, began and "almost tore the school apart." Meanwhile, MES activities continued, but little more was done on IPL.

During 1987–88, the reorganization began. That, and associated central office interventions, placed nearly everyone at the school under great stress. People said: "A really difficult year . . . completely bedlam . . . I'm totally frustrated and blown out . . . it was physically a night-mare . . . it's a zoo — disorganized and mismanaged . . . I feel ashamed and worthless that I can't do something [to improve things] . . . it was the worst year in 36 years of teaching."

The new plan involved 3 houses and clusters of 125 students, with a team of teachers from English, Math, Social Studies, and Science work-ing together. Each was led by a vice-principal, with an assistant. This part of the reorganization went relatively smoothly — in the sense that students seemed to like the setup and reportedly adapted well.

But there were many problems and stresses. The critical role of the vice-principal for central support services was never really defined clearly, so that attendance, discipline, student activities, and security were managed in an uncoordinated, decentralized way — although cen-tralized records were still necessary. Other problems that teachers com-plained about included physical movement of offices, files, and materi-als; new roles to learn for most people; a secretarial revolt (who could legitimately give them work?); poor guidance functioning (in the face of 300 new students); continuing ambiguity about behavioral expectations for adults; poor fit of facilities to the house plan (no science labs in some houses); much-reduced contact between teachers and department chairs (who felt a loss of power); increased conflict among staff and among supervisors; mistrust among supervisors and V.P.'s.

As if these problems were not enough, the central office reduced staffing from six V.P.'s to four, and disciplinarians from four to two, and would not replace people who left. A central office supervisor, assigned by the associate superintendent for curriculum to assist the school, be-gan to visit the school daily. It was almost as if he took over the manage-ment of the school: He made a wide range of decisions, including when to schedule High School Proficiency Tests, the introduction of Saturday detentions, the assignment of V.P.'s to central office committees, and a requirement that all administrators do periodic cafeteria duty. Protests by the principal were overruled on several occasions.

MES received a one-year extension, and its activities continued during 1987–88. Little was visible on the IPL front.

How the Program Stands Now

MES's extension ended in the summer of 1988. Though some say the incentives/rewards activities (T-shirts, awards, scholars' banquet) have been helpful, the silk screen shop for job printing is a success, and the time-out center and computer facilities are useful, the high school staff, responding to a district questionnaire, ranked MES activities low — 12th on the list of 15 key areas in terms of their importance to students. (By contrast, elementary staff gave MES a high rank of 2.5; junior high, 8.5; and administrators, 2.) A key district office administrator commented that MES had solved some problems through hiring extra staff — but that these positions were difficult to institutionalize. As of now the central office MES manager "has nothing to do."

There is little overt IPL activity ("it was treated as an option"), no support has been provided, and central office and school priorities are elsewhere. Classroom scanning, as predicted, has not been implemented at all, and the teachers' union has filed a grievance against it.

Even so, there are some useful IPL residues: continued coordination of testing and the curriculum; widespread use of quarterly lesson plans for 1986–87 (and in some departments during 1987–88). Forty-nine percent of the high school staff said the quarterly planning idea was well implemented (a figure very close to what others at all system levels said).

Outcomes

It is fair to say that student learning has probably not been directly affected by the MES/IPL program. The curriculum alignment procedures undoubtedly helped clarify educational goals, but those goals must be achieved by instructional change — and that is not particularly evident. Though writing scores on the state's proficiency test are up in 1988 for the high school, reading and math are down. About one-third of students are said to need remediation, which is similar to the figure at the end of 1986.

For many schools in our survey it seemed relatively easy to affect school climate for teachers and students in a short period of time. But even here Chester Central cannot be said to have improved. The morale problems among faculty and administrators are in abundant evidence in the descriptions presented above; a sense of low self-esteem permeates both adult and student groups in the school.

The positive impact of the reorganization's first year is also hard to judge. A report to the board by the principal noted some short-term benefits (better articulation between junior highs and senior highs, earlier program selection, less traffic in hallways after the bell, fewer post-September schedule changes, on-paper decentralization of instructional leadership). It also said that longer-term benefits such as reduced dropouts, better test scores, more college acceptance, more vocational education enrollment, fewer students in basic skills classes, and reduced "transitional" house students would occur "in time."

It does appear that the school is more responsive to student needs than before. But attendance this year is about the same as before (85%), and a central office study of "school leavers" shows a dropout increase: Altogether, 26.5 percent of Chester Central High students left during the 1986–87 school year. Discipline is said by several people to be worse than before.

In summary, although much effort has gone into renewal at Chester Central over the past four years, students cannot be said to have benefited visibly, and there is abundant evidence that the work climate for administrators and teachers has deteriorated.

Why Did This Happen? A Reflective Review

Early Implementation

Why did early implementation go as it did? Certain pre-conditions seemed important: the prior history of follow-through failure on improvement projects; distant, top-down school–central office relationships; and a school that was quite "loosely coupled" to begin with, with a climate of blaming and powerlessness. The fact that both MES and IPL were initiated top-down did little to build program ownership or initiative taking at the school level.

Program design posed a different set of restraints on success. Both programs were largely technical in nature, and did not address the inevitable organizational issues they generated. No one seemed to have a very clear vision of what sort of change process would be required to move toward effective implementation. The invisibility (and complexity) of MES and the fact that IPL violated norms about supervision and was poorly adapted for high schools increased resistance.

Although both programs encountered many problems, the school received little beyond initial assistance from state or central office, and — given lack of ownership — coped with the problems in a generally superficial way, often delaying or avoiding problem-solving efforts, and coordinating efforts only weakly. Influence over the programs in the school was thus not widely shared; the collaborative work and interaction that had been inspiring in previous change projects were mostly absent. The interference effects of other state-mandated programs and the district-initiated reorganization were substantial.

Later Implementation

Why did things go as they did during 1986–88? Chester Central High's reorganization efforts appear to have been unusually difficult because they were done too soon, with a weakly managed "band-aid approach" that left many issues ambiguous and confused. In effect, the change activities exacerbated already existing problems at the high school rather than solving them.

The central office had many other priorities (desegregation, state monitoring of program adequacy, a new dropout prevention program, the basic skills program), and key administrators felt that the high school *should* be more controlled than it had been, and be more cost-effective.

The tendency to blame rather than search for solutions contributed to a sense of being out of control at all levels. Though a high school administrator said, "They have their nose in here too much . . . they should let *us* have egg on our face," a central office person said, "Sometimes things have to come top-down, especially if there's resistance . . . maybe some of them should go sell newspapers."

Why the Outcomes?

The results for students and staff at Chester Central High were not promising. What might account for the disappointing outcomes?

The reorganization (itself, like MES and IPL, pushed from outside the school), was approached with good will and energy by high school staff (and the principal did make an effort to share influence and involve people more fully). But the combination of the severe problems any reorganization involves, along with the central office's simultaneous withdrawal of financial resources and addition of control, and the state proficiency test-driven basic skills program, appears to have induced a very high degree of stress, a deteriorating central office–school relationship, and a considerable loss of hope in many people at the high school.

We can also note that MES and IPL, both of which had noble goals and were reasonably well planned and designed, were, with some exceptions, never really well implemented. We can hardly expect non-implementation to change things positively for staff and students — and, as Chester Central High's history shows, non-implementation, after initial arousal of expectations, makes for a continuing cycle of discouragement and cynicism.

The Chester Central High story is not a happy one. But it has no villains, nor any fools. Well-intentioned, capable people found themselves in a set of circumstances that was like a web they could not or would not escape from. The challenge for Chester Central, and for many urban high schools in similar odds-against predicaments, is to cut the web and move out of it.

In the next part of this book, we begin looking across our five cases and the survey, describing the key issues that make the difference between success and failure in improving urban high schools.

NOTE

1. This report is drawn, with additions, from the original case study (Miles & Rosenblum, 1987). Quotations come directly from the case.

Part III

LEADERSHIP AND MANAGEMENT: WHAT MAKES FOR SUCCESS?

In this part of the book, we are working to draw lessons from our cases and the survey. What key factors seem to have brought about successful improvement efforts? We will be dealing with five major issues, chapter by chapter: the importance of the school's external and internal context as conditioners of change; how planning proceeds most effectively; vision-building and the empowerment that goes with it; getting and managing the resources needed; and the day-to-day problem finding and problem coping involved in the change process.

For each major issue, we will compare what happened in our A, B, and C schools to see what the correlates of success seem to have been. We will also turn to our survey in a similar quest, comparing more and less successful schools to see what worked, and documenting with specific examples from the cases and survey. As we proceed, we will mark off clear conclusions, cast in the form of general guidelines for action.

We will also link our findings as carefully as we can to the existing literature on school improvement and organizational change. Much is known about the leadership and management of change, and we need to see how relevant it is to the problems of improving big-city high schools.

In our final chapter we reflect on what it takes to put our findings to use. Moving from ideas – even those expressed as practical guidelines – to productive action takes both courage and specific skill, and we identify what may be required.

7

In the Beginning
Looking Out and Looking In

You wouldn't understand what it's like out there. This [the school] is heaven, a kingdom by comparison.   (Bartholdi's principal)

We have seen the enemy, and they is us.   (Walt Kelly's "Pogo")

Praise Allah, but first tie your camel to a post.   (Sufi saying)

Urban schools find themselves beset by a large number of difficult contextual conditions that may undermine administrators' and teachers' belief that they *can* make a difference, making the odds seem great even for those who are willing to give reform a try. We found that the realities our schools faced before they began their efforts were all difficult, and varied only in degree rather than in their basic nature. Before turning dreams of a better school into a major change program, the key actors — administrators and teachers — need to tie up their camels by making a realistic assessment of the obstacles they will face. Acknowledging obstacles does not mean that the journey toward improvement will stop, but it will help to pinpoint where special leadership and management skills may be called for.

We will focus on two types of contextual influences on the change process. *External conditions*, or the nature of the community and district setting, were shown in Chapter 3 to generate "rare but intractable problems" for a small proportion of the surveyed schools. Our cases let us elaborate on just how external conditions affected school-based efforts to improve. *Internal conditions* of the school also exerted a powerful effect — both positive and negative — on reform. The pre-existing school characteristics we will look at include staff cohesiveness, the results of previous school improvement efforts, the stories that staff tell about "what it used to be like" in the school, and the structure of the school. As this list shows, we consider "context" to be not only geographical, but social and historical: Contexts deal with place and with what goes on in that place, conditioned by what has gone before.

All five schools were in difficult, demanding contexts, but many of their other basic characteristics differ. And, although we sought schools where reasonably successful improvement efforts were going on, as we've seen, there proved to be real differences in success among them. These differences are very useful, in fact: We can make some comparative generalizations about what contextual features help to shape the outcomes of a major change program, and why.

THE EXTERNAL CONTEXT

The Community

As we noted in Chapter 3, our case studies, like those in the larger survey, examine schools with typical inner-city student populations, and typical urban problems. All of them had a history of poor student achievement and of difficulty and disruption. Compared with suburban districts, however, their most unique feature is the turbulence of their community settings.

Problem Communities

The description of Bartholdi's location gives a general flavor that applies to many inner-city schools. Although the focus is on the physical quality of the environment, there is a clear juxtaposition of school (which aims for stability, concentration, and a belief that hard work can pay off in student success) and community (which has a volatile and changing population, believing education to be largely irrelevant to the press of safety and survival).[1]

■ The immediate community setting is one of working-class homes but many buildings were burned in the '70s and there are many condemned buildings. When David Martinez, the present principal, came to the school on his first day, he walked out to find his car's battery stolen. The area is dangerous . . . there's a wry saying that new teachers in New York are allowed to refuse only two assignments: to Riker's Island [a prison] and Bartholdi.

In Burroughs and Agassiz, a different but equally familiar pattern occurred: Students were not drawn from the neighborhood at all, but bused in from other parts of the city. Few cities that have operated under a court order to desegregate can claim that the social disruption has passed.

■ The dramatic and devastating recent history of [the Cleveland schools] . . . has not been told. But press files and personal accounts suggest that it may rival . . . Boston and New York for its nasty politics, overt racism, and shocking disregard for educational quality. . . . The turmoil of these years was not helped by the fact that Cleveland's white establishment does not live in the city. . . . The current superintendent, with four children, lives in the suburbs . . . simmering racial and social class animosity . . . characterize relations between ethnic working-class and black communities. . . . According to the educational writer of . . . the [local] newspaper, a project to develop a story on race relations in the schools had to be shelved when few high school students were willing to talk about it.

While Chester's situation was not as severe, the community problems were reflected in the students.

■ Many have serious home problems: lack of money, abuse by parents, pregnancy, illiteracy. One estimate is that 20 to 30 percent of the students have children . . . they come to school for security, companionship, food, and heat rather than education — "which won't pay off for them anyway," according to many educators [because of the high local unemployment rate].

Only the unified district where Alameda was located appeared to be somewhat different. This large southwestern area, composed of three distinct cities, lacked the visible inner-city urban blight of the Northeast and Midwest. Because of its geographic expanse, the consolidated district contained sizeable pockets of more affluent schools and a magnet examination high school that helped to prevent middle-class parents from fleeing. More accustomed to mobility and ethnic diversity, the community context seemed less hostile. Nevertheless, until the reform effort began at Alameda, there was widespread public concern about gangs, graffiti, and vandalism at this high school, located next to a barrio community, and drawing many students from mixed housing. Middle-class district parents viewed Alameda as a choice only for those who were not clever enough to get their child assigned to another school.

Community Support

Our two "A" high schools are both situated in communities where (despite past disruptions) there was a strong local push for improved education, and a willingness to put some community effort behind it.

The Alameda story emphasized the community's concern to "do something" about the high school; the reform- and open-minded nature of the school board was clear. The surprisingly long tenure of the innovation-minded superintendent is another indicator of local support; he would not have stayed as long if the community had not been behind him.

Boston's tradition is less proud. However, the Agassiz story reflects relatively stable leadership (three years of superintendent Bud Spillane, who was a dynamic and nationally visible figure), during which there was a fairly open reform mandate and little direct interference from the School Committee due to court-ordered supervision of the school system. In addition, the strong support and pressure for reform from the business community was a clear factor in filling an innovation vacuum at the school level. Finally, although conflict between blacks and whites over the schools was profound in the mid-'70s, there appeared to be an uneasy truce when this story began.

In contrast, Cleveland, New York, and Chester had continuing instability in local responses to the schools. In New York, schools and education have often been a football in the continuing battle between city and state. For the mayor, the schools were no more important than the public transportation system. Educational priorities do not come out clearly in the case, perhaps because of the politicized environment. Chester and Burroughs were both disasters in terms of community context. Both were plagued with divisive leadership, conflict between the superintendent and school board, and widespread rumors of corruption. In both cases there was a struggle between the black and white communities over school control. There was little clear pressure from community leaders for reform, and no apparent business involvement. Both cities, like the sending area for Bartholdi, had lost their middle-class families, although some were drifting back in Chester.

Note that size does not seem to be a critical factor. Of the two least successful schools, one is located in a large city, one in our smallest city. Of the two most successful, one is big city, and one is semi-urban sprawl. Neither do other characteristics of the community context (such as racial mix, desegregation effort, or parent activism) appear important.

CONCLUSION: Strong support from the community at large, coupled with pressure for improvement, seems to be an important stimulus and helps to maintain program activities. Highly politicized community contexts, or those with little consensus about the main educational priorities, provide poor contexts.

The Role of the State

State influence was modest in three schools (at least for the time being), although all of the states claimed to have significant reform programs. At Bartholdi, the recent proposal for state reform measures had little clear effect on the way staff thought about the school and what they were doing; the long-standing Regents' examination program, which had provided graduation standards in the past, was irrelevant to a school population as severely disadvantaged as theirs. In New York, schools have been largely insulated from direct state pressure by a tradition that reluctantly gives the city autonomy which other districts do not have. In Agassiz and Burroughs, state influence was almost nonexistent: School people simply didn't talk about the state, its programs, or its staff. Agassiz, for example, is located in the state capital; the governor of the state was widely viewed as "pro-education"; and a recent school-focused improvement program was passed by the legislature. Yet the only discussion of state programs revolved around a generalized irritation at the increase in mandated testing.

State influence was strongly negative in another case, Chester, where the state provided money and a program framework, but the program was not designed to fit the school's context, and the support was erratic and insufficient, except in the dollar funding level. What we observed in Chester was the piling up of mandated programs, mostly based on testing and individualized remediation. Each of these programs had *prima facie* validity as a mechanism to stimulate improvement and attention to Chester's many at-risk students, but collectively they exhausted the staff, increased central office bureaucracy, and distracted attention from the efforts to implement the state's targeted (and much touted) Urban Improvement Program.

In the single case of Alameda, we saw the state playing a positive role through two well-designed programs that were integrated into the school's activities. But the analysis in the case indicates that one was incorporated into the school only as an add-on to a district effort that was already implemented, while the California School Improvement Program was not really a direct state intervention, but a form of revenue sharing that had only a few planning strings attached to it.

There are four different kinds of state contexts in the study, if we use two dimensions to classify the historical relationship between state and schools (Dentler, 1984). The first dimension is the traditional state stance on *regulation* (for example, how deep and penetrating the state rules are). The second concerns the traditional posture of the state on providing support and *assistance* for local districts. New York has traditionally been both highly regulatory and supportive. The recent program (CSIP) targeted at the most poorly performing schools *required* them to work on a detailed improvement plan that mandated and monitored specific improvements, but "Bartholdi is among the 30 schools with the most severe problems where a board-assigned facilitator has provided help." New Jersey has traditionally been regulatory, but not terribly strong in initiating support. Chapter 6 notes that the state's Urban Improvement Program was initially designed to provide not only money, but technical assistance from the state; the technical assistance disappeared, however. Many state regulatory initiatives made for work and pressure at Chester Central High School, but resulted in little indication of actual improvement. California has a relatively weak position in terms of regulation, but has traditionally initiated many supportive programs — including the two that formed the basis of Alameda's improvement effort. Massachusetts and Ohio are low on both dimensions, providing little regulation and little assistance.

Four of the states may be characterized as relatively stable in terms of leadership and policies (Ohio, California, New York, and Massachusetts), while one is unstable and rather politicized (New Jersey). New Jersey's historical and continued instability in terms of reform measures is reflected in the Chester case report, where we see the negative results at the school level in an array of reform initiatives that never seemed to be funded for long enough, or to be guided by a consistent policy direction.

CONCLUSION: Direct and positive state influence over the kinds of major school reform efforts that we are studying is negligible. Our cases don't support the idea that increased state influence over activities at the school level – either through regulation or support – will produce significant effects in the absence of much more powerful local factors.

The District Office

Only the Alameda district seems to have had an effective relationship between school and central office administrators. Here, the superintendent's door was open to Cara Mosely, the principal. He was enthusiastic about her suggestions for using the state programs for a broad improvement program, and gave her a great deal of latitude.

■ The superintendent has also been a strong advocate for staff development and recognizing skilled teachers. "Teachers are usually underutilized," he said. . . . Stressing the importance of leaders, he said, "Change very seldom begins at the teacher level without leadership" . . . [he] supports school-based management, and empowerment of staff down the organizational line.

Most of the schools had a mixed relationship with district office personnel, in which the schools faced with a negative district context found one or two people in the central office who can "do things for us," or "help us out." Bartholdi got modest levels of support from the district office on a continuing basis for a variety of things; perhaps the most important support was the "at-the-elbow" assistance that a retired principal provided to the newly appointed David Martinez. On the whole, however, the district office was viewed as remote, and 110 Livingston Street — the New York City central office — was as distant and inaccessible as the White House. Agassiz got some support (program and moral) from the personnel department. The city-wide office responsible for designing and managing the Boston Compact was viewed as largely irrelevant to their work. But the district's Compact design provided resources (the business and university partners) and a legitimating framework for action. Even Burroughs could point to a single stalwart friend in court in the guise of a specialist who was willing to provide advice and assistance to the improvement effort. Chester's relationship initially appears to have been an unmitigated disaster — yet the district did write a proposal that provided them with lots of money. Thus, in many respects the district offices served as a useful stimulus for change in our sites.

But the instances of interference — both direct and because of conflicting demands — are legion in every case except Alameda. Unlike states, whose direct influence tends to be very limited, districts can make life difficult for schools on a daily basis. Interference is rarely intentionally disruptive to a school improvement effort; rather, it disrupts because it has not taken the school context or needs into consideration. Relationships between urban high schools and their district offices are like enduring bad marriages. Although the relationship is rarely uniformly positive or negative, on balance it tends to cause the improving school a lot of trouble. Yet, there is no possibility of divorce, and opportunities for positive mutual influence tend to be very limited.

Engagement and Bureaucratization

Let us provide more detail on school–district relationships.[2] Two dimensions affecting the quality of the relationship between school and district are the degree of *engagement*, and the level of *bureaucratization*. By engagement we mean a relationship that has some shared goals and objectives, reasonably clear and frequent communication, and mutual coordination and influence. By bureaucratization we mean control through rules and regulations, rather than through individualistic relationships, or through goal-based accountability.

We can probably assume that some level of engagement between district and school is a good idea; after all, districts and schools are legally and historically intertwined in the same enterprise. But the cases present a dismal picture of that possibility. As defined, engagement is dependent on consistency of communication and policies. This is not possible in systems that have high levels of turnover in key administrative positions.

Furthermore, district offices, at least in larger districts, are viewed as very remote from the school. School people rarely know more than one or two district people well; they use their contacts with these few individuals to get what they can from the system. Research suggests that an important aspect of open and honest communication is trust. But trust does not typically exist between strangers; rather, it must be built up over a period of sustained interaction. Turnover of staff in the schools and central office, and frequent reorganizations (so that people who remain are in different positions) decrease the potential for developing sustained relationships, and lower the level of trust and subsequent communication.

Look at New York: five chancellors since 1980. Cleveland: seven superintendents since the mid-'70s. Boston: musical chairs at the top between 1974 and 1982. Then, after three years of stability, another new superintendent, very different in style and programmatic emphasis from the last (and who, during his initial reorganizations, dismantled the school improvement office that sponsored the Boston Compact program). Only Chester and Alameda have the kind of administrative stability that could permit close engagement.

The role of districts as bureaucratic rule makers has been increasing rapidly over the last 20 years, possibly as a function of increasing size. Has this change also been in response to increasing regulation from state and federally funded programs? Probably: It's a form of protection to have explicit interpretations of rules. A rules-based approach to running the district is also a consequence of civil rights suits, because court-ordered desegregation requires many things that were previously within the discretion of individual staff members and schools to be covered by clear, district-wide standards.

But is a rules-based relationship between district and school necessary? We doubt it; Alameda is an example of a relatively non-bureaucratic district, with lean staff and a non-regulatory posture. In Boston, superintendent Spillane was trying to introduce minimized central control and emphasize school-based management, but didn't have a strong program, and was hampered by a bloated bureaucracy and an intrusive court-supervised desegregation plan.

We observe three different contexts at work in our cases, only two of which seem to permit effective school improvement. The first type is exemplified by Cleveland, Boston, and New York, which are *bureaucratic but disengaged* systems. In these systems there are plenty of rules and regulations. Just because the system is in turmoil and/or is ineffective on some dimensions does not prevent that. In fact, in this kind of system, with rotating people at the top for short periods of time, there is rarely an opportunity to "clean up" the rules and throw out conflicting ones, or ones that don't make sense given new programs and priorities. (This is probably particularly true of New York City, where rules can come from any one of the four levels between chancellor and principal.)

Reliance on rules is also exemplified by union contracts, and the vigilance with which the unions often insist on the "letter of the law." Because of the district's rule orientation, teachers feel they must defend themselves against exploitation, and develop their own formal system to parallel the bureaucracy. Union issues were at the fore in Cleveland, and the case attributes them to district problems. Union issues were a minor factor in New York; in Boston, staffing and staff rotation issues were a result of prior union grievances.

But with the exception of "sent rules," in these three cases the district and school often seemed to operate virtually in isolation from each other — that is, they were not engaged. At the most extreme (Cleveland) the district provided no support (except for one dedicated individual), no leadership, no new ideas, and no programs, except for the new district-wide curriculum. And the curriculum caused one of the more important components of Burroughs' improvement effort to fail.

■ The faculty . . . had designed a program to provide more attention to students . . . by clustering them in small, stable groups that were taught by cross-disciplinary teams. . . . Teachers felt that the new curriculum was [so] restrictive that they could not continue team teaching across disciplines without risking low test scores for failure to cover prescribed content . . . teams continued to meet, but rather than working together on cross-subject lesson plans and student problems, they organized awards assemblies and recreational events.

In two less extreme cases of bureaucratic disengagement (New York and Boston), there were new ideas and programs — even some support — but they were largely imposed rather than responsive to actual school needs. In New York, the borough superintendent can respond to specific school situations (for instance, sending the retired principal to help a new principal learn the ropes), but the office did not seem to have the resources to mount more comprehensive programs or assistance. In New York (as in Boston), the district superintendency seemed a weak position that added another layer rather than helping to make the system more locally responsive. (Note that in the smaller Boston system, the principal almost always talked directly with "Court Street," although there was a district superintendent to whom he nominally reported.) In the New York City case, the principal seemed confused about whom he should go to — probably with justification.

Though New York change programs almost invariably came from 110 Livingston Street, and Boston ones from Court Street, the new programs tended to get set up in ad hoc offices (the New York DRP program and the Compact), which were not always well coordinated with the rest of the bureaucracy, adding to uncertainty.

In a disengaged but regulatory system, the district/school system becomes nothing but a pesky set of constraints and conflicting demands: It offers no real support, and the principals — even strong ones like those at Burroughs and Agassiz — don't even bother to try to exercise influence over the district, or do anything but work more or less within the rules and try to manage competing programs that are "sent."

Passive rule evasion is not rare, which decreases engagement, because communication upward becomes a facade. And because of limited support and understanding at the central office level, and conflicting demands, even potentially good district programs may not work out well at the school level. If they do, it is for other reasons, as in the case of Agassiz, where the principal probably spent up to 25 percent of his time managing central office–school relationships.

Note that these were the three largest districts — by any standards "big city," and more than twice as big as Alameda or Chester. Creating effective engagement *is* harder in big systems. But it is also clearly possible: One would have to say that the parts of a company such as 3M or Hewlett Packard (larger and physically scattered) are more engaged (Kanter, 1983; Peters & Waterman, 1984). Size may not be the issue for regulatory stance, either: Chester is just as regulatory, and the smallest of our districts.

At least in the regulatory/disengaged situation an effective principal can actively buffer the school, and be a careful outlaw with regard to central regulations. (This cuts both ways, of course. Conservative or ineffective principals can block central office initiatives that are well conceived and desirable.) A second (but even less promising) type of school–district relationship appeared in Chester: *engaged and regulatory*.

The superintendent's original intent at Chester was to combine pressure and support, by having each school have a central office person as link between the school and the demands of the mandated change program. But Superintendent Bartlett, who was to be the link to Chester Central High School, never really followed through. In Chester there were "plans" for increasing the engagement between the superintendent and the high school improvement effort — which never materialized. Both sides blamed each other for the lack of mutual influence.

■ The principal says, "I've had four different supervisors during my four years as principal . . . " and complains that she does not know to whom she should report. . . . From the district side . . . the high school is seen as an enigmatic entity, hard to influence. One central office staff member stated that their hopes for changes in the cluster program had been sabotaged by uncooperative high school people.

Although Bartlett did not become personally engaged, however, his staff eventually assigned an individual from the district office to monitor the school in a highly intrusive fashion.

Bartlett did not support any request for increased autonomy from principal Hayes even when these were made to promote his own reform program. For example, he refused to permit the use of district staff development days for the More Effective Schools program implementation. Later, there was interference (board-imposed reorganization, in the middle of a major change program), which escalated later to micromanagement interventions — how testing should be scheduled, for example.

The evolving relationship between school and district showed the pathology of close engagement and regulation. Hayes apparently felt it was useless to continue to try: In exercising real leadership, she would just be setting herself up for failure. Yet, lack of leadership apparently led the central office to become more and more involved in "micromanaging" Chester Central High.

Let's imagine another scenario for Chester: Bartlett is appointed superintendent, and puts the mentoring of Hayes and high school reform simultaneously high on his agenda. He meets with her regularly, and makes sure that new high school efforts are co-announced, even if many of the ideas have come from him. He finds a consultant from a local college who can do for Hayes what the retired principal did for principal Martinez at Bartholdi. He helps Hayes to focus on organizational design issues, especially the role of vice-principals and department heads. When he sees IPL, and/or writes the MES proposal, he makes sure that she is responsible for the key elements of program design, along with several other high school staff members. Would engagement of this sort have made a positive difference, both in the structure of the relationship between district and school, and in Hayes' behavior and potential? That seems a reasonable speculation.

The third and only clearly positive district context was Alameda's, which was *engaged and non-bureaucratic*. The district staffing was thin — tiny, compared with the others. The limited staff size meant that any district-wide effort had to involve contributions from other administrators and teachers. Essentially, the picture was one of co-management, with good levels of engagement and less reliance on formal rules. Of course, one could not simply introduce the idea of co-management into Chester without making other changes — any more than the idea of school-based management could work in Boston within the system as it exists.[3]

The experience in our cases makes us seriously question the function of the district as a "manager of school improvement," especially in light of the increasing role of states in stimulating improvement and regulating local education. When state and district each become more involved with designing and managing school improvement activities, there is a sharp increase in the likelihood of conflicting demands on schools.

CONCLUSION: The best district contexts for school improvement may be characterized by the adage "less is more," at least on the dimension of bureaucratization. In general, high engagement is better for school improvement, coupled with fewer rules. In bureaucratic districts, school administrators must actively negotiate for latitude, or even "go outside the rules" if effective school-based change is to take place.

Policy Design Strategies

The district–school relationship is connected with another issue: what we have called open versus closed program design. We may distinguish four kinds of centrally initiated school improvement models.

1. A *top-down* implementation strategy (strong central control over both the process of change and accountability for well-defined outcomes).
2. A *goal-based* accountability strategy (weak control over the change process, strong accountability for outcomes).
3. An *evolutionary planning* strategy (strong control over the change process, with school-level definition of desired outcomes).
4. A *professional investment* strategy (weak central control over both process and outcomes).[4]

Evolutionary planning models look very promising, as in Agassiz and Alameda: The next chapter will explore the characteristics and activities of evolutionary planning that made it so effective. But schools are often bombarded with a mixture of *externally initiated* improvement programs based on different models. For example, in Agassiz we have the evolutionary planning model embedded in Spillane's school-based management program, the goal-driven accountability model of the Boston Compact, and the top-down implementation model of the new district curriculum. Some programs, such as MES/IPL in Chester, have different components that are based on different models. Look especially at poor principal Hayes: On the one hand, she was expected to be leading a participatory planning activity; on the other, she was faced with many top-down demands for concrete implementation.

In order to cope with such demands, the school and principal have to figure out which underlying model is most acceptable to the district administration if any progress is to be made at the school level. For example, implementation of and compliance with the central office's initiatives seemed to be required in Chester, no matter what the rhetoric; Agassiz's principal Cohen took a bet that he could get away with using any kind of planning model he wished as long as he met the district's requirement to turn in a formal annual plan that included the district's goals; Bartholdi's approach started out by emphasizing program implementation, but as the program steering group gained confidence and skill, more attention was paid to an evolutionary planning process and less to specific goals set from the outside.

In this way, district assumptions and norms become a filter for all kinds of action within the school: The real questions are often, "What can we get away with?" or "What should I do that will cause least trouble for the school?" Perhaps this is one of the real bases for the confusion of schools: It is not just a matter of multiple programs, but multiple conflicting *assumptions* about the role of the school and the people in it vis-à-vis the district. A clear example of this can be seen in Bartholdi: Some of the sub-programs in CASA were based on a top-down implementation strategy, while others were locally invested (an evolutionary planning strategy). The state's comprehensive improvement program was also based on an evolutionary planning strategy.

What implications do district/state leadership and management of change have? In successful Alameda we saw stable leadership coming from the superintendent (and the state's chief school officer too): They set goals and standards, and designed big frameworks for program efforts. But there was little or no attempt to actually manage schools in terms of procedures: They were held accountable only for their improved *performance*, not for how they got there.[5] Some of the most clearly defined programs in Alameda High School (for example, the MIRT program) were still very flexible and were revised based on suggestions from teachers. Evidence suggests that individual schools in the Alameda district were also treated differently.

In Boston and New York, on the other hand, the central administration continually set precise goals like "5 percent reduction in dropout rates for the next five years for all schools," not acknowledging that schools have different populations, different needs, and different constituencies.[6] This is good public relations, but not helpful in getting schools to become more goal achievement-oriented themselves, and creates the Catch-22s that are noted in both cases.[7] The fact that Agassiz did well and Bartholdi reasonably well is traceable more to the *de facto* autonomy the schools had during implementation to check, revise, and improve what they were doing than to the externally set goals.

CONCLUSION: District programs that give more latitude to the schools in tailoring and developing improvement objectives *and* strategies may be more effective than those that provide very detailed mandates for goals and/or change processes.

THE INTERNAL CONTEXT

As we've seen, the external context is often difficult to manage or change, and also quite critical in determining the success of school change efforts. The internal context also contains a few important organizational characteristics that strongly condition improvement ventures. Some are also hard to alter, at least in the short run. We'll discuss organizational sagas[8] and school structure.

Organizational Sagas

"Deep history" is revealed by the spontaneous stories that individuals in the school offer as explanations for the organization and functioning of the school. When taken together, these stories form a saga that helps to define the culture of the school. The overall saga is usually unique and focuses on specific individuals or events in the school's past that have shaped its goals or character. In some cases, however, similar themes can be noted across schools. We saw three: staff cohesiveness, innovation history, and the "golden age" myth.

Staff cohesiveness was pointed to in both the Alameda and Agassiz cases as very high—in Agassiz, the class of '69; in Alameda, the close social relationships among staff ("we grew up together"), and the commitment to caring for students. In these two schools, new teachers were selected because they "fit" with the existing culture and goals of the school. Cohesiveness seems, in Chester's staff, to be particularly low, although the staff was exceptionally stable. There were many conflicts, both stated and unstated, and a tendency to blame everyone in sight for the problems in the school.

The two schools in the middle (Bartholdi getting better at managing its own school improvement activities; Burroughs deteriorating) show a more mixed pattern, largely due to staff instability. In Bartholdi, most conflicts seemed to be centered in the management team. There were some problems between departments, but at least a proportion of the teachers felt a "special sense of community." This, however, was limited to the stable group of teachers working on contract: The high proportion teaching on a per diem basis were not part of a solidary group. Burroughs presented a similar problem: High staff instability from district retrenchment and reassignment made cohesiveness, except among the small stable group of senior teachers, difficult. In these two cases we see the effects of district policies on staff cohesiveness.

Stories about *previous innovation efforts* are also very revealing. Two of the schools, Bartholdi and Chester, had disappointing previous results. Based on these cases we hypothesize that previous program failures can have two effects. First, a failed program produces a sense of loss and skepticism about future results. This was explicitly articulated in Chester, where people really worked at the Program Achieve effort, and in the more recent school climate improvement initiative, and then felt that nothing came through. Heightened expectations were dashed. Poorly implemented or ineffective prior programs can also produce a "so what" response to innovations, which seemed to be the case in Bartholdi. Here a sequence of similar programs produced the sense that there was "no follow-through." There was no sharp cynicism, as in Chester, but no sense of excitement either. The "so what" attitudes represented a major barrier that needed to be overcome before this program, originally classified as a "C" effort, could begin to succeed.

The three remaining schools tell no stories about past innovations; in fact, they seem almost "innovation-free" in their sagas. They also have no attachments to past efforts, or major cynicism. Alameda's district has been innovative for some time, but one gets no sense that Alameda itself had any significant improvement efforts (at least any that are remembered) going on prior to SIP. Agassiz's past is similarly innovation-free, at least in terms of what people remember. The staff there was reported to be skeptical and burned out, but a substantial number were pretty easily convinced to join the effort with just a few key early successes. Innovation freeness seemed to be a less important factor in Burroughs, but there is no evidence that previous innovations had a negative impact or a positive one.

Perhaps it is significant that in our five schools we have no instance of a school with a successful innovation history. We may guess that (1) successful reforms are rare in urban high schools; and (2) they appear only in the few schools that have maintained a steady habit of improvement initiatives over a long period of time.

A *"golden age" mythology* has been noted in other studies, especially in secondary schools (Deal & Rallis, 1981). The faculty looks back to some period — usually at least 10 years ago — when the place was, as they put it in Chester, "a paradise; how could they pay you to teach here?" This may be contrasted most clearly with Agassiz, where the local mythology accepts the fact that the school had a long history of mediocrity, and with Alameda, where staff believed that they had always nurtured their students, but didn't seem to believe that they were ever educationally effective prior to SIP.

A "golden age" mythology impedes change in two ways. First, it typically masks a set of teacher assumptions that are primarily student- (or community-) blaming: The golden age occurred at a time when students really wanted to learn, and so on. Recall that our survey suggests that nearly a quarter of the principals find teacher attitudes of this sort to be one of the few serious barriers to planning. Second, the myth typically acts as a barrier to real innovation in the school: It is essentially a conservative view, which emphasizes wanting to go back to the old ways. This is the downside of staff stability: A stable staff may be necessary for change, but it is also more likely to lead to a "golden age" framework.

Changing demographics that increase the number of low-SES students are part of the story, but can't be all of it, because they have affected every single one of our schools. Note, however, that the transition has been particularly sharp in Chester, where the school turned over from middle-class/professional kids to lots of welfare kids. The other schools either have been mixed for a long time, or were primarily working class from the beginning, as in Agassiz and Burroughs.

CONCLUSION: The "deep history" of each school dominates the story of what has happened, and includes attention to the contextual factors discussed above. Characteristics of the school's "deep history" that seem particularly important across cases are: (1) staff cohesiveness; (2) the absence of recent disappointing school improvement efforts; and (3) the absence of a "golden age" mythology.

The Existing School Structure

Our cases suggest that certain structural features — authority, role clarity, and school autonomy — were pre-conditions for getting things off the ground. Their absence produced major implementation problems for both Chester and Bartholdi. In Chester the lack of perceived autonomy at the school level was a major source of low morale for both teachers and administrators. But the problems did not lie only within the central office: Within the school the question of "who is responsible for what" was apparent at every turn. One of the problems with the More Effective Schools program in Chester was that it "didn't belong anywhere," and no one had clearly delegated responsibility for managing it. But this was not just a problem of change management: Lines of authority and responsibility for any aspect of school functioning were generally unclear. Thus, it was hard for people in the school to know where to turn when they had problems with the improvement efforts. In Bartholdi, the new principal was not a strong leader and, at the beginning of the program, no other experienced and well-respected staff person was in charge of the program either: There was no tradition of strong staff leadership in the school. The problems in Bartholdi were compounded by the difficult scheduling, including the "crazy 10-period day." The Bartholdi epilogue shows that, along with the increasing success of the improvement effort, clarification of roles and responsibilities, and the development of leaders among the management team and staff had occurred.

In contrast, authority, role clarity, and school autonomy were viewed as so important in Alameda and Agassiz that, although these schools looked pretty good on these dimensions even at the beginning of the program, both were actually incorporated as part of the overall strategy for improvement (the SIP, MIRT and Key Planners groups at Alameda, and the cluster team, the Student Support Team, and the scheduling changes at Agassiz).

CONCLUSION: The structure of the school will affect the change process and outcomes. Key structural features are the presence of clear lines of authority and responsibility, a clear role structure within the school, and school autonomy in relation to its district context.

CONCLUDING COMMENTS

What implications do these findings on the importance of context have for those directly involved in implementing school improvement programs?

First, it's useful for implementers to analyze the external pre-conditions for school improvement in the community and district; for example, the level of "politicizing" of education, support for real school improvement, administrative stability, the presence of some school autonomy, the opportunities for negotiating the rules or ignoring them.

Without appropriate pre-conditions, it is probably better not to launch a major school improvement effort. The chances for failure are high; and such a failure will affect future opportunities for success. It may be better to temporize with smaller-scale innovations that may keep the staff interested and mobilized, while parallel negotiation occurs to improve the pre-conditions, where possible.

The internal pre-conditions for school improvement are equally critical, specifically the organizational sagas and structure. If they are not promising, altering or dealing with them should become part of the design of the improvement program. Internal pre-conditions are difficult, but not impossible to change — usually easier than community and district factors.

The lesson from our successful cases is: Always keep one eye on the district. Be prepared to negotiate steadily but discreetly for special status, especially in a rule-oriented bureaucracy. Extra visibility for the school and program seems to create opportunities for extra resources and/or needed flexibility. It also appears that negotiating autonomy for the school and the staff is well worth the effort. In many cases what is asked for will be received.

NOTES

1. Throughout Chapters 7 to 11, quotes used are drawn from the longer unpublished case studies rather than from the previous three chapters. These include: Louis & Cipollone, 1986; Rosenblum, 1986; Farrar, 1987b; Miles, 1986; and Miles & Rosenblum, 1987.

2. The arguments made in this section are similar to those presented by Chubb (1988) based on analysis of a quantitative data base. Our arguments were developed independently (see Miles et al., 1986); the congruence of the conclusions increases our confidence.

3. As we write, Boston is on the brink of moving into school-based management, sparked by the mayor and superintendent. It has required substantial structural changes: Adding local school councils of teachers, administrators, parents, and external business or university partners with large autonomy in planning, fiscal, and hiring issues has been accompanied by reorganization of districts into four zones and decentralization of many Court Street staff to the zone offices, where school-based management assistance staff will work.

4. This framework was developed in Louis, 1989.

5. This is also true of the state programs that we studied. The California School Improvement Program, for example, specified that there should be a sip council, but gave schools a great deal of leeway as to how it should function, how the program should actually be managed, or what kinds of activities should be funded. Alameda, for example, was one of only a few schools that chose to support a sip coordinator nearly full-time, and in which the representative sip council was responsible for all dollar allocation decisions.

6. Elmore & McLaughlin (1988) indicate that the slow work of school improvement varies depending on the characteristics of local schools.

7. See also Metz (1988b).

8. The term "organizational sagas" was first used by Clark (1972).

8

Planning Improvement Efforts

> There are many ways to plan effectively, but not all ways of planning are equally effective.[1]

Can planning work? School-based educators occasionally look at district, state, or federal administrators and wonder what it would be like to spend one's work life planning and monitoring rather than doing. Not far behind is the realization that a substantial chunk of their own time is required to tinker with programs that have been planned at the district or state level, but don't quite seem to "fit" their own school or classroom.

Planning—particularly planning for change—has also been carefully scrutinized by educational researchers, many of whom believe it makes an insignificant contribution to real school improvement. Whether or not *real change and improvement* occur depends more on implementation, or what happens after a reform actually gets put to the test in classrooms (Berman, 1981; Berman & McLaughlin, 1974; Louis, Rosenblum, & Molitor, 1981). Studies of unsuccessful experimental programs initiated in the '70s implied that planning, along with a "top-down, technological" model of change in education, should give way to a more fluid model, in which the ideal of planning for school-wide goals is abandoned in favor of letting "a thousand flowers bloom" (Clark, McKibbin, & Malkas, 1980).

But in our view, the role of planning is not as easily dismissed as these critiques imply. Furthermore, there are many different ways to go about planning. Our study suggests very strongly that the presence of *good planning* helps to determine whether urban schools actually change for the better. To give an example from our survey of principals, there is a strong statistical association between the use of *good planning techniques* and *cross-role involvement* on the one hand, and the actual *quality of the plan* that was produced and the *consensus* in the school about the goals expressed in the plan. These in turn affect the number of *implementation problems* that arise, and the level of coping effort that school people make to grapple with and *solve* those problems (Figure C.1, Appendix C).

Yet, our study also suggests something else: "Good planning" in the high schools that we studied looked very little like the planning models that are most commonly advocated in textbooks on administration and management. The goal of this chapter is to look at the reality of planning in urban high schools, and to derive some principles for action from what we observed.

ALTERNATIVE PLANNING MODELS

The paraphrase at the beginning of this chapter reflects a confusing reality. There is no single right way to plan, but there are a great many ways to go wrong. The choice of how to plan, however, is not something that needs to be left to chance. The most appropriate model will depend on a range of factors discussed in previous chapters, including

- The amount of consensus within the school and among the school, the community, and the district about the nature of the school's problems and desirable strategies for solving them.
- The complexity and difficulty of problems facing the school.
- The level of energy for change.
- The turbulence of the school's context.
- The amount of autonomy and flexibility available to the school.

We'll review some common, familiar planning models, and some promising newer ones.

Common Planning Models

Long-range Planning, or "The Blueprint Model"

This model views the human actor as rational, but imperfect (Allison, 1971). Ideally, planning involves regular analysis of performance problems, careful setting of measurable goals both annually and for the long range (a five- to ten-year period), exhaustive search for alternative ways of meeting the goals, and a reflective selection process resulting in a detailed plan for implementing the chosen alternatives. Because human beings are not machines, we fall short of the ideal planning model: Constrained timelines, difficulties in getting (and processing) information, and the need for immediate response to unanticipated pressures from outside competitors or regulators throw our decisions off course. Nevertheless, effective leaders should attempt to approximate the approach of the rational planner.

This model does not always apply very well to real organizations and people. For example, studies of decision making in successful organizations indicate that strategic decisions are often made without a careful, analytic process (Daft & Lengel, 1984; Donaldson & Lorsch, 1983). In schools, the blueprint model usually means that planning — particularly long-range planning — is done in the district office, which may make principals and teachers feel disenfranchised, and slow their acceptance of the changes.

"Muddling Through"

A second common model involves an incremental strategy: making only decisions that cannot be avoided, letting each decision be made at the lowest possible level, and even then making a plan that has the least chance of rocking the boat (Lindblom, 1959).

There are three arguments in favor of incremental planning. First, those who believe in teacher empowerment point out that an accumulation of decisions made by intelligent professionals is just as likely to result in a good direction for a school as any centralized plan. Because incremental plans are short term, and confined to a small part of the school, there is opportunity to ensure that they "work" before they are used more broadly (Weick, 1976). Second, there may be no viable alternative: Because long-range planning is largely a myth, it is preferable to accommodate to the essential non-rationality of life in organizations rather than to perpetrate false standards (March & Olsen, 1986). Finally, decentralized decision making helps to promote creativity at all levels (Kanter, 1983).

"Muddling through" may work for a school performing reasonably well in a relatively stable setting. However, it is often insufficient when schools face pressure to make major shifts in policy or practice. The more complicated the demands, and the larger the number of outside constituencies, the less likely it is that letting individual professionals plan for themselves and their units will result in productive change (Anderson, 1989).

Newer Planning Models

Strategic Planning, or Renewing Commitment to Mission and Goals

The burst of interest in strategic planning (McCune, 1986; Steiner, 1979; Tichy, 1983) is a response to the problem of how to shift an organization's course relatively rapidly. This model departs from the previous two by emphasizing the involvement of key administrators in realigning mission and goals to the claims of relevant constituencies and trends in the environment. Emphasis is placed on creating a unified understanding among organizational members of an image of "what this organization should look like." The emphasis is on a middle-range plan — generally less than five years — and on decision making by intuition rather than by detailed quantitative analysis. Finally, strategic planning moves beyond just acknowledging environmental pressures to proactive design of strategies to enhance the organization's ability to deal with them. When a strategic plan is in place, other levels in the organization engage in traditional planning activities to carry out the centrally determined mission.

Emphasizing coherent strategy works well where the organization is able to choose distinctive strategies to increase its competitive position in the environment. But it does not necessarily have the same effect in organizations that are highly regulated, like schools (Snow & Hrbiniak, 1980). Schools also have many legitimate goals that are difficult to prioritize, which makes it hard for top administrators to develop a clear vision that is sufficiently specific to be meaningful, yet accepted by all.

Evolutionary Planning, or "Getting There Is Half the Fun"

The newest ideas about planning try to strike a compromise among the previous models. The evolutionary perspective rests on the assumption that the environment both inside and outside organizations is often chaotic. No specific plan can last for very long, because it will become outmoded either due to changing external pressures, or because disagreement over priorities arises within the organization. Yet, there is no reason to assume that the best response is to plan passively, relying on incremental decisions. Instead, the organization can cycle back and forth between efforts to gain normative consensus about what it may become, to plan strategies for getting there, and to carry out decentralized, incremental experimentation that harnesses the creativity of all members to the change effort.

This approach is evolutionary in the sense that, although the mission and image of the organization's ideal future may be based on a top-level analysis of the environment and its demands, strategies for achieving the mission are frequently reviewed and refined based on internal scanning for opportunities and successes. Strategy is viewed as a flexible tool, rather than as a semi-permanent extension of the mission: If rational planning is like blueprinting, evolutionary planning is more like taking a journey. There is a general destination, but many twists and turns as unexpected events occur along the way.

No one planning model will ever suit the needs of a school under all conditions. However, our cases suggest that the evolutionary model may be the best for schools undertaking a major renewal and change effort.

GETTING STARTED WITH PLANNING

Our advocacy of new and less rational models does not provide an answer to a very reasonable question: *How should we start?* How can a major improvement program begin under the difficult conditions discussed in Chapter 7? More specifically, how can a demoralized and often apathetic staff come to feel that they can control the fate of the school and the students who move through it? Even more specifically, what should we do first?

Finding Energy: Building an Initial Team

Planning experts in education frequently advocate the use of a broadly based, representative planning team. Some go so far as to advocate the involvement of every employee in planning (Lotto, Clark, & Carroll, 1980).

The requirement for broad participation was, for example, built into the California School Improvement Program that formed the initial basis for Alameda's activities. Let's look more closely at Alameda in order to see how planning is "supposed to look" from the perspective of an ideal process.

■ A first step was to constitute an ad hoc School Site Council with representatives from administrators, teachers, other staff, parents, and students. . . . The first coordinator . . . proceeded [with] formal elections for a site council. . . . The procedural plan . . . was to have the entire faculty meet as a large body. [Planning] was not to be an isolated process engaged in by a small group. . . . A list of task groups were set to plan in different areas, and faculty joined up. . . . These groups met monthly for one-and-a-half hours of planning. . . . Simultaneously, a goal-setting process was conducted by the Site Council based on surveys of students, faculty, and parents. . . . In this process, the faculty developed ownership of the program.

This description illustrates elements that are believed to lead to good planning activities: a coordinating group representing all stakeholders in the school, a broadly based process in which most school members have the opportunity to contribute, and a clearly defined planning period focusing on the development of specific goals and action steps. In Alameda, many proposed activities were generated from this process, and were blended together to form the plan for the first year of implementation. As one person put it, "everyone worked without hidden agendas."

But a broadly based, participatory planning process does not always work so well in a school where faculty are divided and skeptical about change. Chester is a case in point.

■ A district-wide steering group was appointed to develop a plan for the proposal to the state's More Effective Schools program. The district's group included 87 people, representing all schools and community groups. During the planning period task forces . . . met as often as twice a month to develop ideas. However, commitment of energy was low, and actual planning documents were usually prepared by the central office staff.

■ The high school's chronic mistrust of the district office increased when the superintendent chose a major component of the program before the participatory planning process was completed: Comments from the school indicated widespread agreement . . . that "downtown is ramming this down our throats." Although there was supposed to be a school-level task force . . . low morale at the school level made it difficult to sustain involvement.

On the surface, the initial approach to planning in Chester appeared to be rather similar in design to Alameda's. However, broadly based planning is not a panacea in a school with a history of conflict. Chester was full of teachers who were interested in change, but the long list of recently failed innovations made them skeptical about making a commitment to the district's planning effort. They also perceived that district office planning and any planning that they might do were largely decoupled — which reinforced their sense of powerlessness and lack of interest in getting involved.

The paradox is that participation can increase alienation under less than ideal circumstances, by increasing the profound conviction of many urban teachers that they are manipulated by administrators who do not understand the circumstances of their work.

Survey evidence about the effects of broadly based planning activities in urban high schools also shows mixed results. Schools that included more diverse groups on their planning committees tended to encounter more problems during the planning process. (Of course, the involvement of many stakeholders may have been a response to a divided or conflictful situation rather than a cause.) Planning group diversity is also associated with reduced influence of both teachers and principals over the final shape of the plan.[2] As we will discuss in more detail later in this chapter, reduced influence of school-based participants has serious consequences for implementation and change.

But there are alternative approaches to developing an initial plan that do not require broadly based intensive participatory planning. One strategy used in three of our schools — Agassiz, Burroughs, and Bartholdi — was to find a small group of people who, for a variety of reasons, were committed to school improvement and saw themselves as able to carry out some coordinating activity. In these schools, energy had to come from a few people who had *time* as well as *interest*. Rather than beginning with a school-wide activity, the initial planning in these schools began small — even invisibly.

In Agassiz, it is not surprising that principal Cohen turned toward the "class of '69" when he took over the principalship. After all,

■ most of the "old team" had hung on through the bad years, in part because of strong interpersonal loyalties. As one administrator said, "During our darkest hours we gravitated toward collegial networking. We had a hard basis of caring and respect to see us through. We could share our goals, support each other."

Using a small team was responsive more than strategically planned: The district's planning institute (an eight-day kickoff event for the Boston Compact program) occurred during the summer. Thus, the initial plan was drawn up with staff that were available — mainly "class of '69" administrators and department chairs.

A small group of volunteers also dominated Bartholdi's initial planning events — and for much the same reasons. The district's program required a multi-role planning group, whose members attended a summer planning institute. As their initial work was later fleshed out, core planners were winnowed down to the program coordinator, the program supervisor, the principal, and the A.P.'s. In Bartholdi, unlike Agassiz, the early planning group meetings were rarely attended by principal Martinez, although he remained informed about their activities.

In Burroughs, the impetus for involving the school in E2 clearly came from Margaret Storm, the principal. As Storm began to plan, she turned toward faculty volunteers.

■ Storm told her faculty about E2, and "eight people stepped forward who were really willing to put forth for it. I felt that was enough support to go ahead." During the early months, E2 consisted largely of that committee . . . meetings scheduled after school hours . . . were attended by few faculty.

Miss Storm was reflective about the reason why she chose to run fast with a few players.

■ "The number one thing is to build a support base. You can't think you have a fantastic dream and expect people to accept it. You have to have gradual movement; you have to build support. . . . You have to know your staff, who are the good teachers, who are interested in working with children and parents, who are committed and non-punitive." And when she had identified those staff, she gave them major responsibilities as well as rewards.

Although Burroughs relied on teachers rather than administrators as the early source of energy, it is not surprising that most of them were un-married, and had fewer conflicts with the many late afternoon and evening meetings.

EARLY PLANNING:
SCHOOL-FOCUSED, ADMINISTRATOR-DOMINATED

Our study began by assuming that principals are rarely charismatic leaders who become "turnaround managers" based on personal magnet-ism and vision. Nevertheless, in three of our most successful schools, the early planning process was dominated by the principal, while in the two schools that were initially less successful, principals played a less dynam-ic and central role. Let us begin by taking a look at the latter.

In both Bartholdi (originally rated as a "C" school) and Chester, where early planning was controlled outside the building, there were real problems in implementation and gaining consensus. However, the role of the principal in each of these schools, and the consequences for planning and program outcomes, were quite different.

■ Chester's principal, Carol Hayes, took little active initiative in plan-ning for or coordinating the school renewal program, nor did she actively invite other school administrators to take charge. . . . But [her] tendency to avoid a visible leadership role was not due entirely to her somewhat tentative management style: The decision to adopt the Instructional Program Leadership program as a major component of the district's improvement effort was made [by the superintendent] without any enthusiasm on her part; she was also aware that some components of the program, such as classroom scanning, were very controversial among her teachers.

In Bartholdi, the principal also exhibited low investment in the district's change program, and did not participate in the initial summer planning sessions.

■ New to the job, principal Martinez was struggling with the need to learn a variety of new skills in addition to change management.

Unlike principal Hayes, however, he clearly delegated responsibility for the program to another experienced administrator.

■ The first person appointed to the task was unequal to it, but when Martinez was faced with the need to restaff the position he chose a respected associate principal, who was encouraged to take on a strong planning and coordinating role.

Thus, although his initiative in the early planning efforts was limited, attempts were made to compensate for this later in the program.

In both schools, however, there were noticeable results of limited administrative leadership in planning. Neither Bartholdi's nor Chester's staff viewed the program as legitimate: It was initially an "outsiders' program," regarded at best as irrelevant to solving problems that teachers thought were most pressing, and at worst as a significant distraction from the school's main job.

Similarly, in neither school was there a clear mandate for any individual or group to resolve conflicting views about the program, or deal with problems of coordination among related efforts. People at Bartholdi and Chester could recite long lists of innovation efforts that were logically connected to the planned reform that we studied, but no early effort was made to consider how these could work together to meet school needs.

In contrast, the principals of Agassiz, Burroughs, and Alameda gave active sponsorship to the Boston Compact, E2, and the mentor teacher program — all of which also originated outside the school. Teachers — even the skeptics — *knew* that the school's leaders cared about the program and actively engaged teachers in planning that would make it fit the school's agenda and needs. These programs could be grumbled about, but they could not be ignored.

Early principal involvement has enduring consequences for school improvement that are demonstrated through our survey data. In schools where principals reported that they had a great deal of influence over the school's plan for change, 55% also indicated that they grappled with implementation problems in a wide variety of ways. Among the principals who reported that they had less influence on planning, only 35% reported a wide variety of coping activities.[3] Wide-range coping, as we'll see in Chapter 11, is one of the main determinants of program success.

In most schools it is the top administrators who must spend the most time coping with unanticipated problems: If they don't "own" the plan, perhaps they feel less inclined to invest their time this way.

CONCLUSION: Effective evolutionary planning must be built on the direct involvement of the principal or some other key leader in the school. The involvement of official leaders in planning gives value to the expenditure of effort on the part of others, increases the legitimacy of those who argue for change, and increases successful problem coping.

ACTION BEFORE PLANNING: DEFUSING SKEPTICISM

Active principal sponsorship of the program and the recruitment of a small enthusiastic team were not always enough to galvanize broad action in the depressed settings. Planning theory suggests that there should be a number of distinct stages in a change effort, and planning (or mobilization) is considered an antecedent to actual implementation or activity. But in Agassiz and Burroughs, we see the opposite. First there was action, and then detailed planning began. In Agassiz, for example,

■ Cohen . . . realized that if the Compact . . . was to succeed he would need to "deliver to the skeptics." . . . The school was not ready for a real commitment to program change. Rather it had to be encouraged in that direction: "In the first year, my main concerns were with safety and climate." One of his first . . . battles was with . . . the physical plant staff over the use of a budget for repairs.

> . . . The central office proposed replacing the heating plant, wiring, and pipes, but Cohen reasoned that these would hardly boost the morale of the staff and students. . . . After a hard fight the school received all of the internal cosmetic repairs. . . . Cohen utilized the victory to its fullest advantage, holding a special dedication ceremony in the newly redecorated auditorium.

The case goes on to describe other programs and activities that were initiated during Cohen's first year — a new magnet program, junior ROTC, a special program for teenage parents, and various efforts to reduce truancy. All began without the benefit of any formal school-wide planning at all. Although Cohen was verbally committed to participatory planning, the second year of his tenure also involved more action than planning, as a variety of new activities were initiated by various faculty and administrators.

At Burroughs a similar process unfolded. The school received a small planning grant from the supporting foundation at the end of the school year, and the summer was devoted primarily to reading and locating possible consultants. In the fall,

■ project planning continued, but Miss Storm and the E2 committee also began to implement some of their ideas. They used some of their [planning] money to contract with a professor at [the local] state university to conduct seven workshops during the year on reading in the content areas. And Miss Storm organized a seventh grade team of . . . teachers and arranged their teaching schedules so that they could meet together to coordinate their curricular units and discuss problem students. Weekly meetings began with a guidance counselor and Miss Storm participating. . . . Planning and implementation were all of one piece during E2's first years at Burroughs.

Even at Alameda, where the state School Improvement Program resulted in extensive planning documents, changes initiated in the broader Staff Development project were begun with limited or no planning. When Cara Mosely came to the school,

■ her first step was to work on campus climate and to restore pride to the school. . . . Rules were tightened, the schedule was changed to stagger arrival and departure, but with no free periods . . . discipline was enforced . . . including temporary out-transfer of violators, the elimination of in-school suspension, and implementation of Saturday work days . . . the students were back in class remarkably quickly. . . . The next issue to be addressed was curriculum . . . during [the second year] Mosely also initiated . . . a series of intensive staff retreats, during which . . . substantive training and development took place.

In each of these cases, major activities, including restructuring and the initiation of significant (and sometimes costly) new programs took place without committee meetings, and with no written plan supporting that action.

Was this bad administration? An error in judgment on the part of the principals and cooperating teachers? Our cases suggest not, and there is theoretical evidence from other settings to support this assertion.

Action to Create Energy

Many educational researchers agree that starting an innovation program with an effort that centers on curriculum and instruction is the most effective strategy for getting teachers interested and involved (Crandall, Eiseman, & Louis, 1986). Even where organizational variables, such as morale or climate, need to be worked on, these should usually come *after* teachers have been excited about an innovation that reaches into the pedagogic core. In the urban high schools that we studied, however, the collective sense of efficacy on the part of teachers was exceptionally low. The "depressed" quality of the schools required a frontal attack on organizational problems first.

Early activities should not, under these conditions, require *broad* teacher involvement. Making the transition to a teacher-owned effort from an administrator-owned effort is critical, but sometimes very slow. Notice that in both Agassiz and Alameda, the attack on morale and energy was not initially direct: Training programs to improve these were not instituted until the program was under way for some time. Rather, the importance of giving the whole school a sense of "being a winner" — new facilities, improved climate, and more order — is critical.

Action to Create Learning

A profound transformation in a school usually precedes increases in achievement, retention, or other outcomes. People in the organization need to learn how to act in different ways to produce the desired results. Old patterns need to be changed, new ones learned. The greater the anticipated behavioral change, the more learning must occur and the more difficult the process. More important, the development of a consensus in the school that a new way of doing things is "right" cannot occur until the new behaviors have been tried and tested. This observation does not mean that planning is irrelevant to learning. Instead, it means that in some circumstances planning cannot be carried out very effectively until people already find themselves in a "learning mode." *Change is learning.*[4]

Learning occurs when we gather information and reflect on it. Donald Schön (1987) argues that the most effective professional learning occurs not through logical analysis (plan-then-do), or random accumulation of data (trial-and-error) but through *reflection-in-action*, a more intuitive way of analyzing and dealing with issues that face us in our own behavior. Other research suggests that where *doing* comes before *planning*, it takes the organization longer to produce results, but that there is more collective commitment than when classical plan-then-do models are used (Miles & Randolph, 1981).

Thus, in some (perhaps even many) circumstances, rational planning theory and even strategic planning models are simply inappropriate. If we know the general direction we want to go in, we may discover more if we start walking than if we spend the morning studying maps, listening to weather reports, and plotting out the precise route.

A note of caution: This works only if the do-then-plan action takes place at the school level, and at least a core group of faculty are already supportive of change. In Chester, district action and training on Instructional Program Leadership preceded planning at the school level, and this was viewed as a threat. Action in the district office does not produce learning in the school.

How Important Are Data for Planning?

As a sympathetic codicil to our assertion of the primacy of action, we note that effective planning strategies are supposed to involve active data collection on the part of schools' staffs. Traditional rational planning models and strategic planning models put much emphasis on formal data collection and feedback—"finding the best information to help analyze your problem and develop the most appropriate solution."

The more successful schools in our study sometimes collected data in a formal way—but in no case was it considered very important in planning, and in some cases people didn't tell us about the data collection effort until we had interviewed them about planning on several occasions. (As we'll see, data were sometimes important in assessing the effects of action, however.)

In Burroughs, for example, significant data collection efforts accompanied planning. The first, which occurred at the beginning of the 1982 foundation-funded planning period, involved "a faculty-wide needs assessment keyed to the characteristics of effective schools." Although that school year was full of action, there was no apparent tie between activities—which focused on reading across the content areas, parent involvement in supporting reading and study skills, and rewards for student reading—and the assessment. In the next school year,

■ a school-wide assessment (Middle Grades Assessment Program) [was] carried out by a faculty/parent group trained . . . at the Center for Early Adolescence in North Carolina. . . . MGAP . . . is a diagnostic-prescriptive tool to determine how well a school is responding to the academic and social needs of teenagers. . . . The results . . . indicated that the school needed more structure and clearer limits for students; increased parent participation; closer personal relationships between staff and students; teacher training in a wide variety of instructional methods; better coordination within and across departments; and more faculty effort to promote student competence and achievement. . . . According to one teacher who conducted the assessment, "We didn't systematically do something about these results once the study was released. But everyone got a copy of the report and used it for their own purposes."

MGAP was saved from obscurity in Burroughs because the assessment was accompanied by suggestions for activities to remediate areas of weakness, a number of which were incorporated into the school's future plans. It was not exactly the data (which reportedly confirmed what the staff already knew), but the "how to do it" tips that helped the school.

A similar but even more extreme phenomenon can be observed in Agassiz, where a needs assessment was conducted during Cohen's first year as principal, but never analyzed or explicitly used in the later planning process. Cohen was certainly analytical, spending his years as an assistant principal observing the needs of the school: "When I came back (after the appointment of an interim headmaster), I had a good idea of what needed to be done." In fact, in Agassiz the main focus of the reform effort after the first two years was on improved "bottom-up planning." As the business liaison to the school stated,

. . . before the Compact there was no planning . . . the focus has been on improving long-range planning and strategic planning. . . . I have been trying to move people away from thinking only about money, toward a research utilization perspective in the school.

This is not an ironic comment on the disjuncture between what the actors in the school wanted to happen, and what was actually happening. Agassiz *was* moving toward a research utilization perspective; it *was* incorporating planning activities at all levels. But good planning practices in this and other schools diverged from popular planning theories.

We might compare our findings with those of recent advocates for school-based review as a precursor to a major change effort (Hopkins, 1985; Hopkins & Bollen, 1987). In contrast to data-for-planning models, school-based review portrays the teachers in a school as researchers, formulating and collecting data that will help them to think about action. In this way the data collection is an important symbol — and support — for the teachers' engagement with the reform effort. The goal of school-based review is not simply to produce technical information to undergird a plan, but a way of organizing and celebrating the need for all staff to reflect upon common practice, and to contrast it with an emerging shared image of ideal practice.

It is significant that both Bartholdi and Chester were plagued by a repeated history of prior data-collection and planning efforts that went nowhere. Data collection energized faculty, named school problems, and aroused hope that "this time things would be better." But when no action ensued, despair and cynicism grew. The issue is connecting understanding (based on formal data or not) to action in the service of a shared vision.

CONCLUSION: In "depressed schools" one of the few ways of building commitment to a reform program is for successful action to occur that actualizes hope for genuine change. Effective action by a small group often stimulates an interest in planning rather than vice versa. Collecting data about school problems and new programs to solve them may energize people and provide a vehicle for a group's reflection about practice, but does not automatically lead to a better plan. Making the data-planning-action connection is critical.

SETTING GOALS—OR FINDING THEMES?

Strategic planning manuals advocate developing a strong statement of mission prior to program planning (McCune, 1986). In later planning, all possible strategic goals and courses of action should be assessed against their potential for achieving that mission. In general, while the mission statement should reflect the broad, long-term objectives of the system, change goals should be explicit and concrete.

But in *none* of our schools did planning behavior correspond exactly to this image. That does not mean, however, that these schools were operating under a "goal-free" or ad hoc approach to planning. Let's look at the way in which goals and school missions seemed to operate in the five schools.

Goals for Change

The main differences in the schools lie in (1) the specific change goals; and (2) the scope of the goals and program. The contrast among Bartholdi, Burroughs, and Agassiz is instructive.

- *Bartholdi* began the program with decidedly narrow goals. The main focus was on dropout prevention, and the intervention was expected to be focused on students who were chronic absentees. The claim to be improving Bartholdi as an overall system was not supported with school-wide activities, nor did most staff view the program as anything other than a dropout program.
- *Burroughs* came closest to designing a major reform effort around a mission, due to principal Storm's unswerving commitment to the middle school concept. In her mind, the program centered on changing the teachers' role patterns of student guidance and grouping. At Burroughs, however, middle school objectives were mixed in with the language of the effective schools research (the basis for the foundation support). And even at Burroughs other themes, such as reading improvement, which were not explicitly linked to either the middle school or effective schools thrusts, were prominent.
- In *Agassiz*, goals were broad and poorly specified. The initial planning document conformed to the umbrella Compact program, including specific statements about reducing truancy, increasing achievement and graduation rates, and other critical student outcomes. There were also unrecorded objectives that were known only to the headmaster (although some were shared with close colleagues, and some were widely recognized within the school after a few years). These ranged from improving social services, to curriculum reform, to changes in planning and supervision in the school. Unstated goals provided more drive for the school than did the Compact-related goals.

The conclusion that we draw fits with other studies of implementation (Farrar, DeSanctis, & Cohen, 1980). But it also goes against the thrust of the planning literature.

CONCLUSION: The more narrow and specific the goals, the more likely the school is to run into problems in creating an environment for school reform. In schools with broader or vaguer goals, the multiplicity of moving parts and the overarching nature of the reform movement permits lots of positive action to generate support for reform.

The need for specific goals is probably true where the "innovation" is a single program. But if broad reform of the school is needed, it may be more appropriate to think about "targets of change" — classroom teaching, department functioning, whole-school climate — rather than about "goals."[5]

Mission — or Themes?

The more successful of our schools had no *a priori* mission statements for the program or the school itself. Instead, multiple improvement efforts coalesced around a theme or set of themes only after activity had begun. The themes, as they became linked, gradually reflected an image of what the school could become, and thus served to motivate staff members.

We use the term "theme," rather than "vision," deliberately. Themes in the more successful schools were typically not as specific and vivid about the desired future of the school as is usually implied by the term "vision." Themes were, in effect, interim change goals that helped to organize and direct energy. They were more general than specific program activities (such as implementing an in-school suspension program), but certainly were not "end-state" goals (such as "reduce dropout rate"). A "theme" is an answer to the implicit question, "What are we trying to do to improve things right now . . . what are we working toward?" Figure 8.1 shows the themes from each of our sites, arranged in rough chronological order as they emerged over the period of our study.

Thus, themes served as vehicles to coordinate disparate improvement efforts within the school. Rather than being deduced from an explicit examination of values and goals, themes were arrived at intuitively and inductively, by looking at what needed to be done in the name of reform. And they shifted over time.

In Agassiz, for example, themes reflected a maturation of the improvement program: Initial themes focused almost exclusively on superficial improvements in facilities and school climate, then moved to programs to serve the needs of the "whole child," incorporating social service, self-esteem, school-to-work experience, and dropout intervention. As staff became more accustomed to the program, and as principal Cohen became versed in planning theories, they shifted toward a general vision of school-wide decentralized planning and accountability. Each alteration in the main themes involved more staff, beginning with administrators, then a small number of teachers, and finally moving to the whole staff.

In Chester, on the other hand, the themes began with the need to implement the externally imposed MES change program and its partner, IPL; the curriculum alignment work proved to have usefulness and meaning. Subsequent change themes were driven by state testing and remediation requirements, the district remediation program, and the incredible demands posed by the mandated reorganization. None of the themes really added up to a vision, and most were reactive rather than "owned."

A critical point may be drawn from the above discussion.

CONCLUSION: Effective school improvement involves a succession of change themes that are interim goals growing out of the effort itself. Sometimes these are derived from a general "vision" of what the school should become; more often, a vision emerges as themes become more linked, successful, and owned by people at all levels in the school. Themes that result from programs imposed from outside the school may galvanize effort, but leave little in the way of coherent improvement.

Perhaps this is at the heart of the failure of Chester's renewal program to thrive: even in this suspicious, highly centralized school and school district, teachers didn't want to be treated just as "implementers" — yet the whole thrust of the Instructional Program Leadership effort was just that. Resistance was expressed even though many teachers were initially positive about some of the specific activities and goals of IPL, such as curriculum alignment. Although it is often easy to attract teachers' interest with a good program or new idea (Louis & Dentler, 1988), if a great deal of effort is going to be demanded, there is also a need for them to believe in the efficacy of the themes.

Figure 8.1 Improvement Themes in the Five Sites

AGASSIZ

Fix what looks bad cosmetically
Get attendance working better
Get discipline under control
Get specific success in small programs
  (ROTC, health services, parenting)
Build staff and student energy
Empower administrators and staff
  (e.g., through coordinator jobs)
Provide social services for students
Get good goal setting and planning
  going at the department level
Build community involvement, raise
  image of school through publicity
Expand cluster program
Develop new curriculum

ALAMEDA

Empower staff, mobilize faculty
Get innovative projects,
  new courses, going
Clean up environment, fix graffiti
Bring order, better discipline
Go beyond just caring to
  effective teaching
Do goal setting and strategy
  planning with entire staff
Get good staff development on
  teaching content and skills
Model improved supervision/teaching
Build internal cadre of staff
  development managers
Get staff ownership of change
Build culture of communication
  and sharing
Empower students
Decentralize decisions
Push for steady curriculum
  change and development

BARTHOLDI

Improve attendance
Get social services to students
Get student jobs
Link to public-sector organization
Get at-risk students into
  the program
Improve organizational functions:
  attendance, security
Make the pieces work, coordinate
  new and old programs
Develop new programs (both at-risk
  and across whole school)

BURROUGHS

Build staff planning group,
  empowered cadre
Emphasize student skills and
  attitude development
Mobilize faculty interest in
  improvement
Improve reading in the content areas
Improve faculty's ability to work
  with young adolescents
Initiate and support teaming
Develop faculty knowledge about
  testing
Improve math in the content areas
Change toward a middle school
  structure (team teaching,
  attention to student problems)
Improve student motivation
Do faculty advisory groups (improve
  self-esteem and motivation)
Add new courses

CHESTER

Implement the MES program pieces
  (attendance, computers, career
  resource room, etc.)
Specify curriculum objectives in
  quarterly lesson plans, align
  curriculum with testing,
  improve remediation
Implement student incentives/awards
Deal with state requirements
  (testing, remediation)
Plan to reorganize
Carry out reorganization

THE PROCESS AND CONTENT OF
EVOLUTIONARY PLANNING

Arriving at the conclusions "first act then plan" and "themes are more important than missions and goals" does not provide school-based change agents with a very specific handle on what they should do to improve the planning process. As one writer puts it,

> Normative vision is ethereal; it is a mental event. Action is concrete; it is effort in the manifest world. The interpolation of these two realms is vital for change in social systems. These are reflective processes thematic fitting. (Pava, 1986, p. 617)

In the remainder of this section we will review some of the adjustments that need to be made between the mental and the concrete.

Letting the Themes Form the Program

As we have suggested, following a "good planning process" is not too important. None of the schools that we looked at are textbook cases of good planning—if, by good, we mean the rational, explicit model. But an alternative view that incorporates the evolutionary planning approach we have begun to describe is worth looking at. One of the best ways of illustrating the management of evolutionary planning is to look at how the schools adapted their programs during the first few years.

All of the reform programs we studied were initiated outside the school, but the degree to which they were specified in detail varied. In Agassiz, we described the Boston Compact program as an "empty vessel," which imposed a few goals for student achievement, but said nothing about how the school should achieve those goals. In contrast, Alameda's two state programs specified some of the *process* of change (having a school site council for planning, using mentor teachers), but left the school improvement objectives up to the school.

In the other three sites, the outlines of the change program were initially clearer, and were derived from outside the school. In Chester, the program was designed in some detail at the district and state level. The Bartholdi program was locally designed, but within a specific district-generated framework. In Burroughs, the basic thrust of the middle school concept was derived from the extensive literature on middle schools. In none of these cases were all staff comfortable with basic program assumptions.

Where a program doesn't "fit" initially, there is a great deal of extra coordinating work to keep it alive (Bartholdi); or it will simply be put off (Chester), or perhaps "downsized and blunted" in some aspects (Burroughs).[6] Where the program is controlled outside the school (Chester), lack of fit is more likely, but may not be addressed. But no program fits perfectly. What do schools have to do to adjust over the longer haul?

Segmentation and Experimentation

It has been noted that schools are "loosely coupled" or segmented — what happens in one classroom or department may have little or no impact on what happens in the rest of the building (Weick, 1976). This has the advantage of permitting small-scale innovative activities to flourish without requiring shifts in the whole school. On the other hand, when incremental planning processes dominate, moving to the large-scale improvement effort that is necessary to truly reform high schools may be impeded.

It has also been noted that the field of education is very uncertain; that for many of the most difficult problems that schools face, we cannot choose remedial strategies that have a known probability of succeeding. This uncertainty has a negative effect on motivation (Brunsson, 1985).

In Alameda and Agassiz, we saw common patterns of dealing with this double-edged problem. In both schools, program descriptions involved a long list of different efforts. For example, Alameda's first year in the California School Improvement Program culminated in funding 30 separate curriculum development proposals; in Agassiz, the first year of action generated efforts to refurbish the school, improve attendance monitoring, reorganize the disciplinary and guidance system, develop a health services magnet program, and introduce Junior ROTC and a teen-parent counseling program. For the most part, early efforts were spearheaded by a single individual, or a small group of highly motivated staff. This may be contrasted, for example, with Burroughs, where early planning occurred all at once.

■ The planning process and the first phase of implementation dropped an avalanche of new ideas and activities on the school. It was the biggest event to hit Burroughs since the school library burned down. Among some of the faculty, it was just about as welcome. "There was a great deal of resistance in the faculty," one said. "They just wouldn't get involved."

The "start small and experiment" approach has another important evolutionary planning feature: It permits schools to take advantage of unanticipated opportunities that might be overlooked or viewed as distractions if a master plan were being followed. Agassiz, for example, made little progress in thinking about inventive programs to support students with college potential. By happenstance they learned of programs in two branches of the state university that gave students opportunities to spend time on campus and, for successful participants, preferential admission status. These became a main thrust in their efforts to increase college application rates.

Expanding the Successful, Contracting the Less Successful

When the "incubation period" for new projects was well underway, schools were able to assess the value and potential impact of what was being done in the segmented activities. Rather than facing high-risk public scrutiny, the program components would be locally (and rather invisibly) tested, and evidence of their potential value could be produced on the basis of effective fit with the school as well as impact. In Alameda,

■ Faculty were skeptical that students could do well in Advanced Placement courses. In one department's experimental AP courses it became apparent that students were passing the exams, and the program was expanded to include five departments. At the other end of the student spectrum, a rock climbing/wilderness course initiated to deal with gang violence was expanded, with faculty support, to include positive as well as negative student leaders, and is viewed as a symbol of their success in creating a climate of cooperation among the student body. Other, less successful programs were not continued or remained small in scale.

CONCLUSION: The objective of evolutionary planning is to capitalize on the "low-risk" quality of smaller-scale innovation (acting) to increase certainty (a mental event). This in turn increases motivation and the possibility of concerted, more "tightly coupled" action across the school.

Creating a Story

The potential danger of segmented experimentation and sifting through the success and fit of each piece is that the reform effort will deteriorate into a hodgepodge of unrelated efforts. Use of unanticipated resources can, if unchecked, become simple opportunism. (Indeed, the Alameda case makes it plain that teachers, especially the SIP coordinator and the school site team, were aware that many of their colleagues wanted to use the project in part as a slush fund for field trips and supplies.) Thus, an important part of change management is to create a post hoc saga of how various improvement efforts fit together into a reasonable (if slightly untidy) whole. This involves returning to the school's improvement themes, and demonstrating how new plans and activities can potentially contribute to them. The development of a coherent story was particularly in evidence at Agassiz, where the program had so many new components every year that few people in the school could name them all spontaneously. Yet, when prompted about each component, staff could explain how it contributed to the overall school improvement themes.

Revising the Story

Themes are dynamic shorthand descriptions of the change program, and require revision as action and reflection induce creativity in the school. In this case, changes in the story that explains the themes should not be viewed as signs of purposelessness. Instead, the evolution of themes is a normal part of the effort to create and recreate a value consensus in the school. As one eminent management theorist of the 1930s has pointed out, one of the major functions of leadership in organizations is to reinvent and restate organizational purposes regularly, and invite members of the organization to reaffirm their commitment (Barnard, 1938).

Linking the Past and Future

In order for the thematic development-action-reflection pattern to persist in a school, the effort must not only evolve and "fit," it must have a deep meaning to the teachers. One way of creating meaning is to present the story of reform in idealistic terms that appeal to most educators (Louis & Dentler, 1988). But idealism is not enough in many schools: The actions and themes must be tied to the staff's collective understanding of their organization.

In the two least successful schools—Chester and Bartholdi—there were strong memories of recent failures in reform. Programs that had only recently captured the imagination of many faculty members—60 faculty had become involved in Chester—had not yielded significant change, but the failures were not due to resistance or lack of caring on the part of the staff. In both schools stories about the value of the defunct programs' concepts still circulated.

One of the problems that seemed most critical in these schools was that recognition was not given to the good components of these recent programs — the goals that motivated staff, the efforts that, in slightly different circumstances or with more time, might have succeeded, providing a basis for more forward movement. To build on past change efforts, even those that have not been entirely successful, acknowledges the fact that change and improvement are a continuous (and difficult) process. Evolutionary planning must celebrate the energy and hope that still exist, and involve key people who can be counted on for new projects. Throwing out or ignoring previous efforts during the planning process, as we have seen in Chester and Bartholdi, causes doubt and cynicism.

CONCLUSION: A saga that provides justification for the particular mix of actions, evolves as the program themes change, and ties current efforts to staff understanding of the past helps to integrate disparate efforts into a coherent whole and reinforce the meaning of the change effort.

BEHIND THE CLASSROOM DOOR:
THE IMPORTANCE OF SHARED PLANNING

As we noted in Chapter 3, few urban school reforms today are grappling with issues of instruction and teaching. Teachers, like those in Chester, are often fearful of programs that attempt to open the classroom door and look at teacher behavior — the instructional program leadership scanning component was expected to "rip the school apart."

We believe that teacher engagement in planning is crucial. Even the most burned-out staff wants to see good and new things happen; the key is to provide easy working channels where their energy can be mobilized and made most effective. The important point here is that a principal-dominated activity (early planning) needs to become more widely shared. Although the use of cross-role groups may not be essential in the earliest planning phases, it becomes increasingly critical as evolutionary planning proceeds. We will explore the reasons for this in somewhat more detail in the next chapter, where we deal with the importance of sharing ownership of the themes. Here we will show how shared planning may feed the potential for real instructional change.

The depth of the shift to shared planning varies even in the more successful schools. In Alameda, the goal was to design a school that was controlled by the teachers, and the efforts were largely successful. Agassiz, located in a more bureaucratic district that was dedicated to hierarchical control procedures, did not make such a complete transition. Nevertheless, the control structure of the school did become more decentralized. Both department heads and teachers talked about their accountability for improvement.

Changing the focus from principal-dominated to shared control with strong teacher influence over change planning does not ensure impacts on teaching and instruction, but it is a necessary pre-condition. Discussions about instruction, which necessarily include discussions of individual and collective weaknesses, are more likely to occur when effective and successful planning has created an open and trusting environment. We note the success of the active cadre in Burroughs as implementation proceeded, and the increasing confidence of the cross-role steering group at Bartholdi in dealing with instructional issues that used to be "the domain of the A.P.'s." In Chester, though the engagement of teachers in curriculum alignment work bore some fruit, the fact that the classroom scanning was to be imposed on them simply led department chairs to walk away quietly from the effort.

Our survey also supports the importance of creating participatory planning rather early in the program. For example, where initial planning is well carried out and effective, it results in a clear understanding of what teachers and administrators *should* do, and it corresponds with what teachers are *able* to do. In these circumstances teacher commitment to the change process will be high. Seventy-four percent of the schools with high quality planning claimed to have high teacher commitment, contrasted with 23% of the schools that had poor planning quality. Teacher commitment seems to promote more active efforts to engage in continued effort to deal with implementation problems: Only 38 percent of the schools where teacher commitment was low had active and successful efforts to cope with later problems, as contrasted with 78 percent of the high teacher commitment schools.

CONCLUSION: Evolutionary planning, particularly in "depressed schools," requires a gradual shift of control from the administrator to department heads and teachers. This later participation is essential to carry out the other elements of evolutionary planning such as the action orientation, a focus on reflection, and the collective development of themes and sagas.

THE ENDURING EFFECTS OF PLANNING

This chapter has spun out several arguments. First, we claimed that it is not necessary to abandon school-wide planning just because of the messiness of the real world and the lack of rationality that often characterizes educational decision making. Instead, schools wishing to make major shifts in their operations and effectiveness must recognize that they are embarking on a long journey during which their goals and activities—and the nature of the school itself—will evolve. Major reforms are not planned, and then implemented. Nor, as we tried to show from looking at our less successful schools, is a simple modification of this linear model of change, which advocates planning, implementing, testing, and "mutual adaptation," an appropriate model when large changes are envisioned.

Second, we showed that evolutionary planning departs from most other descriptions of planning in three significant ways.

- The first premise of evolutionary planning is *act—then plan*.
- The second premise is *pay less attention to missions and goals and more to inspirational themes* to guide the change process.
- The third premise is that evolutionary change requires *reflection on the relationship between action and improvement*, including the careful effort to renew staff commitment to both.

Finally, we discussed two key problems in reform-like school improvement efforts: the need to tie what is being proposed to people's images and constructive past change efforts, and the need to increase interaction among staff members in different roles and departments to promote an instructional emphasis.

But the reader may still be left with a "so what" feeling. Does planning really make a difference in most schools, or are these case studies unusual? This chapter has emphasized the process of planning, but if we turn to our survey data we find an answer to this final question.

We used multiple regression analysis, a statistical technique that allows us to look at the influence of a wide variety of different factors that may affect whether or not schools actually become more effective.[7]

No matter what we looked at — whether it was the initial emphasis of the program, the implementation problems that the schools encountered, or the pressures and support from the district office and state — consensus and good planning contributed to the movement of schools toward improved teaching effectiveness (see Table C.8, Appendix C). The analysis also supports another argument made above: that the process of planning and the way in which it affects commitment are more important than the exact planning steps followed or the "goodness" of the first plan. In the case of our survey data, a factor strongly affecting the school's movement toward improved outcomes — for students, teachers, and the organization — was the *level of support* for implementation of the change effort.

This finding highlights the centrality of *themes* for improvement, and suggests that finding the right one(s) and encouraging ownership of them are at the heart of school reform. In the next chapter we will explore this topic in more detail.

NOTES

1. This is a paraphrase of a statement made by the well-known organizational theorist Jay Galbraith about organizational design.

2. The Pearson correlation between the number of outside groups represented on the planning team and the degree of consensus within the school about the plan is $-.16$, and between the number of outside groups and implementation problems is $.20$. The relationship between the number of different groups from inside the school and teacher influence over the plan is $-.22$, and with principal influence is $-.18$. These are all significant at the $.05$ level or better.

3. This difference is significant at the $.05$ level, using the Tau statistic. The number of principals reporting that they had a great deal of influence over planning was 151, while 27 indicated that they had lower levels of influence.

4. See Miles & Louis (1987) for a brief review of the organizational learning literature as it relates to change programs.

5. A look at change efforts in business suggests that urban high schools are not unique in this regard. See Kanter (1983) and Iacocca & Novak (1984).

6. The terms "downsizing and blunting" are borrowed from Huberman & Miles, 1984.

7. Specifically, we used multiple least squares linear regression, with the SAS analysis package.

9

Vision Building
in School Reform

A vision statement is an expression of hope, and if we have no hope, it is hard to create a vision.   (Block, 1987)

The best leader doesn't say much, but what he says carries weight. When he is finished with his work, the people say "it happened naturally."   (Lao Tzu)

The previous chapter argued that successful planning centers on the development of themes that represent different thrusts to the program of change. Themes are the threads that hold together the disparate and scattered experiments that occur in departments, in individual classrooms, and among small groups of teachers. An accumulation of improvement themes can either reflect a collective vision of where the school is going — or can help the school to arrive at such a vision through inductive reflection. However, we need to understand more about what themes and visions are, how they work in a school improvement project, and how they can be orchestrated, or we risk introducing abstract concepts that have little practical meaning for educators.

Writers on management are currently fascinated with the notion of vision as a critical ingredient of successful leadership.[1] This interest, further stimulated by Peters and Waterman's (1984) *In Search of Excellence*, has resulted in more rhetoric than usable advice. Few authors give practical, experience-based examples of how organizations drifting without a vision can develop one. Those that try to do so often offer routes that correspond poorly to what we have observed happening in schools.

The business management view of vision, for example, often has two key components. First, it is assumed that a vision of the future is presented to the chief executive of the organization as revealed truth, a keyhole to the future that has "personal meaning." In contrast, we found that visions in the case study schools were often emergent and flexible. Second, the spread of the leader's vision is often assumed to be, in large measure, a function of a mystical charisma.

> Leaders are like mediums. They act as channels of expression between
> the down-to-earth followers and their otherworldly dreams. (Kouzes
> & Posner, 1987, p. 113)

The practical core of charisma — much needed when the vision is developed by one individual — is seen as communication skills, for it is the chief officer's obligation to *persuade* others in the organization to "share" his or her dream.

We, on the other hand, assume that personal charisma is a rare phenomenon, and we also know that many educators are skeptical about charisma and "strong leadership" (Corcoran, Walker, & White, 1988). In addition, hanging the fate of school reform on the communication skills of principals or superintendents seems to us a frail strategy. If the magnetic quality of personal leadership is absent, is a school condemned to being "dull, boring, and stupid?" We argue that it is not, and will show how more typical schools and leaders are able to develop consensus and a collective excitement about the task of reform.

The main questions we address in this chapter are (1) the nature, origin, and development of visions; (2) some pre-conditions for effective vision building; (3) principles of good vision building; (4) how vision building actually works, and what some practical strategies look like. However, before we turn to these questions, we need first to clarify some underlying assumptions regarding the concepts of school mission and leader vision.

THE ORIGIN OF VISION

Recent strategic planning literature in education (McCune, 1986) typically assumes that the process of change (identifying new strategies to align the school with the changing environment) begins with a re-examination of the *mission*, or the ultimate purposes of the school or district. Like the rational planning model discussed in Chapter 8, strategic planning is assumed to be a goal-directed process in which different strategic approaches are judged according to how clearly they would contribute to the mission. Mission and *vision* are often used interchangeably. Block (1987, pp. 107–108), however, argues that they are *not* the same.

> The mission statement names the game we are going to play . . . a
> vision is more a philosophy about how we are going to manage the
> business.

What Is a Vision?

We need to be clear about the nature of visions, what some of the pre-conditions are for their development, and how they develop over time in a school. Block goes on to suggest other important characteristics: A vision is both strategic and lofty, the "deepest expression of what we want . . . [a] declaration of a desired future." Goals and objectives, he notes, are only "predictions of what is to come." A vision is strongly value-laden, alluding optimistically to possibilities of "greatness." It's a "dream created in our waking hours of how we would like the organization to be."

Do visions of this sort exist in schools? Yes: The Alameda vision of "a school for students and a university for teachers" has these qualities. So does the "demanding and caring" vision that gradually emerged at Agassiz. So does the vision that has animated many inner-city schools using effective schools programs: "We are a place where all children can learn." As these examples indicate, a good vision can often be expressed succinctly, in motto or slogan form. Many schools don't have visions, proceeding with day-to-day business without much of a guiding dream. But we suspect that few schools with a strong improvement push lack them — and that few really excellent schools lack them.

What Visions Do

Visions, as we've suggested, can serve important functions in school improvement. Assuming that they are well shared within a school, they provide mobilizing, energizing foci for the difficult work of change, and help to create coherence among the diverse themes discussed in the preceding chapters. Visions also provide a sense of values, and some security in the confusion of activities involved in any change effort.

It's also clear that a vision is an important bridge between planning and implementation. A vision that begins to emerge during planning has driving power, energizing movement into actualizing initial plans. Even more crucially, it supplies clear criteria for choosing what is more and less important in the way of change activities.

Block (1987) also notes some important effects of visions: They "signify our disappointment with what exists now" (thus supplying a driving force for change); expose the desired future and how it may conflict with others' hopes; and require us to be accountable for vision-congruent action.

Thus visions are highly relevant to school improvement efforts. How might they be developed, if they don't exist in a school?

Pre-conditions for Vision Building

There are a few contextual conditions that make vision building easier, though they certainly don't seem to be all-determinative. Three stand out in our cases and the survey.

First, as we'll see shortly, the presence of a principal who is willing to "think vision" and share with others the extended process of vision development, ownership, and use makes a substantial difference. Although the principal plays a central role in developing a mission or vision for a school, he or she does not work with a *tabula rasa*, and a collective vision is therefore deeply affected by the school's recent past and current environment. Some of the greatest leadership may be provided by individuals who do not simply *provide* others with a vision of what they could be, but who coach members of the group to begin to articulate their own individual and collective wisdom (Block, 1987, p. 123).

Second, our case studies suggest that reasonable *staff cohesiveness* is required in order to begin the task of spreading ownership and understanding of themes and vision. Cohesiveness in a school is not typically a matter of personality, but reflects historical patterns of how teachers socialize in and out of school, what they talk about when they are together, and the opportunities they have had to engage in meaningful joint work. For example, Agassiz had a head start on collective work because of a core group of faculty and administrators who were building leaders and who liked and respected one another. In Alameda, teachers also cared for each other, which made them immediately open to the emphasis on collective work and staff development proposed by principal Mosely.

■ For the most part, the staff is very collegial. . . . There is substantial mixing between departments . . . interactions occur formally, on staff committees, and also informally in the staff lounge. All staff are on a first-name basis, including the principal. . . .

These schools stand in sharp contrast to Chester, where faculty and administrators were largely estranged, and spoke disparagingly about each other.

■ The principal alluded several times to "polarization" and a desire to "avert problems" . . . conversations with people at the school often contain a good deal of complaining and blaming, and a sense of powerlessness . . . "every department has clinkers . . . and some chronic absentees" . . . the time clock is crowded at 3:00 as people punch out; after-school meetings are difficult to arrange. . . .

In Bartholdi and Burroughs, the sense of social alienation was not so great, but a high proportion of the faculty were on temporary assignments, or had been recently reassigned and were likely to be reassigned again. The ability of a faculty or a principal to create a climate of participation, connection, and cohesiveness is more limited in those circumstances. Still, direct climate-change efforts, for example, through organization development interventions (Schmuck & Runkel, 1985), are feasible and often effective.

Third, in order to reinforce and maintain a vision there needs to be some *school-based control over staffing.* In many urban schools, principals have very little control over which teachers are assigned to their building. Yet, as principal Cohen pointed out, each year there were eligible teachers seeking assignment to Agassiz whose educational philosophies and working styles were simply incompatible with the emerging vision. Burroughs' principal simply gave up on trying to involve the new, uninitiated teachers in her efforts: It was simply not possible to motivate people who might be gone in a year to dramatically alter their ideas about how instruction should be organized for early adolescents. The two most successful schools had managed to negotiate greater control over staffing, either formally, due to district policy (Alameda), or informally, through getting to know the personnel department and actively discouraging eligible teachers who didn't seem to "fit" (Agassiz).

Although it is more difficult for principals to manage cohesiveness and staff allocation issues, these are so critical to developing coherent themes that can become a vision that they must usually be addressed and planned around before effective change activities can take place.

How Do Themes and Visions Get Developed in Schools?

Sometimes a new principal brings a vision to the school. More typically a vision is generated out of the planning process, rather than prior to it. Under this scenario, members spend more time thinking about what they want to do to remediate their weaknesses and capitalize on their strengths, and only when these deliberations have become quite concrete do they turn their attention to the implications for basic organizational principles such as vision and mission (Steiner, 1979, p. 25). This view is consistent with the idea of evolutionary planning set forth in the previous chapter.

Second, we can also say that both themes and visions usually emerge gradually. In only one case — Burroughs — were the main aspects of the change effort evident from the very beginning, in the principal's aspirations for a child-centered middle school. Even in Burroughs, however, teachers were permitted to add curriculum themes to the principal's vision of an affectively supportive school. Allowing vision to emerge slowly seems particularly important where the school begins its efforts without a great deal of hope among the staff, as in the case of Agassiz.

Third, in school-wide improvement efforts, developing a vision usually involves braiding hopes and aspirations from previous, ongoing, and emerging activities with those generated around new programs. In Alameda, Cara Mosely, the new principal, imported her own (personal) vision of the school as a university, but she was wise enough to permit the popular theme of improvement through teacher-developed curriculum (embodied in the existing School Improvement Project) to remain on the front burner and retain its own identity. The new MIRT program was well linked to it. Schools need to acknowledge their own history, and build a consensus about various strategies for making the future different, while preserving those aspects of the school that they like.

Fourth, in more successful schools, disparate themes become integrated into a vision through *informal* planning and articulation. While this integration of themes may center on the ideals of the principal, it also incorporates the preferences and contributions of others, both inside and outside the school.

To illustrate these points, let's go back to the origins of the five schools' improvement efforts. In every case, the school was working within a program that was initially designed *outside* the school, and where the outside agency — state, district, or foundation — provided resources to carry out its goals. Our survey suggests that this is typical: Three-quarters of the survey respondents reported that their improvement efforts were stimulated by district and state mandates.

The schools were attracted by the money, but did not try to turn it only to their own purposes. They adopted the objectives of the external programs that provided them with funding or support, but built at least a few of these goals into improvement themes. For example,

- In Agassiz, the Boston Compact's emphasis on ties with business and universities became a major theme in the school's approach to improvement.
- In Alameda, the theme of participatory decision making was internalized from the School Improvement Program's process.

■ In Burroughs, the local foundation's emphasis on the effective schools model was incorporated as a sub-theme (although less substantially than the themes in the two "A" schools).

But in *all* the schools there was a variety of other improvement efforts, some of which predated the opportunity to get involved in an externally funded effort and some of which emerged later. Again, the case study schools are not dissimilar from the survey schools, most of which reported that one or more additional state efforts to improve education had affected them in the past five years; many of these provided additional themes.

Themes that emerged early in the reform effort usually combined a set of educational beliefs espoused by the principal and other school leaders with the formal objectives of external funding agencies, and the implicit objectives of other activities that were going on in the school. In the more successful schools, the process of creating a story about how activities fit together helped administrators and teachers to understand what they were doing, and how apparently distinctive elements could add up to a broader improvement effort. In the less successful schools, programs remained unintegrated; somehow the whole was no more than the sum of its parts.

CONCLUSION: In both highly centralized and more decentralized districts, developing a vision in schools typically involves building on a set of mandates or opportunities that come from outside. Leadership involves integrating compatible themes available from different programs.

Perhaps the clearest illustration of this point can be made by contrasting the experiences of Alameda and Chester.

■ In Alameda the improvement program was fueled by two distinct state programs: the School Improvement Program and the Mentor Teacher Program. The SIP "is a practical vehicle for change, but not a mission. It does not have any intrinsic program coherence . . . but the successful planning year of SIP increased the faculty readiness for the kind of comprehensive change program that was envisioned [by the principal]." As interpreted by the school, SIP also focused on curriculum. Principal Mosely's vision of the school as a "school for students and a university for teachers" needed a vehicle of its own to get it started, and she used the MIRT program as a source of enthusiasm and funding. Mosely reoriented the mentor teacher concept to focus on "a team who plan and implement staff development. . . . Here it has created an environment where improving instruction is a focus." Under Mosely, SIP and MIRT, while still distinct, have become merged. The curriculum focus of SIP has become linked to the instructional focus of MIRT. Both have been tied together under another component of the "school as university" — staff empowerment in decision making, both in determining the projects that will be funded under SIP as well as administering the program, and in having the inservice activities be responsive to teacher-expressed needs, and designed by other teachers. The MIRT and SIP programs are also integrated in that MIRT-designated staff serve on the SIP School Site Council, and a core group of faculty tend to be actively involved in both programs.

■ In Chester, the More Effective Schools (MES) program was intended as a comprehensive umbrella under which a wide variety of improvement activities addressing the five state goals could be grouped. During the planning phase, however, MES became viewed as "just another program — not *the* program" that would turn Chester around. One of the main factors that contributed to this was the district's choice of IPL, a program with a distinct identity and many highly specified goals, as a main thrust, with little justification for how it was connected with the broader reform goals of MES. Because IPL was more visible and initially more demanding, it became increasingly separate. Teachers were barely able to describe MES, although they were familiar with the major requirements of IPL.

   In addition, perhaps because principal Hayes was not involved in the major MES design decisions, existing improvement efforts in the school (which focused on improvements in climate and behavior rather than curriculum) continued to exist as a laundry list of efforts unconnected to MES. This included many programs that bore a resemblance to those in Agassiz — student award and incentive programs, Junior ROTC, a partnership with a local college to improve inservice, a coaching program for students who could not pass the state's minimum standards test, and a peer leadership program for seniors, among others. Although there was a reform slogan (*The Chester High* School — TCHS — standing for Together, Commitment, High Expectations, and Success), it was not a vision, and even the principal had difficulty remembering what the letters stood for. In summary, all the pieces that existed in more successful schools were present in Chester, but they did not cohere.

An additional conclusion may be drawn from the above discussion.

CONCLUSION: The more narrow and specific the objectives of external programs that stimulate an improvement effort, the more likely the school is to run into problems in creating its own vision for school reform.

SPREADING THE THEMES AND VISION: KEY PRINCIPLES

An Integrative, Internal Process

Although themes can be adopted from outside sources, *vision cannot be mandated, but must be generated within the organization that seeks reform.* When externally derived reform programs are characterized not by tight goals, but by broader and more vision-like objectives (such as partnership between schools and the business community, or professionalizing schools), there is room for the school to elaborate a vision of its own.[2] This fits with other studies of schools (Farrar et al., 1980), but counters the thrust of the literature on effective planning and management, which suggests that relatively detailed visions should come "from the top."

This argument for a loose vision-development process that fits external pressures, opportunities, and interests to the unique characteristics of the school and its staff is consistent with a basic assumption that organizations "learn" just as individuals do — and that they learn most effectively (although not necessarily most rapidly) if they make and correct their own mistakes (Miles & Louis, 1987; Miles & Randolph, 1980). Organizational learning and change is *hard work*, but it is the kind of work that begins to give themes and emergent visions a tangible shape.

Vaill (1982), in analyzing high-performing systems in a variety of sectors, distinguishes *purposing* (or vision development) from *goal setting*. While goal setting may be an armchair activity that occurs outside of the context of action,

Purposing refers to that continuous stream of actions . . . that has
the effect of inducing clarity, consensus and commitment regarding
the organization's basic purpose. (p. 24)

This description of high-performing systems in the private sector suggests that the thematic development and understanding of basic purpose
cannot be separated from activities within the organization.

An Active, Participatory Process

Another conclusion may be drawn from the Alameda-Chester contrast.

CONCLUSION: Shared development of themes and vision is
more likely when teachers have active influence over program
planning and implementation. Master teachers, department
heads, and regular classroom teachers must share the overall
concept in order to generate activities and ideas that are consistent.

Perhaps this is at the heart of the failure of Chester's More Effective
Schools Program to thrive: Even in this highly centralized school and
school district, teachers didn't want to be treated as "just implementers" — yet the whole thrust of the Instructional Program Leadership
effort was just that. Resistance was expressed even though many teachers were initially positive about some of the specific activities and goals
of IPL, such as curriculum alignment. Although it is often easy to appeal
to teachers' idealistic side with a good program or new idea (Louis &
Dentler, 1988), where a great deal of effort is demanded the direct
opportunity to influence the change process is more compelling than
philosophical attractiveness.

To put it more strongly: Vision spreading involves empowerment.
Real ownership of a coherent, value-laden dream for a school arises not
from elaborate "communication" exercises, or from formal participation on voting committees, but from day-to-day work on the planning,
implementation, and management of change efforts.[3] Sites that had
serious steering groups with control over implementation (especially
Agassiz and Alameda, but to some degree Bartholdi and Burroughs)
tended to converge on visions. In Chester, where steering groups rarely
met, no coherent vision emerged.

SPREADING THE VISION: PRACTICAL ADVICE

Rules of Thumb

Knowing that the theme must be shared—and felt—by staff in order to make a major improvement effort work does not provide a great deal of guidance on *how to do it*. Block (1987, pp. 109–115) has some useful tips that seem as relevant to schools as to private industry.

- "Forget about being number 1"—the urge to "compete and win" is less motivating than the desire to contribute to a group effort.
- "Don't be practical"—practicality works against vision by emphasizing things that can be done within a normal planning period.
- "Begin with your customers"—both external (students, parents) and internal (teachers and departments). It is important to establish a preferred future of how you will relate to them.
- "You can't treat your customers any better than you treat each other." A vision must include idealized scenarios governing interpersonal relationships within the school.
- "If your vision statement sounds like motherhood and apple pie, and is somewhat embarrassing, you are on the right track." Vision is not emotionally neutral but reflects things that we care about with passion. Few of us are used to sharing dreams with co-workers.

These general rules of thumb, while helpful, don't really tell educators how to move from centralized ownership of a vision to a broader affirmation. Our data reveal some clear strategies that are useful in high schools.

Cross-Role Interaction

The survey data suggest two important outcomes of good planning that contribute to broad ownership of an emerging vision (see Fig. 9.1). The first is the *quality of the plan*—whether it fits well with the school's needs, whether it is do-able with existing or achievable resources, and whether it has a sufficient number of action steps spelled out so that people know what they should do first. The second is more strongly related to the idea that planning can be rewarding in itself.

One of the great motivational outcomes of good planning is consen-

Figure 9.1   Planning, Vision, and Implementation

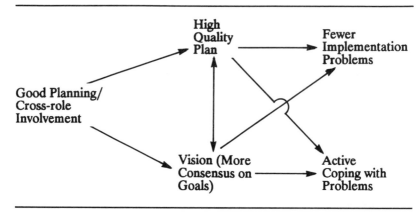

Fig. C.1, Appendix C, shows this Figure with appropriate correlations.

sus about where the school ought to be going, and at least some tentative ideas about how it ought to try to get there. This consensus becomes the embryo vision.

In addition, an enduring finding of social science is that people who interact frequently tend to (1) like each other more, (2) understand each other's needs better, and (3) exercise greater potential influence over each other (Riecken & Homans, 1954). Thus, cross-role planning, which involves administrators of different types, department heads, and teachers from different departments, may itself be used as a means of increasing cohesiveness and coherence within the school while also encouraging the segmented experimentation that is a necessary component of evolutionary planning.

- In Alameda it was considered important to have teachers from all parts of the school participate in and value the school improvement effort. Cohesiveness in Alameda was an essential pre-condition of the staff's willingness to make instruction visible and open to peer review.
- Efforts to involve a broad spectrum of the staff moved more slowly in Agassiz, where burnout and low morale were serious problems. However, by the end of the second year, one critical cross-role event — the staff training for a group of teachers and administrators in the Investment in Excellence program — provided a unique opportunity for

sharing and theme building around the notion of improving self-image and sense of efficacy.

Cross-role groups that came together in the early phases of program development placed their stamp on the nature of the emerging themes. First, they served as a screen through which the multiple potential projects or activities supporting change had to pass. The School Site Council in Alameda, the "class of '69" in Agassiz, and the group of eight teachers who formed the planning team in Burroughs sifted through the things that could be done, and selected those that were most consistent with the emerging themes and vision of the school — as defined by them. In contrast, in the lower-performing schools the early months of the program involved either conflict (Bartholdi) or no interaction (Chester) within the group of key players that had responsibility for planning.

Second, through the sifting process, the character of the themes emerged and/or became refined.

- Agassiz began without any themes, but early decisions to use available money to fund a cluster for at-risk ninth graders, to apply for a grant for a social services coordinator, and to utilize the business partner's planning expertise later evolved into the vision of the whole educational process as focused effective planning at the personal and organizational level.
- In Alameda, the annual review of teacher proposals for use of the School Improvement Program funds permitted the School Site Council to consistently reinforce the theme of curricular improvement, which became meshed with the principal-initiated vision of "a school for students and a university for teachers."

CONCLUSION: Consensus on a vision is increased by cross-role involvement and influence on planning: administrators, teachers, and department heads are all involved. Consensus, in turn, helps the school to reduce later implementation problems of all types.

The case studies suggest that implementation problems are not eliminated because "the plan" has anticipated them and built in compensating mechanisms. Rather, consensus expands staff commitment to dealing with problems—to *coping*—a finding that is also strongly supported by the survey. (See Chapter 11 for more on this.)

The Principal: Active but Not Dominating

The need for cross-role participation and involvement does not mean that leadership from the principal is unimportant. On the contrary, in all three of our more successful schools the principal's emerging vision of what the school might become was a major influence on the direction of decision making. Principal involvement and leadership served to develop themes and spread them broadly throughout the school.

Two aspects of the principal's leadership are important as we look over the cases. The first concerns *symbolic behavior*, or actions that convinced faculty and staff of the importance of the themes and vision. The second concerns actual *strategies for involvement*.

Symbolic Behavior

Does the principal have to be a "charismatic leader," a "man on a white horse," or a "strong instructional leader" to influence the development of a significant improvement vision in a school? We do not believe so, based on these cases. (For one thing, two of the vision builders were women.) Except for Alameda, no one who visited these schools would come away with the sense that the principals who set planning into motion were "movers and shakers."

- Principal Cohen at Agassiz, far from playing an instructional leadership role, acknowledged openly that his background as a health teacher and basketball coach did not give him the authority to speak about curriculum. Nor did he pretend to be a planning expert, but rather learned while moving forward.
- Although principal Mosely in Alameda had a reputation as someone who could inspire as well as manage, the program that she helped to initiate was not dependent on her continuing presence, but was deeply embedded in the culture of the school.

One author has isolated three non-charismatic elements of leader behavior that contribute to the development of thematic consensus: time, feeling, and focus (Vaill, 1982). The symbolic importance of these elements of principal behavior is reflected in our cases.

Spending *time* is important for symbolic reasons as well as practical ones. If the principal is insufficiently invested in the innovation effort to devote substantial amounts of energy to it, the rest of the staff receives a not-so-subtle hint about priorities. In the three higher-performing schools, the principals were viewed by all of the staff as centrally involved, hardworking, major actors, while in the two lower-performing schools there were questions about the energy given to the reform activities (Chester) or responsibility for the program was delegated to another person (Bartholdi).

Our survey data corroborate this conclusion from the cases: The percentage of time that the principal commits to the improvement program is directly related to the school's active attempts to cope with innovation problems.

Feeling, or a passionate belief in and caring about the school, is also critical. The principal's style may be nurturing (principal Mosely in Alameda) or more hardnosed (principal Cohen in Agassiz), but staff in the school must be able to sense the commitment to the underlying values — the vision — emerging from the theme.[4] Conversations with the principals of Alameda, Agassiz, and Burroughs are punctuated with statements revealing the depth of their feeling about the school and its success.

Focus involves helping faculty members and others to sift through the variety of activities in the school, drawing explicit attention to those that matter and those that are most consistent with the emerging vision. Focusing is at the heart of the reflective matching process discussed in the previous chapter; it also lets the principal indicate to the staff *what matters most* to him or her. For example, Cohen's willingness to reorganize the schedule at Agassiz so that intensified departmental planning could occur in the English department was a stronger signal about his commitment to that than anything that he said. Similarly, his efforts to increase cohesiveness within the staff, and between the school and community, were manifested in selective and targeted actions.

■ Cohen actually places a great deal of emphasis . . . on symbolic events that denote cohesiveness. Perhaps the foremost among these was the effort expended to bring parents in for the . . . back-to-school night. In the past these events brought in a handful of the most concerned parents: Last year Cohen barraged parents and kids with reminders, and put a great deal of pressure upon kids to show up with at least one relative. The results were outstanding: More than 400 people showed up. The effect on the students and parents was probably good, but Cohen's real target was the staff, whom he felt would be deeply affected by the evidence that the community cared about what was happening in the school.

The above example shows how the time-feeling-focus activities of principals can mold the improvement program's themes and vision.

Strategies for Involvement

As we indicated at the beginning of this chapter, recent leadership literature suggests that effective strategies for "spreading the vision" rest on the individual's communication skills: effective use of language, positive communication styles, the ability to project conviction and optimism (Block, 1988; Kouzes & Posner, 1987). In contrast, the five school case studies reveal actions that are far more strategic, which involve increasing involvement among all members of the school. These include power sharing, rewarding staff, encouraging openness and inclusiveness in the change program efforts, expanding leadership roles, and patience, or a hands-off approach to bottom-up change.

POWER SHARING. As we have seen, leadership in the more successful schools involved finding staff who wanted to work on reform, and giving them lots of responsibility and freedom. Voluntarism and serious influence by teachers pervaded the early planning efforts in all three of the most successful schools. In Agassiz, for example, principal Cohen staffed the new ninth grade dropout prevention program with a dynamic teacher, asked for volunteers from the rest of the staff, and then turned them loose to flesh out the design with very minimal supervision. In Alameda, teachers pointed to the fact that the School Improvement Program committee had turned down several proposals submitted by administrators as evidence of their legitimate authority. The group of eight staff at Burroughs who were most involved in the E2 program described their position as follows:

> We're not exactly setting policy for the school, but . . . how to put it. If you come up with a good idea and present it to the committee, before you know it, the school is doing it. For example, we came up with a library use policy, so that each teacher now takes classes to the library twice a semester. [The principal] would make a policy statement and we would work out the actual plan and schedule for doing it.

A department chair at Burroughs said,

It's important for teachers to know that other teachers are involved
with the administration in running the school.

In Bartholdi and Chester (for very different reasons) teachers did
not feel they had been given the opportunity to work on an important,
school-wide effort that could be made *better* and *more significant* if
they participated. (Later, as the Bartholdi planning group, which included some teachers, gained confidence and influence in the school,
implementation improved considerably, and the program's themes became more coherent.)

REWARDS FOR STAFF. Planning can be perceived as rewarding in
and of itself. Making choices, designing new programs, and working
together to think about what the school can become instilled hope and
energy in Alameda, Agassiz, and Burroughs, where early planning was
carried out well and was perceived by teachers as genuine. In addition,
decisions about program activities during the early phases of the program resulted in rewards for many teachers who were not among the
early volunteers — staff retreats that worked on teacher self-esteem, and
in-service activities that spoke to the expressed needs of teachers. As the
Alameda case says,

■ [The program's] success and popularity are enhanced [because] it
. . . provides concrete and visible rewards to teachers and the school;
it provides a forum for different constituent groups of the school to
really get together. . . . In some way or other . . . everyone at the
school benefits from [the school improvement program].

OPENNESS, INCLUSIVENESS. Block (1987) points out that effective
leaders need to manage those who initially oppose a reform program
with the same kind of respect that is accorded to the enthusiasts, and we
independently reached this conclusion from our cases. Although Burroughs started out well, the demands placed on involved teachers by
principal Storm, and the poor results of outreach to get other teachers
involved, led to a situation where the planning group seemed increasingly cut off from the rest of the school. In contrast, in Alameda and
Agassiz, anyone could get involved in planning at any time: Volunteers
always felt welcome, and there were many planning activities that they
could engage in that did not require extensive commitments of time. For
example, in Alameda,

■ The number and variety of proposals submitted to the [School Improvement Program] committee have increased. . . . SIP appealed to faculty in most quarters of the school . . . [only] the industrial and vocational departments tend not to participate [as] they claim their needs are "too big to be funded by SIP."

Leaders can create opportunities to increase involvement in planning. In Alameda and Agassiz, for example, resources were rearranged and reallocated so that more and more staff were drawn into the planning process. In Agassiz this occurred through the increasing focus on department-wide planning; in Alameda, through changing the priorities of the SIP project so that as wide a variety of staff could be drawn in as possible. In both of these schools, the pervasive climate suggested that almost every good idea that was consistent with the school's themes would be explored.

Efforts to be open and inclusive do not always succeed fully. Though the Alameda process had these goals, the MIRT teachers were sometimes envied or criticized for their ambitiousness, and there were tensions between "true believers and resisters." The E2 cadre at Burroughs was seen as a "clique," an "in-group of big shots." Such perceptions are in fact a measure of how well empowerment of planning and steering groups has proceeded. Both openness and inclusiveness, and the introduction of early and rewarding planning and in-service activities for teachers increased staff cohesiveness in Alameda and Agassiz (and in Burroughs among the smaller group of involved teachers). The sense of *collective engagement* with the task of school reform that is evidenced in the above quote from the Alameda case helped to promote a consensus about the nature of the school.

EXPANDING LEADERSHIP ROLES.   In both Agassiz and Alameda, increasing cross-role interaction involved significant changes in the role of department heads, who came "out of the closet" and into the classroom.

In Agassiz, teachers and administrators began to discuss different approaches to changing and improving instruction through planning and more use of observation and coaching. Prior to the Boston Compact, the full-time department heads were largely viewed as curriculum specialists and paper pushers. As part of the planning thrust, however, department heads were expected to work with teachers to develop clear annual department goals, and also to help teachers develop individual goals. Finally, along with their departments, heads were to assess how well both individuals and the department were measuring up. The planning brought together department members who had previously interacted briefly, and rarely saw themselves as having a common job. While these changes in role relations were challenging for all (and the idea of department chairs doing classroom observation and feedback did not catch on with every chair), there was also a sense of optimism and excitement about forming active working relationships at the department level.

In Alameda, the department chairs' role change was not so dramatic because they were not full-time nor were they considered administrators. Still, cross-role work was encouraged when the chairs were given released time to do peer coaching. This was consistent with the principal's general thrust toward utilizing a variety of forms of career ladders that kept good teachers in classroom roles.

PATIENCE. Planning manuals often counsel people not to spend too much time on initial planning. We agree, and have noted the "do then plan" approach taken by the more successful schools. Still, the evolutionary planning process in most of these schools stretched out not over a period of weeks or months, but *years*. Thus, a principal or a change team that expects to get an early fix on the nature of planned reform activities in a school will be very discouraged — and may react by centralizing decisions to make the change process more efficent. What we observed in the more successful schools was patience with slow movement. Agassiz is a case in point.

■ Problems encountered in both early and later planning stemmed from the extremely low morale of the staff prior to Cohen's appointment as principal. Few of the regular teaching staff believed that the school could be turned around; few were willing to commit time and energy to improvement projects . . . planning also had to move very slowly because the staff had few planning skills. Although Cohen wanted more involvement from departments, it was not possible to design and implement a decentralized planning strategy very quickly. . . . The hardest parts [of the change program] were deliberately not introduced until there was concrete evidence of success in areas that are easier to change.

Agassiz was not alone. As we saw in Chapter 3, the survey showed that those principals who had been involved in a major change effort for several years were more likely to believe that achieving their goals would require many years. In contrast, those in the early stages of improvement tended to view it as a two- or three-year effort. If one sees reform as a process that evolves over a decade or more, short-term setbacks are viewed as a problem to be coped with, and not a crisis. Patience is particularly important in reinforcing the norm that it is all right to experiment and even to fail — a norm that reinforces both individual and organizational learning. We may summarize the findings of this section briefly.

CONCLUSION: Principals must give up some of their singular "authority" within the school if they wish to have real influence over the innovation process. By expressing enthusiasm and confidence in the change program, but slowly promoting the assumption of genuine leadership roles by others, principals of secondary schools can build a network of influence that permits them to become "instructional leaders" in all departments.

CONCLUSIONS

Only three of our five schools can be said to have had anything that resembled a vision by the time that our initial study was completed. These three were the most successful schools, which implies that vision is associated with the effective leadership of a reform process. Our analysis, however, leads us to several conclusions that challenge the facile application of the business management literature to school settings.

The shape of our arguments can be briefly summarized as follows: Although we have no quarrel with the need for leaders to articulate collective purpose, and agree that effective leaders can and do elevate the commitment of groups to higher or moral purposes, they do not do this alone. We agree with Burns (1978) that there is no leadership without followership, and that good leaders not only reflect the needs and wants of others, but are also engaged with them in constant communication and exchange. Thus, although leaders may take the initiative for both planning and visioning, followers are not "sold" a vision, but know they have helped to create it.

More specifically, our analysis leads us to the following conclusions: First, visions are not fully articulated (or even articulated at all) at the beginning of the change process. Instead, visions develop over the course of the evolutionary planning process.

Second, visions are not generated solely by the principal or another individual in a leadership position but, even where the principal is strong, are developed collectively, through action and reflection, by all those who play active roles in the change effort. Visions become strong not because faculty believe in the principal, but because they believe in themselves and their ability to *really* change the school for the better.

Third, visions are not a simple, unified view of "what this school can be," but are a complex braid of the evolving themes of the change program. "Visioning" is a dynamic process, no more a one-time event that has a beginning and an end than is planning. Visions are developed and reinforced from action, although they may have a seed that is based simply on hope. However, vision building is not like a garden party, where participants can pick and choose from the food and conversations they prefer (Farrar, DeSanctis, & Cohen, 1980). Although flexible, it has shared meaning: People talk about it, use the same language to describe it, and believe that they are engaged in a common task.

Fourth, although themes and the resulting vision tend to be generated with a small group of people, the principal plays a significant role in spreading the vision to a broader group in the school. The process of spreading the vision is, however, less dependent on the articulateness and persuasiveness of the individual than on his or her willingness to structure opportunities for all interested faculty to discuss their aspirations for the change program and the school, and to be patient in trusting that staff members will take on the collective responsibility for refining the vision through shared action.

A final note of caution to school leaders who hope to embark on the vision-development process: Even in our most successful schools — Alameda and Agassiz — the reform vision did not penetrate every corner or classroom. In Alameda, staff members estimated that only about 25 percent of the teachers were enthusiastic about the learning/curriculum development/professionalization vision embodied in the SIP/MIRT programs, another 50 percent were supportive, and 25 percent remained skeptics or passive opponents (active opponents had, for the most part, been convinced to leave). Our observations suggest that this distribution would apply to Agassiz as well, and both Burroughs and Bartholdi were changing with even lower levels of support. Schools *can* and *must* move forward without everyone on the train — but there will be more people on the train if it is clear where it is going.

NOTES

1. This interest is quite recent. For example, most popular books on leadership published in the early '80s contain no reference to vision at all. It is likely that the origins of the current interest can be traced to the highly influential study by Burns (1978) of the moral dimensions of leadership.

2. This, of course, implies a strong argument against having superintendents attempt to play a visionary role in larger districts. In general, schools are
too segmented from the central office to perceive the district as a "real" organization: Instead, it is their environment.

3. See also Louis & Smith (1989).

4. Other writers support the importance of "feeling." Block (1987), for
example, advocates using emotionally charged words to talk about a vision, and
the exploration of metaphors.

10

Getting and Managing Resources for Change

Who would say no? If I'm drowning and a toothpick goes by, I'll grab it.   (Bartholdi's principal)

Do whatever you can to make things better; don't worry about the money—I'll take care of it.   (Alameda's principal)

In this chapter and the next, we turn from the tasks of leadership— working the context, planning, vision building—to the day-to-day tasks of managing change: getting resources, managing their use, and coping with the daily flood of problems.

The resources to run schools—money, staff, equipment, build- ings—are a routine part of school life. They're often considered insuffi- cient, especially in big cities. But the scale is substantial. To keep a moderate-sized urban high school open usually costs about $4 to 5 mil- lion a year, most of it salaries. Building maintenance, equipment, and materials may add hundreds of thousands more.

But that's just keeping school as it is. To carry out a change or improvement always involves an increment of *extra* resources—for training, released time, new materials and equipment, often new space, and staff time for coordination and management. Change, by defini- tion, cannot be managed through the status quo level of resources. It makes new demands, creates unsolved problems, and is resource hun- gry. In study after study of people involved in change efforts, insuffi- cient resources of time and money are cited as a prime problem. In our own survey, for example, 76% of principals said fiscal resources were a major or minor problem, and 88% named lack of teacher time.

In this chapter we discuss sources and types of resources (ranging from time and funds to information, services, and psychosocial support and influence), providing examples from our sites and the survey. We also review key resourcing processes, including scanning, acquiring, reallocating, and supporting use, and capacity building, showing how they can be more or less successful.

We argue that, over a certain floor, the level of resources supporting a change effort is less important than *how* resources are acquired, and *where* they are applied. Critics of Great Society social programs were always fond of pointing out that "you can't just throw money at problems," ignoring the fact that a great deal of money was being thrown at new weapons systems, space exploration, and failing automobile companies — and not at, for example, educational reform. Still, the critics were partially right. It depends where you throw money, and how.

WHERE DO RESOURCES COME FROM?

The environment of schools can be described as including both a *demand* system and a *resource* system. Demands come from central offices and the local school board, citizens and parents (individually and through organized groups), business organizations, state and federal agencies, reform groups, accreditation bodies, unions — the list, while not infinite, can get very long. (We should also note that demands can come from within the school itself: from students, teachers, and administrators.) Demands can range from rule enforcement to standard setting, exhortation or requirements for better output, calls for new curricula, methods, restructuring, better working conditions, less boredom — again, a long list.

To continue functioning well, a school normally has to "buffer" its operations somewhat from the demand system, so that pressures are not too disruptive. Parents are placated, the forms are filled out for the state department, a breakfast meeting is promised with the Lions Club, the board member is reminded that she should consult the superintendent before visiting a school unannounced.

But the main importance of demand systems is that they are often part of the resource system as well. Demands can be accepted, and turned on their originators. If IBM is concerned about entry-level office skills, it can be asked for curriculum development assistance. Parents concerned about day care can lobby the board. State departments mandating a new test can legitimately be expected to supply technical help on its implementation.

The resource system thus often includes players from the demand system. But many other parts of the resource system often bring funds, educational content, assistance, or support, while making few demands. These include special funded programs (dropout reduction, desegregation), business or university partners, service agencies (such as intermediate units or regional educational laboratories, publishers, equipment vendors, professional associations, information retrieval systems [ERIC, Dialog], etc.), consulting firms, and networks of one's professional colleagues.

TYPES OF RESOURCES

In our cases and survey it was clear that a wide range of resources were in play. We'll define and illustrate these, and show their importance for successful improvement.

Money

Money is a master resource, since it's used to buy other resources: staff, released time, technical assistance, materials, and equipment. But money for change was in short supply in our survey schools. Though the range was from zero to $1 million, the typical total was only $800 over the school's regular budget. The case study schools, however, had much more.

- Agassiz usually spent about $100,000 of new funds a year, which it raised from the Private Industry Council, the Boston Compact, the army, the district, and the state. It was largely spent on new positions—Compact Ventures and the social services coordinator, for example, and on assistance. (Prior to our study, principal Cohen had also spent nearly $1 million on court-ordered facilities renovation.) Agassiz also "leveraged" many non-dollar resources from its business and university partners.
- Alameda had annual dollar support of $100,000 to $125,000, largely through the $70-per-student, state-funded SIP program, plus the mentoring and Instructional Resource Teacher programs ($22,800 a year). A third or more of the SIP money was used for coordinator salaries, a quarter for add-on staff positions, a quarter for special innovative teaching projects, and the remainder for a great deal of staff development through workshops and retreats. Most of the MIRT funds were for direct teacher help and coaching.
- Burroughs averaged about $7,000 a year in its grants from the Clark Foundation (more at the beginning, less at the end), spending it mostly for in-service training, visits, summer reading camps, and consulting.
- Bartholdi spent $539,000 of district-brokered Dropout Reduction Program funds in its first year, and similar amounts for two more years. Nearly two-thirds went for add-on salaries, including the

social service staff, 20 percent for student stipends, 10 percent for equipment, and the rest discretionary. Almost nothing was used for in-service.

■ The figures at Chester are hard to come by, but were in the $250,000 to $350,000 range for the three years of MES/IPL, supported by the state department of education. Most went for add-on staff, equipment (computers), and materials. Only 1 to 2 percent was under discretionary control. Little or no money went for training or technical assistance.

As we have seen, the large funding effort at Bartholdi bore little fruit at first, until serious energy was given to coordination and change management. There and at Chester, the money for add-on positions proved to be project-bound; the jobs did not become institutionalized as they did at Agassiz and Alameda. The heavy funding at Chester had few durable results.

How much money is "enough" to support substantial change? Burroughs got as far as it did with $7,000 annually only because it spent nearly everything on assistance; it could not afford new coordination positions, and the stress on the E2 group was very high. We believe something in the range of $50,000 to $100,000, located either through new funds or reallocated from other parts of the regular budget, is needed for sustained and substantial improvement.

CONCLUSION: Effective improvement efforts in urban high schools may need a "floor" of $50,000 to $100,000 a year for several years, though moderate changes can be achieved with less. Much more critical than absolute amount is where resources are allocated. More change is likely when funds go for assistance and coordinative effort, not just for add-on salaries or stipends that will not continue after the improvement funds stop. Leveraging additional non-dollar resources helps.

A parenthetical note: $50,000 to $100,000 sounds like big money. But that is an illusion. We are speaking, in most big-city high schools, of 1 or 2 percent of regular expenditures, or the equivalent of one or two salaried positions. That does not seem much if one is aiming for serious improvement. It is a considerably smaller percentage of income than most firms spend on training and change management, let alone research and development. Trying for serious change with the "$800" that our average survey principal reported spending over the regular budget seems unlikely to help. That is only enough to pay for two hours of whole-staff in-service in our typical school, and it's less than 1 percent of what our successful case study schools spent.

Structural Resources

Under this label we include time, personnel, space, and equipment: the nuts and bolts of resources.

Time

As we've seen, time for change projects is a serious concern. The principals in our survey also noted that the average teacher who was closely involved with the change project spent 70 *days* work (in planning, developing, training, monitoring, and evaluating) over the life of the project — which typically lasted three to four years. (That helps to explain why the schools got as far as they did with little new money.) The median administrator most closely involved spent 29 percent of his or her time, which figures out to 70 days *annually*.

Thus we can see that change projects are labor-intensive for closely involved people. That is confirmed in our sites.

- At Burroughs, for example, the nine-person E-2 core group spent more than 900 hours of contributed time in the first project year. In a later year, one member said: "A tremendous amount of time and energy is required to keep this going. Sometimes we've been able to get subs, but that's infrequent. It really zaps your energy."
- At Agassiz, it appeared that the program involved 4.5 full-time equivalent positions, most of them put into internal assistance and coordination. Much work time, including that of the New England Telephone and UMass liaisons, was contributed by partner organizations.
- At Bartholdi, there was a total of 16.8 positions: eight social service staff, job developers, mentors, and attendance staff — managed with difficulty by a part-time supervisor and part-time coordinator.
- At Alameda, the sip Council met monthly, and the coordinator was half-time. The change effort also engaged the MIRT team participants very actively. Some MIRT team members spent so much time out of their classrooms that their teaching suffered. And some regular staff members felt "overcircuited" by all the improvement activity; a few left the school.
- By contrast, at Chester, the supposed steering group never met.

There were monthly regular one-hour department meetings to work on IPL curriculum alignment. Many sub-programs of MES had no coordinators. The principal, nominally coordinating the MES pieces, did not know the status of some of them when asked. The actual time investment was minimal.

Is time expenditure important? Yes, judging from the cases. And the survey data show us (see Chapter 11) that where administrators spent more time, problem coping and thus program success were fuller.

How was time used? The survey data indicate that 84 percent of principals said "a great deal" of time was spent on task force work. Similar time went into classroom observation and coaching (73%), training and staff development for teachers (68%), collecting and feeding back data about school functioning (64%), and short-run action projects (60%). Less frequent were training for administrators (51%), developing new special programs (48%), and changing the curriculum (37%).

What uses of time helped implementation, specifically? Appointing a coordinator was said to help implementation "a great deal" by 83% of those who did it (the large majority of sites). Monitoring the process and feeding back results to staff was rated as similarly helpful by 67% of those who did it. The parallel figures for other frequent uses of time are: use of task forces, 78%; frequent discussion at staff meetings, 77%; staff development on project-related skills, 64%.

CONCLUSION: Time is a crucial resource for improvement, and is most typically used for change management, and for training and assistance to staff. Centrally involved people can expect overload.

Personnel

Money pays for people. The issue, both in our survey and the case study sites, was the quality of people, and the congruence of their ideas with the emerging themes and vision.

■ At Agassiz, principal Cohen paid careful attention to the choice of people he asked to become program managers. The energy and imagination of Kent Jansen were important in ensuring success for the Compact Ventures cluster program. Each year Cohen, like few other Boston headmasters, attended the "excess pool" and interviewed candidates, encouraging the best and discouraging those he felt would not fit.

■ Principal Storm at Burroughs told her faculty about the E2 program, and "eight people stepped forward who were really willing to put forth for it." She further ensured quality and congruence through involving them in the summer planning effort, reading, visits, and E2-relevant workshops.

The choice, and the out-transfer, of school staff were also matters of close concern in our sites.

■ Administrators at Bartholdi worried about the "bag ladies" they were sent by the central office, and exercised informal refusal. They could also transfer out temporary per diem teachers.

■ Margaret Storm brought new teachers into Burroughs who had elementary credentials and were more child-centered, fitting her middle school concept. She noted, "You have to know your staff, who are the good teachers, who are interested in working with children and parents, who are committed and non-punitive." She also succeeded through her knowledge of the transfer process in getting back an E2 veteran. And as the restructuring proceeded, she said: "I was very, very selective in who went and who stayed. I made decisions on the basis of teacher quality, not on what subjects they taught. [As for E2 participants] . . . whatever I need to do and can do to keep them, I will."

■ In Chester, on the other hand, the existing faculty was treated as a "given." In any case, there was no particular shared vision to supply criteria for who might be added or subtracted from the staff. The central office's aggressive cuts in the school's administrative staff worsened existing overload.

We should also note that Agassiz staff were cut by one-third after several years of Compact work, but the process was well enough managed that the improvement effort did not suffer.

Only a minority of principals in our survey (17%) said they had arranged for the transfer of staff who did not support the project. But 70 percent of them said it had helped implementation a great deal.

CONCLUSION: Purposive hiring and transferring of staff, particularly those in steering, managing, or training positions, but also faculty in general, can be useful in supporting implementation.

Space and Equipment

Corcoran et al. (1988) have documented serious space and equipment problems in urban high schools (insufficient classrooms; inadequate, deteriorated buildings; no teacher work space; poor maintenance; limited or no access to copiers, phones, computers), and our sites and survey respondents were no exception. Two-thirds of survey principals said constraints of the school's physical plant were a major or minor problem.

In our sites, the improvement effort was occasionally hampered by space limitations. At Bartholdi there was initially "no space" for the eight new social service personnel to sit, and it had to be stolen from other programs and special education. Finding space for the career resource and computer projects at Chester wasn't easy.

But more important was the poor condition of physical plant, which was usually an early key target for improvement efforts, where an "early win" was symbolically important, and helped mobilize hope and energy in staff.

- At Agassiz, where a visiting foundation official said "students couldn't learn" because the building was so bad, principal Cohen on his arrival bucked the central office and deliberately diverted nearly a million dollars of repair funds into painting halls and lockers, redecorating the auditorium, and getting glass backboards for the gym. These were essentially cosmetic issues. "I knew if the boiler failed later they would have to fix it anyway."
- At Alameda, removal of graffiti (and re-removal at 6 AM if they reappeared), along with repainting from "institutional green" to more pleasing colors, served a similar function.

It's of some interest that both these "cosmetic" efforts were accompanied by tightening of discipline procedures and structures. It was as if efforts to "get the school in shape" had to proceed in both the physical and social realms. Purely cosmetic changes probably wouldn't have had the same impact — and probably would have deteriorated again without a more orderly climate. As the Alameda case noted, improving climate was not only a non-threatening endeavor, but one that bid well to improve school pride.

Equipment resources were not asked about in the survey, and probably play a small part in most effective schools improvement programs (with the probable exception of photocopy machines, as the data collected by Corcoran et al., 1988, suggest). It's a telling point that a list of effective schools characteristics was tacked up over the photocopy machine at Agassiz — the place where many faculty found themselves each day.

Other equipment issues were noted in our more programmatically oriented sites. At Bartholdi the automatic telephone answering machine and the ID-checking robot for taking attendance were part of the program, but were mainly notable for delay in arrival and installation. The same was true for computers at Chester. Neither were serious problems.

CONCLUSION: Space and equipment limitations can usually be worked around. Directly addressing deteriorated physical conditions, however, may be important in the early stages of a serious improvement effort, especially if accompanied by systematic efforts to bring more order to the school.

Educational Content Resources

We have emphasized the process of educational reform so much that it is easy to forget that schools require educational content resources as well. Their "core technology" is that of bringing about learning, a complex task that needs sustained attention. Here we will be mainly illustrative.

Big Ideas

A major set of educational content resources involves well-worked-out frameworks. Such frameworks often supply raw material for visions, inspire hope, and add coherence to dispersed, segmented programs.

■ The effective schools framework proved to be rather central for the staff development work at Alameda, organized a good deal of effort at Agassiz, and was important in the early mobilization at Burroughs. John Goodlad's ideas about school reform were well internalized by Cara Mosely at Alameda, strengthening the collaboration with UCLA and suggesting a clear vision.

- John Goodlad's Middle Grades Assessment Project (MGAP) conception was a very important resource for Margaret Storm and her restructuring efforts at Burroughs.
- Even at Chester, the time-on-task and curriculum alignment concepts underlying IPL helped bring some coherence to that part of the program.
- The relative lack of framework behind MES at Chester and the DRP program at Bartholdi often seemed like a real hindrance.

Practices and Materials

"Information" is often said to be a resource needed for school improvement. But if we set aside internally derived information (such as that obtained from data collection and monitoring efforts, which we've already seen can be important for success) and turn to external information resources, they turn out in most cases to refer to educational practices and supporting materials.[1]

- The important resource in the well-worked-out MGAP materials used at Burroughs was not so much the general ideas, nor even the confirming results of the assessment the teachers and parents carried out after MGAP training, but the proven practices, which didn't just tell the E2 group what they needed to do, but how to do it.
- Similarly, the well-developed program Investment in Excellence, aimed at increasing self-esteem, motivation, and personal goal setting, proved a key resource at Agassiz. The stories of impact that circulated through the school led to enthusiasm, further use, and the widespread adoption of the student version, Keys to Excellence.
- The materials supporting the IPL program at Chester were a useful resource in helping departments carry out the curriculum alignment work. But as it turned out, the "scanning" aspect of IPL, though it was well specified in the materials, went nowhere because of teacher, department head, and union resistance, coupled with minimal or poor quality assistance.
- Alameda was simply practices- and materials-rich, with new teaching programs on topics ranging from outcome-based education to critical thinking, learning styles, ESL teaching, composition, and business education.

Finally, we can note that 65 percent of principals in our survey said their improvement program involved use of programs or curricula initially developed "in another school district, in a university, in a regional laboratory or some other setting." No major school reform program can rely totally on materials and practices developed elsewhere, but *selective* use can produce important and timely results.

CONCLUSION: Educational content resources are critical for school improvement. For success, practices and materials need to be well developed – that is, be "well in hand" and likely to produce clear results – connected to a coherent general framework, and accompanied by training and assistance. It also appears that locally active, enthusiastic users help a great deal.

Assistance

One of the clearest findings in recent research on educational improvement (Crandall et al., 1982; Huberman & Miles, 1984; Louis et al., 1981) is that it benefits sharply from assistance, either from outside or inside the school. Effective assistance is intense, relevant to local needs, varied, and sustained.

The importance of assistance is confirmed in both the survey and case studies. In the survey, 49 percent said they were "very satisfied" with help received from outside the school, and 47 percent were fairly satisfied. Outside help that was most strongly associated with good project outcomes came from outside program developers or other principals — not from the district office. The total number of days of outside help made a clear difference in achieving improved school organizational functioning, especially in coordination, communication, and school climate. For example, in schools where less than 50 days of help had been received, 41 percent had above-median organizational improvement outcomes. For more than 50 days, the figure was 50 percent, and for more than 100 days, 61 percent. (Recall that project length was typically 3 to 4 years, so these figures are more striking: using, say, 30 days a year of external assistance improves success probability substantially.) Similar findings occurred for teacher classroom practice outcomes and (less strongly) for student achievement outcomes. As another indication, only 26 percent of those administrators whose satisfaction with external assistance was below median reported above-median organizational improvement outcomes. Highly satisfied administrators had a 64 percent figure, more than double the success rate for those who were less satisfied with assistance received. As we'll see in Chapter 11, assistance had its main impact on outcomes by improving successful coping with problems — itself the main determinant of overall school improvement.

In the case studies, the findings were even more striking.

- At Agassiz, the best estimate was that about 4.5 new full-time equivalent persons were involved in assistance giving (in addition to "an incalculable amount of administrative energy from existing staff"). They included local project coordinators, the PIC coordinator, the UMass and NE Telephone liaisons, and the internal development officer. They supplied a range of well-tailored assistance (coaching, planning help, identification and operation of specific training packages, coordination and orchestration, training local trainers). The collaboration between insiders and outsiders was strong.

- Alameda was also assistance-rich, using the SIP coordinator, the nine MIRT team members serving as a strong cadre, many external consultants, district personnel, and department heads, who did a great deal of clinical supervision and coaching. The "university for teachers" model was clearly working.

- Burroughs had fewer add-on funds, but put most of them into consultants and outside training, and got free central office help as often as possible. Even at the start, Storm felt, "Here's a chance to get some consultants to work with us on reading." As E2 developed, more and more of the training was run by teachers themselves.

- By contrast, Bartholdi, whose success was in doubt early in the program, was struggling under the assumption that money should go into *program* expenses, not into helping people implement programs. Though 16.8 FTE's were involved, many were regular high school staff being funded by DRP, and they were doing sub-program pieces, not assisting others. The assumption seemed to be that appointing good people would obviate the need for assistance, after some modest front-end planning help. Principal Martinez benefited from his long-term coaching, but CASA staff got almost no ongoing help in spite of serious implementation problems — and had not built assistance into their budget in the first place. The CASA coordinators were part-time, and felt constantly overloaded.

- At Chester, the state department assistance hoped for as part of the massive MES program never materialized. Top management members were successfully trained in IPL methods, and were supposed to pass on their knowledge and skill to principals, who would in turn supply

assistance to department heads and teachers. But the training sessions for principals were done in batches of 45 people on a one-way
lecturing basis; those limitations, and the resistance of faculty to IPL
classroom scanning, almost guaranteed defeat for IPL at the high
school. The MES program pieces languished through lack of coordination and management.

CONCLUSION: Substantial amounts of assistance, well tailored to
local needs, are required for successful improvement outcomes.
Successful sites are more satisfied with external assistance, use a
lot of it (at least 30 days a year), *and* develop local staff members' abilities as internal assistance givers.

In the rest of this section we review four major types of assistance:
training, ongoing consulting and coaching, managing/coordinating, and
capacity building.

Training

Training implies a systematic effort to familiarize people with new
concepts or practices, and enhance their effective use. It's often done at
the start of, and recurrently during, improvement efforts. In our survey,
68 percent of principals said training/staff development for teachers had
received "a great deal" of emphasis, and another 28 percent said there
had been "some" emphasis. (The corresponding figures for administrators were 51% and 33%, still high.) Staff development focused on project-related skills was done in 92 percent of schools, and said to help "a
great deal" in implementation by two-thirds. Furthermore, training
teachers in specific project-related skills was reported as "some" or "a
lot" by 79 percent of schools, and made a stronger contribution to the
effort than most other types of assistance. Of schools doing a lot of
training, 65 percent said it made a strong contribution.

We've already noted the range of training events that occurred at
case sites. The styles of training delivery also varied considerably.

- At Agassiz and Alameda, training had several important aspects: It
  was sustained and regular, not only at the onset of the program; it
  was hand-tailored to immediate needs and settings, not done monolithically; it occurred on many fronts at once, on different topics; and
  above all, it was intensive enough to do some good.

■ Burroughs' training was thinner (sometimes only a staff meeting a month, but sustained and focused on priorities — reading, math, assertive discipline). And (as in the MGAP work and the advisories), it was always relevant to the middle school vision.

■ Bartholdi's training was notable for its absence (except for some CASA planning and team-building help). And Chester's training was, like the program itself, managed top-down and carried out monolithically.

CONCLUSION: Training is not a "frill," but a core feature of successful improvement programs. Good training is intensive, needs-specific, diverse, and sustained throughout implementation.

Consulting/Coaching

Focused training events normally need to be supplemented by ongoing trouble-shooting, feedback on performance, support, and advice. This sort of assistance occurred in all sites, but, as might be expected, the intensity varied.

■ Agassiz, for example, essentially had two half-time consultants, from NE Telephone and UMass/Boston, who served as "roving planners," trusted outside advisors, trainers, and resource suppliers. They supplied an immense amount of day-to-day help. The UMass liaison did coaching of department heads on curriculum change and teacher supervision; the NE Tel consultant helped on planning strategies and skills. Their commitment, knowledgeability, and the fact that they were always around to keep the program moving were critical.

■ Alameda built the coaching function directly into the role of MIRT team members, as well as incorporating a clinical supervision model as a central part of the effort. External consultants were used from the state department, the district, the county, consulting firms, and UCLA.

■ Principal Martinez at Bartholdi had a two-day-a-week coach in the person of an experienced former principal. Though this was not part of the CASA program, it was clear that Manny Samson's ongoing help had strengthened Martinez's managerial and educational leadership considerably.

■ The Chester principal and staff were essentially on their own. "We've hardly had any direction other than what's printed on paper. There's been no personal contact or help." The superintendent's promised help never materialized. When a central office person finally did come to the school during the reorganization push, his "help" consisted mainly of directives on minute but deeply irritating matters (ordering all administrators to have cafeteria duty, adding Saturday detentions).

Ongoing assistance data from the survey showed that over two-thirds of schools had involved outside consultants (with 48% deeming they'd helped implementation a great deal). (Use of outside consultants was well correlated with organizational, student, and teacher outcomes.) Three-quarters used organization development activities to improve school climate (61% considering them very helpful). The proportion of schools who said they'd received "a lot" of assistance on ongoing activities varied: diagnosing problems, 26%; facilitating meetings, 16%; feedback on the school's progress, 27%. So ongoing assistance was usually not intense, though very satisfying and useful to recipients when it was. For example, only 17 percent of principals who received little or no diagnostic help said it had made a major contribution, but 76 percent of those getting a lot of help said so. This result is consistent with previous studies, which suggest that a little consulting help may be worse than no help at all, but moderate amounts may make a big difference.[2]

CONCLUSION: Ongoing assistance, responsive to local needs, and available in reasonably high density, aids implementation substantially.

Coordinating and Orchestrating

We will have a great deal more to say about this in Chapter 11, on the subject of "The Importance of Minding the Store." We can summarize our conclusions briefly. Change programs do not run themselves, and normally require a good deal of active monitoring, communicating, "knitting," linking, and managing — usually even more than the coordination required just to "keep school." Our two most successful sites spent about 10 times as much time on coordination as our least successful site did. Normally, the human resources for coordination come from inside the school, though they may be supported by external funds.

Capacity Building

Our last category of assistance involves strengthening the ability of the school to provide its own assistance. We have already alluded to the strong training-of-trainers efforts represented by the MIRT team at Alameda, and the E2 group at Burroughs. In both cases there was good linkage between external experts and internal staff who learned to deliver training and ongoing support to their peers. That strategy was also followed repeatedly at Agassiz. For example,

■ When the Keys to Excellence program was adopted (and after faculty had been trained in the adult version), the Compact Ventures coordinator moved immediately to train paraprofessionals to deliver the program in the classroom.

■ At Chester, the IPL program was designed as a cascading training-of-trainers model: Central office people would train principals and department heads, who would in turn train teachers. But the training was weak, and gave "trainers" no help in *how* to coach subordinates; principals had many other things on their minds as well — including, in principal Hayes' case, considerable doubt about the merits of the scanning portion of the IPL program.

In the survey, 73% of principals said their programs had trained staff to be trainers or supporters for other staff, and two-thirds said it had helped implementation a great deal. Furthermore, 60% of those reporting high helpfulness had above-median organizational outcomes, and 57%, high teacher outcomes; while less helpful training-of-trainers efforts had only 31% and 31% high outcomes, respectively. In short, when capacity building works well, it has impact on both teachers (commitment to achievement, skill development, and use of new methods) and the organization (morale, inter-department collaboration, and staff communication about educational issues).

CONCLUSION: Training internal trainers is not only an economical strategy, making a "critical mass" approach to the use of a particular program easier, but also heightens internal commitment and energy, and responsiveness of assistance.

Psychosocial Resources

Two intangible resources that seemed important in the survey and cases alike were support (encouragement, enthusiasm, sympathy) and influence/power (control over decisions, including the allocation of other resources).

Support

In the survey, 85 percent said support from the district had helped their planning, and 66 percent mentioned "time and energy from school personnel." During implementation, the percentages reporting *strong* support from various groups were amazingly high: 93% from department heads; 92% from teachers; 85% from district office staff; 87% from superintendent; and 83% from parents and community. The support of department heads and staff proved most helpful (86% and 85% said it helped "a great deal"), followed by the superintendent (71%), district office staff (68%), and parents and community (60%). It looks as if support is more critical the closer a group or role is to the actual action of implementation.

- It's clear that Alameda moved as far as it did not just because of the energy and dedication of Cara Mosely, but because superintendent Evans was encouraging, even demanding. He suggested the SIP application, and was instrumental in getting the initial mentoring grant. He has been a strong advocate of staff development, and supports school-based management and empowerment. And the internal support for the program from SIP Council members and the MIRT team has been nothing short of phenomenal.
- By contrast, Chester was very short on external and internal support. The central office was seen as a distant, entrenched, non-responsive, and controlling entity (and in turn itself saw the high school as enigmatic, entrenched, uninfluenceable, and non-responsive to system needs). The faculty's reaction to MES, when they perceived it at all, was not particularly supportive. The department heads were very unevenly committed to doing the IPL work. Principal Hayes in turn did little to support and encourage departments who were working hard on IPL.

Influence and Power

In Chapter 9 we've discussed the importance of empowerment, particularly shared control over the direction and process of implementation, often vested in a cross-role group of administrators, teachers, and sometimes parents and students. The great majority of schools in our survey (86%) had such groups. Program changes were made during implementation by 90% of schools, and the programs were very well

(48%) or well (51%) implemented. Our main point here is that influence and power can be seen as important resources for school improvement. We include both the influence of the school over its immediate environment, particularly the district, and the influence and power relationships within the school itself. An old saying has it that power cannot be given, only taken. For example,

■ The ad hoc site council set up to decide whether to apply for SIP funding at Alameda experienced its first meeting as a milestone event. It was the first time anyone remembered a school-level committee including parents and students that was empowered to make that kind of decision. Once they agreed to proceed and got a planning grant, they in turn produced a "plan for planning" that involved the entire faculty in a series of task groups. As the formal SIP Council worked through the resulting 30 proposals, agreeing to fund them all, basic trust in the planning and decision-making process was strongly developed.

■ At Bartholdi, the CASA steering group originally stayed away from curricular issues, which were "the domain of the A.P.'s." But as the steering group continued, it gained more and more influence ("This same group is really running the school."), and began producing more and more ambitious and successful action proposals. The proposal book got thicker each summer, with the group feeling it had "a license to plan."

■ At Chester empowerment never happened. The school, which had never had much control over MES budget or hiring, became more and more imprisoned in the mandates of the central office. As the principal wearily remarked to the cabinet, "It doesn't matter whether we are pro or con. What we're here for is making it work." And she did not encourage initiative or shared decision making by teachers.

CONCLUSION: Empowerment, in the sense of shared influence over implementation, can be started by structural decisions, but ultimately depends on actual decision making. It's a strong resource for improvement.

RESOURCING: KEY PROCESSES

Our discussion of the importance of various types of resources says little about how they were noticed, acquired, protected, and supported — or how the school's own resource-providing capacity had been improved. We turn to these questions of the resource-using process, which come out most clearly in our cases.

Scanning and Matching

One key process involves alertness to the resource system, with regular scanning to locate resources known to be relevant to the needs of the school. In the survey, 58 percent of principals reported that outside assistance providers helped with "choosing programs to meet your needs." Of those who said "a lot" of such help had occurred, 77 percent said it had made a strong contribution to project success. Where less of this was done, the "contribution" rates were lower (40% for "some help," and 25% for little help).

In our cases, active scanning/matching was a normal and regular activity.

- The MIRT team members were constantly on the lookout for new programs and practices they could introduce at Alameda.
- Principal Cohen looked carefully at the three general improvement programs being pushed by the district, and deliberately chose to put all his eggs in the Boston Compact basket, which was flexible, and would provide enough resources to let him begin on his game plan. Cohen's emerging vision of developing the school's human resources to accompany academic achievement led both to a search for the first human services coordinator, and to training programs for motivation development.
- At Burroughs, principal Storm initially saw the E2 program as relevant to her prior work on improving student attendance and reducing tardiness. A bit later she realized it was a chance to "get some consultants to work with us on reading." More generally, she realized she could adapt the Edmonds effective schools ideas to help with her push toward a middle school concept. And the MGAP program she'd long been aware of was an even closer fit.
- Bartholdi administrators were good at noticing what special funds were available, and there was a history of add-on programs for at-risk youth. When no private-sector firm could be found as a partner, they moved to attract the City Planning Department.
- Even at Chester, the principal was always on the lookout for resources, including the Junior ROTC program, the Peer Leadership program, student exchanges, and others. But there was little evidence of proactive scanning in the MES/IPL context. High school ad-

ministrators and staff simply concentrated on day-to-day functioning, and on responding to external initiatives from the central office, rather than looking for resources that could help.

CONCLUSION: Active scanning for resources is a normal behavior for urban high schools; the issue is how well the scan results are screened against emerging themes and vision.

Acquiring Resources

Once noticed and matched, the important thing is to *get* the resources applied, under local control. This seems to require an assertive, "grabbing" stance, coupled with sensible negotiating skills, and willingness to be creative and "go outside the frame" of usual practice where necessary.

- The Boston Compact actually brought Agassiz few funds directly. They had to be actively acquired through negotiations with the Private Industry Council, the business and university partners, and other sources (such as the army for ROTC). Principal Cohen, according to the site researcher, would "examine any possible source" of resources, and "consider fit between any source and school goals." And he was willing to go outside the frame in attending the excessed teacher pool to get the best people for Agassiz.
- Principal Mosely was an exceptional resource finder. Her message to the staff was: "Do whatever you can to make things better; don't worry about the money — I'll take care of it."
- At Burroughs, 35 faculty stayed after school for 4 hours to plan the coming year's foundation proposal. Later, as foundation support tapered off, Storm was successful in getting the central office to provide equivalent funds.

CONCLUSION: Resource acquisition takes energy and assertiveness, but is far from opportunism. As noted earlier, congruence with vision is a critical screen.

Reworking Resources

In many cases, resources already exist within the school. Naturally, it's important to protect and keep them (as in Storm's fight to ward off transfers of her precious E2 cadre members as school size was cut). But more than this, existing resources can often be rearranged, reallocated, and piggybacked on, without having to add extra resources. Here too creativity is important.

■ Principal Mosely at Alameda changed the schedule to permit monthly in-service sessions *and* monthly department meetings, plus three to four one-day in-service meetings and several interspersed retreats. She was skillful at negotiating with the district to allow her to reallocate funds within her budget to pay for retreats.

■ At Burroughs, Storm once had in-service during school hours, while she, her V.P., and a few parents supervised students during a film showing. As she noted: "If something had happened to students, I could have been cited for insufficient supervision. But I needed more time than the one hour a month the contract allows. There will always be limitations put on you. You have to push ahead." As another example, Storm, based on an in-house study, rescheduled academic classes in the energetic morning and electives in the quieter afternoon.

■ At Agassiz, principal Cohen, with his strong priority for department-level planning, gave the key English department a regular daily meeting slot through relieving them from homerooms. Cohen also went "outside the frame" to reject Court Street initiatives to fix the heating system with the desegregation money, choosing strategically for cosmetic renovation instead.

■ At Chester, when the central office refused to allow use of district in-service time for the IPL curriculum alignment work at the department level, the principal decided to use regular faculty meeting time for it. This showed the principal's support, and aided movement, but effectively cancelled school-wide faculty meetings and other in-service.

CONCLUSION: Schools' resources can often be reworked without adding new ones. The key seems to be unhesitating willingness to step outside the frame in the service of the vision.

Supporting Use

Here we will only note, given the strong importance of assistance — training, ongoing help, and coordination — that resources are not self-using: Even when all the pieces are available, no one may take advantage of them.

- The vigorous training and coaching efforts of the Alameda MIRT team ensured that the many attractive new programs and supporting materials would actually be widely used in the school.
- The fact that every new program at Agassiz had a coordinator/ manager meant that each program had a champion, problems could be identified and coped with, and serious use was much more likely.
- At Chester, lack of ongoing support of MES and eventually IPL efforts meant that the programs languished, and the IPL scanning work was quietly set aside as faculty objections became sharp.

CONCLUSION: Resources, particularly those focusing on educational content, need *other* resources – supportive assistance, both technical and managerial – for full utilization.

Building Resource Capacity

We have already discussed "training of trainers" and similar strategies as an important support for sustained improvement. Resource-getting and using capacity was also important in our most successful sites.

- MIRT team members at Alameda often went to outside workshops or other districts to learn new programs. They learned how to do this more and more effectively. As the MIRT team expanded and developed its work, the bulk of assistance — and resource-finding — expertise lay within the school itself.
- The Agassiz principal paid for a proposal-writing workshop, reasoning that this would help in continuing resource attraction, and it did so. More basically, Cohen had wanted from the beginning to augment human resources at Agassiz. The Health Services program, the ninth grade cluster program, the Student Support Team, and other

initiatives were all designed to give specific staff members more responsibility, and to become permanent elements of the school. Furthermore, as he put it, "I have been trying to move people away from thinking only about money, toward a research utilization perspective in the school."

CONCLUSION: Building internal resource – and resource-getting – capacity in the school is essential for sustained improvement. It usually requires structural changes: cadres, coordinators, steering groups, and the like.

CONCLUDING COMMENTS

Reflecting on the survey and case data and our interim conclusions suggests a few remarks. First, it seems important to "think resources" in broad terms — not only money. Our most successful sites considered services, particularly assistance, along with intangible goods (support, influence) as key resources.

Second, add-on resources are clearly needed for improvement. No new resources, little change. But the absolute amount of add-on, beyond a certain floor of serious effort, is less important than where the resources are applied, why, and how. Technical resources of high quality, congruent with the local vision, need to be found, and supported with strong, sustained assistance to substantial numbers of users.

Third, it is hard to overemphasize the importance of proactiveness and ingenuity, working in tandem. Resource location, acquisition, and use takes tenacity, and cannot be done passively, or always within the existing rules and customary procedures.

Finally, in the case examples we see an interesting but largely implicit phenomenon: Resourcing always takes place in the context of networks of relationships. The key seems to be getting low-energy access to useful resources through trusted contacts. At Agassiz, for example, headmaster Cohen's contacts at Court Street, liaison Ginny Fiske's network of colleagues within the NE Telephone training department, Human Services head Dee Guild's connections to local social service agencies, and Bob Murphy's contacts with the Private Industry Council were all important in garnering needed resources.

NOTES

1. We could argue that "information" about the intentions of the central office, or coming state department mandates, or the political maneuverings around the school board, is also a resource. But the category seems somehow too general and not useful.

2. See Louis (1981) for an overview of the impacts of external consulting.

11

The Change Process Day to Day
Problems and Coping

Q. How do you take a journey of 10,000 miles?
A. First you take a step. Then another step . . . .
— Old Russian proverb

Substantial change in a big-city high school ultimately comes down to what is done day by day. Evolutionary planning, vision, empowerment, and good resources provide a frame. But day-to-day steps are what get there. Those steps must be managed. The leadership skills of vision building, planning, and empowerment must be supplemented by a series of key management skills.

This chapter begins by discussing the importance of "minding the store" — steady orchestration and coordination. Then it sketches the process of problem finding, and reviews a series of typical problems found in the schools we studied. We also found a wide range of "coping styles" — how people dealt with the problems they encountered — and the chapter reviews these, drawing some lessons about more and less effective coping. We conclude with some findings about what leads to "good coping."

THE IMPORTANCE OF MINDING THE STORE

Substantial change programs do not run themselves. They need active orchestration and coordination. That seems like an obvious statement — after all, any organization requires regular management, and so should a change program, which is a special effort housed within the organization. Our survey found that 86 percent had a school-based committee for management and monitoring implementation. But only 42 percent of schools had appointed a program coordinator role, and only 50 percent said the process was formally monitored.

We also saw instances in the schools we studied where this need did not seem to be appreciated.

■ In Chester, the principal was supposedly coordinating the multiple strands of the MES and IPI programs, but often did not know the status of particular aspects when asked. This made for a great deal of vagueness and confusion about who was doing what. Furthermore, only one of the sub-programs involved had a coordinator built into the budget.

■ In Bartholdi, the desk of the supposed coordinator was usually buried in unsorted paper. Between teaching, meetings outside the school, and work with students, he had almost no time to keep the strands of the overall program together. People complained repeatedly that they did not know what was going on. Yet not until late in the year was any effort made to improve coordination through designating an assistant principal in charge.

In both these schools, weak coordination became a sort of mega-problem that made the other "normal" problems of change much worse.

In our more successful schools, on the other hand, active coordination and orchestration were frequent and taken for granted.

■ At Agassiz, the principal met often and repeatedly with a "kitchen cabinet" that included a 25 percent-time development officer and two outside resource people to assess where the change effort was going and what needed to happen next. Most specific sub-programs had appointed managers as well.

CONCLUSION: Change programs require strong coordination and orchestration if they are to succeed. Good coordination typically requires both an assigned coordinator and a multi-role steering group.

What Is Involved in Coordination?

Change programs normally represent an "add-on" to normal life in schools. Thus they require extra energy beyond that normally devoted to keeping the ship afloat. Furthermore, major change programs are not usually a single innovation, but a complex braid of sub-projects and programs.

■ In Bartholdi, the program included sub-parts (remedial teaching, work experience, services to at-risk students, attendance improvement, public awards, mentoring, and community organization linkage). Each of these sub-parts "bumped into" the school's regular organization (attendance, program, discipline, etc.), and into other existing projects (co-op, drug education, after-school tutoring, etc.).

Thus some mechanism — an individual and/or a working group — needs to be set up to carry out some predictable tasks:

- Monitoring implementation efforts
- Transmitting current information on program progress to all concerned parties
- Linking different sub-efforts
- Locating unsolved problems
- Taking clear coping action to resolve problems

These tasks are typically recurrent, persisting throughout the life of a change project. "Coordination" is sometimes seen superficially as a sort of "keeping in touch." But tasks like the above are at the heart of the management of change programs. We estimate that coordination issues in our more successful sites took a very substantial amount of time; less successful schools spent less. The differences are clear in Figure 11.1.

It's clear that the sheer amount of time devoted to coordination varies directly with implementation success. Agassiz and Alameda spent at least ten times as much time on coordination as Chester, and perhaps five times as much as Burroughs and Bartholdi. And many more different roles and groups were formally involved in high-success schools.

CONCLUSION: Coordination includes steady, active work on tasks including monitoring, communicating, linking, problem finding, and coping. A serious, school-wide change program may need at least a half-time person, along with a network of other coordinative roles and groups.

The Right to Coordinate

The time investments in Figure 11.1 also illustrate an important point: Coordination requires legitimacy — the *right*, as well as the sheer time, to take coordinative action. For example,

- In Alameda, the site coordinator was an established job required by the sip guidelines. The sip coordinator, Hernandez, at Alameda also

Figure 11.1   Time Spent on Coordination

AGASSIZ

Portion of PIC (Private Industry Council) coordinator's time, 25 percent of the Development Officer's time, plus daily principal and Development Officer discussion with two half-time external facilitators, plus regular management team meetings, plus work by sub-program managers and department heads. Altogether, 4.5 FTE's were added, plus "incalculable" energy from existing administrative staff.

ALAMEDA

A half-time school coordinator, plus monthly site council meetings, plus department-meeting consideration of proposals, plus monthly MIRT team meetings and daily informal contact.

BARTHOLDI

Supposedly a supervisor and a full-time coordinator; actual coordination time investment only about 20% for each. Steering group met occasionally. Monthly reports to cabinet.

BURROUGHS

Regular attention from the principal, plus meetings of the 9-member E2 committee (900 hours of contributed time the first year; substantially less by the third year).

CHESTER

Occasional attention from the principal, occasional discussion in meetings of cabinet. No sub-program coordinators.

---

oversees the testing program, and can monitor achievement easily to set new improvement priorities and staff development thrusts. He is an adjunct member of the cabinet, and has been close to Mosely and successor principal Jones. The SIP Site Council was similarly legitimized. The MIRT team was seen by all as the authorized body to manage staff development.

■ By contrast, the coordinator at Bartholdi worried that his work would be seen by the assistant principals in the cabinet (where one visitor felt like a "flounder in a shark tank") as infringing on their prerogatives. Only when a well-respected assistant principal was appointed as program supervisor did active coordination proceed. As a Bartholdi administrator said, "We need someone who understands the whole thing, the big picture, and has power."

The issue is not whether the principal — who by definition has the right to coordinate — is necessarily doing so. Rather, in our more successful sites, coordination was shared across several roles, and usually in one or more cross-cutting groups. As we have seen in Chapters 8 and 9, the close interaction in such groups also builds a good deal of cohesiveness, internal trust, and empowerment. The MIRT team at Alameda and the E2 committee at Burroughs even moved perilously close to becoming "elites" or "cliques" — terms suggesting a loss of legitimacy.

CONCLUSION: Coordination requires a "license." Individuals and groups doing orchestration must be seen as legitimate – because to coordinate means to have power.

PROBLEM FINDING

How are problems — which we shall suggest are inevitable — located by coordinative persons and groups? Essentially, it seems, by deliberate scanning on a regular basis. In our successful sites, daily informal base-touching ("management by walking around," and open, regular discussion of problems in meetings) was routine and typical. Problems were seen as natural occurrences.

- At Agassiz, principal Cohen and his planning team of key department heads and external advisors met frequently to assess progress and locate problems. Faced with teacher skepticism, they did not classify it as "resistance," or create a "we–they" situation. Instead, one member said, "They need to know that people working with them identify with their problems, have tackled them before, and know what can be done about them. They need to know that they're not alone with the problems they face."

In less successful sites, problems were either largely invisible to the supposed coordinator(s), or were undiscussed. Often they manifested themselves as overwhelming crises or occasions for blame and defensiveness.

- In Chester, the cabinet meetings rarely included real discussion of the serious department-level concerns about the classroom observation part of the IPI program. Furthermore, many people interviewed about current problems in the school and the change program immediately turned the problem into a blaming complaint: The program was going poorly because the central office was unhelpful, or because the principal was inconsistent ("We're treated the same way as the kids . . . allowed to be absent or late without punishment, get no rewards for doing things right . . . "), or because certain department heads were resisting.

Generally speaking, it appears that problem finding (and subsequent problem coping) is easier when people doing coordination share certain attitudes toward problems. In our more successful sites, a stance like this was frequently in evidence.

1. Problems are natural. They will always come up because we are trying new things that are complicated.
2. Problems are our friends. Only by tracking problems can we understand what has to be done next in order to get what we want.
3. When people bring up problems, they should be taken seriously, and not stereotyped as simply exhibiting "resistance." "We–they" splits should be avoided.

CONCLUSION: Though problems may on occasion force themselves upon the observer, they must more typically be found through regular, active scanning. Good scanning expects problems, treats them as serious, and as occasions for work, not blame.

TYPICAL PROBLEMS IN CHANGING HIGH SCHOOLS

There is no such thing as a problem-free organization — let alone a problem-free change program. As the stance above suggests, there are natural — and multiple — reasons for the existence of problems.

Sources of Problems

Any change program represents not only an energy "add-on" to the way things are normally done, but a potential threat to existing routines. Change also heightens uncertainty considerably, so that normal responses to problems are not made, or don't seem to work. Finally, most serious change programs are quite complex; they have many parts potentially conflicting with each other, and with the "old" organization. It is not surprising that the typical principal in our survey mentioned three to four major problems, and several less severe ones.

More particularly, problems in change programs can be seen to arise from three general sources:

1. The change program itself (its structure and process).
2. The people involved, as they interact in their traditional and change-impacted roles.
3. The organizational setting, particularly its structure and routine procedures, and its relation to the environment (district, state).

Problems can also be seen as more or less tractable or solvable. We shall return to this, but simply comment at this point that *change program* problems are likely to be easiest to solve, because the program is a more or less defined strategy; *people* problems, less easy to solve, because they reflect issues of school culture (attitude, climate, and working relationships); and *setting* problems, the hardest to solve, because they usually refer to well-defined rules and constraints. The survey data discussed in Table 3.2, Chapter 3, showed clearly that most "major" implementation problems were reported in the setting area, fewer in the people area, and least in the program area.

We believed that problems were labeled "major" by principals not only because of their scale and importance, but because of their intractability — difficulty of solution. At the same time, as we also noted in Chapter 3, some problems, though rare and less often noted as "major," are inherently less tractable as far as principals are concerned (for example, district office turnover, political pressures or tensions, and conflict between school and community interest groups).

Still, when major and minor problems were combined, implementation was clearly seen by principals as a problem-rich enterprise. Even the most infrequent problem (too ambitious a project plan) was mentioned by 52% of principals, and the most frequently mentioned problem (money and resources) was mentioned by 95%. Across a list of 13 problems, the median frequency during implementation was 68%.

Examples of Problems

Problems in our five case study schools ranged from a key figure's heart attack to teacher resistance ("the program will tear this place apart") at Chester, to implacable organizational routines, as at Bartholdi ("I have no control over teacher hiring. Last week we got some, I can only call them bag ladies"). They clustered as shown below, and are arranged roughly from most to least tractable.

Program-Related Problems

PROGRAM PROCESS.   Here we saw a wide range of problems, from uncoordinated effort (for example, confusion at Bartholdi over who would supply guidance services to which student groups) to delays (both unanticipated and deliberately staged), conflicts (many Burroughs teachers' opposition to team teaching, for example), and sheer lack of planning (for example, last-minute frenzy in locating Bartholdi students eligible for awards, when the ceremony had been scheduled for weeks).

PROGRAM CONTENT.   In some cases, the content of the program itself made for difficulty. The time-on-task program at Chester ran into severe resistance from high school faculty who said it had no applicability to their daily work; the dropout improvement efforts at Bartholdi ran into a Catch-22: keeping potential dropouts in would make attendance worse; improving attendance through discharging at-risk students would worsen the dropout rate. The various change projects at Agassiz were not fully understood by many teachers, and had conflicting goals as well.

People-Related Problems

TARGET POPULATION.   In more than a few instances, characteristics of the group that the program was aimed at hindered implementation. For example, the hard-to-reach group of near dropouts in Bartholdi proved, in fact, hard to reach. They rarely attended the special supportive classes set up for them, and few qualified for the special incentives (T-shirts, calculators) that had been set up to keep them in school. Similar problems were encountered in trying to involve parents at Burroughs.

LACK OF SKILLS.   Implementation was also hampered by the fact that teachers or administrators did not have the know-how that the change effort required. The Bartholdi cabinet apparently had no idea of how effective group decisions could be reached; the Agassiz leaders knew they were naive in planning processes; the Burroughs teachers had no prior experience in team teaching.

ATTITUDES AND SENTIMENTS. A large number of reported problems boiled down to people's feelings, attitudes, values, and motivations. These ranged from direct resistance and skepticism to lack of hope ("we always start things, never finish them"), to the philosophical arguments Burroughs teachers had with their principal over the middle school concept.

Setting-Related Problems

COMPETING EXTERNAL DEMANDS. A recurring problem was pressures or demands from outside the school that required time and energy that should have been devoted to program implementation. For example, at Agassiz, the staff has had to cope with a new district-originated curriculum, pressure to raise scores on the state achievement test, and a range of new district-imposed tests.

NORMAL CRISES OR EVENTS. As always, unexpected, non-routine events occurred, and required problem-solving action. At Bartholdi, the main coordinator for the improvement program suffered a stroke just before implementation started; a heart attack felled a key vice-principal at Chester.

LACK OF CONTROL, POWERLESSNESS. Program implementation was sometimes difficult because people in the school had little or no control over budget, staff hiring/firing/turnover, or key district policies. At Chester, the time-on-task program was simply mandated for all schools, and the high school could not oppose it directly, even though it fit poorly with high school classroom practice.

PHYSICAL SETTING/PLANT. A difficult, but less frequent, problem was limited or inappropriate space in which to carry out the program. At Bartholdi, for example, there was simply no office space for nine new counselors funded by the program.

RESOURCES. People frequently complained about lack of time to carry out the program, along with feelings of overload. Less often, they mentioned lack of funds.[1]

CONCLUSION: Implementing serious change in urban high schools is a problem-rich enterprise. The chances of a given problem appearing at some time in the life of a change program are well over 50 percent. Furthermore, major or near-intractable problems are nearly as frequent. Problems of the program itself are easiest to solve; "people" problems come next; and "setting" problems of structure and procedures are most difficult to solve.

COPING WITH PROBLEMS

Problems are pervasive, but not all problems get solved equally well. Some are pushed off, others are partially dealt with, and a few get thoughtfully dealt with so that they stay solved and do not recur. This variation in solution quality depends largely, we believe, on *coping* efforts.

By "coping" we mean the pattern of behavior that appears when a problem is noticed or defined. The behavior is not necessarily deliberate, or planful, but it is addressed to — or at least stimulated by — the problem. It usually can be seen as a discernible pattern, a sort of strategy for dealing with the problem, ranging from procrastinating to exhorting to "fixing the system."

Coping Frames

Coping efforts can be looked at as having a general frame or set of basic assumptions that lies behind the pattern. Here we adapt the work of Tichy (1981), House (1981), and Miles, Ekholm, and Vandenberghe (1987), and suggest three general frames. (Of course, more than one can be in play at the same time.)

1. *Technical.* Do it on the merits of the problem; design or allocate social and technical resources to get the problem solved.
2. *Political.* Get people to do what is needed; mobilize and exert the power needed to get and allocate resources; work with the inevitable conflicts; develop coalitions to support your position.
3. *Cultural.* Focus on the shared beliefs, values, and symbols that are key to the problem, give meaning, and hold people together.

We can draw examples of all three frames from Agassiz.

■ *Technical* coping was exemplified by: "[an] effort to ensure that each [identified] problem has a solution perking, or on the drawing board. . . . The key external support personnel feel that it is their role to come up with the support for technical solutions. For example, the problem of staff morale was approached through a direct training program, Investment in Excellence, that focuses on problems of burnout and low efficacy. For another, the English Department's schedule was rearranged to permit brief daily meetings."

■ *Political* coping looked like this in Agassiz: Principal Cohen recognized very early that his standing in the school would depend on his willingness to challenge "Court Street" [the central office] and back his staff. He forestalled the elimination of a key vocational education program (which would have cost staff positions), fought for cosmetic improvements in the building that improved morale more than a new boiler would have, and negotiated for extra time for a new bilingual head to work with the management team.

■ *Cultural* coping is exemplified in certain strategies: Cohen publicizes school successes heavily, keeps a notebook of press clippings for inspection by visiting dignitaries, found money for a lavish Christmas dance and a pancake breakfast to bring staff and parents together, and put pressure on kids to show up with at least one relative for back-to-school night; the staff was deeply affected by the evidence that parents cared. Posters, plaques, student art, and photos of honor roll and perfect-attendance students are prominently displayed.

As these examples show, technical, political, and cultural coping often go together.

■ The bilingual teacher's time was important for good planning, but gaining the time was also a political victory; the poster on the staff's five annual goals for improvement was both technical and cultural; the change in scheduling to accommodate the English department meetings had distinct technical benefits, but its visibility showed the seriousness of Cohen's commitment.

Typical Coping Frames

The principals in our survey were asked about which of a range of coping methods they used, and how helpful they were. The methods are clustered according to frame in Table 11.1.

Technical coping behaviors tend to be more effective than the other two. We can also see that system capacity-building changes (program breakup, coordinator, task forces) tend to be more effective than those focusing on personal capacity building (training trainers, staff development).

**Table 11.1   Frequency and Helpfulness of Coping Methods,
by Coping Frame**

	Frequency of use*	Helped a great deal?*
TECHNICAL		
Break the program up into smaller activities or components	Mod/Hi	Hi
Designate a program coordinator role	Mod/Hi	Hi
Use several task forces to work on specific program elements or implementation issues	Mod/Hi	Hi
Phase in program activities or components gradually	Mod/Hi	Hi
Train staff in your school to be trainers or supporters for other staff	Mod/Hi	Mod
Formally monitor the process and feed back results to the staff	Hi	Mod
Use staff development that focused on staff-related skills	Hi	Mod
Involve outside consultants	Mod	Lo
POLITICAL		
Use a broadly based task force to deal with potential problems	Mod	Mod
Require all staff to participate	Mod	Mod
Provide incentives such as released time or desirable assignments to encourage staff participation	Mod	Mod
Arrange for the transfer of staff who did not support the project	Lo	Mod
Protect the program from community pressures	Lo	Mod
Make some program activities voluntary	Hi	Lo
CULTURAL		
Discuss the program *frequently* at staff or department meetings	Hi	Hi
Have *frequent* informal discussions of the program among teachers	Hi	Mod
Try to increase consensus among staff about program goals	Hi	Mod
Publicize the program broadly to increase support from the community	Hi	Mod

(continued)

Table 11.1 *(Continued)*

Use organization development activities to improve school climate	Mod/Hi	Mod
Motivate staff and/or students with all-school activities (T-shirts, competitions, etc.) related to improvement	Mod/Hi	Mod
Develop teacher support groups	Mod	Mod
Use prestigious or popular external consultants to help sell the program	Lo	Lo

*For frequency of use, Lo=17–50%, Mod=51–69%, Mod/Hi=70–87%, and Hi=88–100%. The helpfulness item asked whether the strategy helped implementation a great deal, some, or not very much. For the percentage helping a great deal, Lo=49–60%, Mod=61–70%, and Hi=76–83%.

Political coping is somewhat less frequent, and typically moderately effective. The frequently used but shallower "easing off" approach (making activities voluntary) does not work very well.

Cultural coping is also moderately effective, though it is about as frequent as technical coping. We can infer that it, like political coping, is harder to succeed at. But Table 11.1 shows that high staff interaction seems to be the sine qua non for good implementation (frequent discussions and consensus building). Here, as in the technical area, the principals doubt that external consultants are useful.

Coping Styles and Coping Depth

The range of specific coping strategies used in our case study sites was so wide that we found it useful to sort them into "styles" or clusters. These coping styles differ in depth. The ones at the top of the list in Figure 11.2 tend to be more shallow, "soft," and informal; the ones toward the bottom are deeper, more deliberately person-changing, and structurally oriented. Altogether we found 23 distinct coping strategies in use. They are clustered here into the nine styles mentioned in Figure 11.2, with specific examples of strategies from our sites.

Do Nothing

NO COPING. No coping or managing behavior is evident, in spite of recurring problem complaints, blaming, and so on. Rarely, there may

Figure 11.2 Coping Styles and Strategies

STYLE	TYPICAL STRATEGIES
Do nothing	No coping (either by omission or deliberately)
Temporize	Delaying, postponing, re-scheduling
Do it the usual way	Firefighting, giving problem to existing group or role, following through, applying a routine
Ease off	Simplifying, aiming for less
Do it harder	Pressuring, supporting, exhorting, adding energy, providing rewards or incentives
Build personal capacity	Training, coaching, giving supervisory feedback, teaching new concepts
Build system capacity	Creating new groups for coordination, vision building, doing "rolling planning," providing assistance
Restaff	Recruiting and hiring large numbers of new staff, to change the mix of attitudes, skills, knowledge, and so on
Redesign the system	Empowering of new roles or groups; changing procedures, time use, tasks, responsibilities; reorganizing

be a deliberate decision to do nothing (analysis suggests the problem will really go away naturally, for example).

Temporize

DELAY, AVOIDANCE. Putting off, procrastinating, postponing. At Chester, the time-on-task classroom observations were put off from January to March, then "later," as faculty grumbling and threats of union grievances grew.

Do It the Usual Way

SHORT-RUN COPING. Improvising solutions, stopgaps, immediate specific actions that will address the problem. The Bartholdi coordinator's day was a whirlwind of phone calls, requests, soothings, mini-meetings, scribbled notes, hallway encounters, student mixups—all dealt with on the fly, sometimes very successfully.

USING EXISTING MEETINGS/ROLES. Giving the problem to some existing group or role. The Chester principal used her regular meeting of vice-principals and department heads to monitor and plan the time-on-task program, but the climate was not open or direct.

ACTION TAKING, FOLLOW-THROUGH.   Being sure that solutions proposed are carried out and followed up on. The new Bartholdi coordinator supplied regular "updates" on the status of each program component to the principal's cabinet and the program steering group. The Chester faculty were intensely frustrated when almost none of the proposals developed by task forces materialized in action.

PEOPLE SHUFFLING.   Moving people around in jobs (for example, if person X has been doing a poor job of coping with the problem, moving X out and bringing in Y, who it is hoped can cope better). The weak coordination supplied by the Bartholdi program director led to the part-time entrance of a strong department head to the job, and eventually to the old director's departure.

Ease Off

PROGRAM MODIFICATION.   Changing the innovative program, usually to make it simpler, easier, less objectionable, smaller. The difficult-to-schedule student mentoring program at Bartholdi was quietly dropped and replaced by two full-time tutors. The Burroughs principal backed off considerably from the time required for student advisory meetings when faculty resisted.

Do It Harder

PROVIDING SYMBOLIC SUPPORT/ADVOCACY.   Stressing the importance or value of the issue in back of the problem, encouraging greater effort and dedication. At Agassiz, a Christmas staff dance and pancake breakfasts, a gigantic back-to-school night, and plaques recognizing homeroom and individual attendance served such purposes.

PROVIDING REWARDS/INCENTIVES.   Reinforcing good performance, or promising rewards ahead of time. The mini-grants available to Alameda teachers were an example, as were the external retreats and training events used at Agassiz. The Burroughs principal rewarded teachers favorable to the program with visits to other schools.

NEGOTIATING.   Altering the rewards/cost balance by bargaining, compromising, making it more likely that people will want to "do it harder." Chester's principal gave up time she had wanted for faculty meetings when departments complained they had no time to do the detailed curriculum work the program required.

PRESSURING. Exerting influence, demanding, or requiring people to do things needed to solve the problem. The Chester vice-principal, faced with arguments, simply insisted that the quarterly lesson plans be done her way.

Build Personal Capacity

TRAINING, DEVELOPING PEOPLE. Carrying out direct person-changing interventions (intensive skill training, coaching, practice) that go beyond sheer information giving. Examples include intensive workshops on self-esteem, motivation, and goal setting for Agassiz administrators, along with training in planning and supervision; and Alameda's intensive staff development work, covering clinical supervision, assertive discipline training, time on task, and cooperative learning.

Build the System

DEFINING A NEW ORCHESTRATION ROLE/STRUCTURE. Creating a coordinator, change manager, or steering group with responsibility for dealing with change-generated problems. The Bartholdi program had a defined coordinator (and a supervisor) from its planning onward. The Agassiz program had 4.5 FTE's working on coordination. By contrast, no one had such a responsibility (except, nominally, the principal) at Chester.

CREATING NEW INTERACTION ARENAS. Setting up cross-role groups that bring together people with different perspectives on the problems of implementation. The SIP program at Alameda is steered by a school council of teachers, administrators, students, and parents, each with equal votes and control over the improvement budget.

VISION BUILDING/SHARING. Articulating and making meaningful an image of where the program is going, and how we will get there. The Burroughs principal helped develop this both through a systematic middle-grades assessment program, and through visits to other schools. The Agassiz principal was able to communicate a vision of shared bottom-up planning toward some well-enunciated purposes. Alameda's principal said, "'POOR' and 'DUMB' are not spelled the same way!" communicating a vision of high expectations.

MONITORING. Tracking carefully how well implementation efforts are going. The Bartholdi program supervisor developed a series of log sheets to record the services received by specific students, and pushed successfully for getting daily attendance reports computerized.

ROLLING PLANNING. Steadily planning, and revising plans based on the monitored success of ongoing efforts. (This is the micro-level counterpart of the "evolutionary planning" discussed in Chapter 8.) It appears to have occurred in Alameda's school council, and in the close working relationship among the Agassiz principal, his "kitchen cabinet," and the business/university representatives assigned to the school.

PROVIDING ONGOING ASSISTANCE. Using regular at-the-elbow help from outside the immediate setting to diagnose problems and support problem-solving efforts. The best example is the Agassiz business and university representatives, who provided sustained, direct consultation; brokered intensive training events; and helped design the bottom-up planning process.

Add New Staff

RE-STAFFING. Moving substantial numbers of people in, out, or across jobs; goes beyond people shuffling to make large changes in the mix of knowledge, attitudes, and skills. The Burroughs principal systematically transferred out teachers who opposed her middle school and team teaching ideas. Alameda's principal made a point of hiring "teachers who know," not just "teachers who care."

Redesign the System

INCREASING RESOURCE CONTROL. Gaining power over the allocation of people, time, and money to the school. Agassiz's principal had no formal control over hiring, but attended the district's "excess pool" meetings (unlike most other principals), and interviewed teachers to encourage (or discourage) their applications to Agassiz. He was also willing to "fight downtown" to retain programs or reallocate resources, and chose his battles carefully.

EMPOWERING/TEAM BUILDING. Giving more influence to roles or groups within the school. Agassiz's bottom-up planning is a clear example, as is the site council at Alameda.

ROLE REDESIGN. Changing or restructuring people's responsibilities (as a strategy, not just as part of the innovative program). The Agassiz program changed the responsibilities of department heads and teachers to include vigorous decentralized planning.

ORGANIZATIONAL REDESIGN. Changing organizational structures or procedures (again, as a strategy, not just as part of the innovative program). Some examples are the movement toward team teaching at Burroughs, along with the intensive student advisory groups; and the mentor-resource teacher teams at Alameda.

GOOD COPING

Was good coping important in our sites? How did it work? And what seemed to lead to it? We discuss these questions below.

The Importance of Good Coping

Our survey data showed clearly that, as might be expected, schools where a wide range of coping was reported were more effective in terms of final project outcomes.[2] We found that in schools with wide-range coping, 76 percent reported above-average changes in the school organization, in such areas as improved communication, problem solving, and inter-department collaboration. For those schools with a narrower coping effort, only 23 percent reported organizational impact. Wide-range coping had the same level of effect on teachers' outcomes, such as heightened morale, changes in teaching methods, and new teaching skills — and on an index of student outcomes such as achievement, attitudes, behavior, dropouts, attendance, and employment.

This relationship between coping and improvement held true even when allowances were made for amount of technical assistance and support, and for the extent of implementation problems (Table C.8, Appendix C). Problems tend to reduce outcomes, but good coping clearly overrides this. In fact, we found coping to be the single most important influence on outcomes. It also had a clear effect on degree of institutionalization of the change program — the degree to which it became "built in" and continued as a regular part of the school.

In our cases, we found a clear and strong relationship between coping *depth* and implementation effectiveness; good implementation was in turn closely associated with outcomes.

First, it was quite apparent that most of the instances of "shallow" coping (none at all, temporizing, using "normal" routines) appeared in two less successful sites, Chester and Bartholdi.[3] Coping at this level did not seem to lead to implementation success, at least in these two sites where implementation was still at an early stage.

Second, it was also clear that the deeper managing and coping strategies (improving capacities of persons and the system, re-staffing, and role/organizational redesign) were used mostly by more successful sites. Except for the new orchestration structure and the monitoring strategy in Bartholdi, such strategies were mostly absent in both Bartholdi and Chester. Burroughs employed a few "deep" strategies, such as empowering, increasing control, and re-staffing, but fewer than those at Alameda and Agassiz. We saw too that serious *assistance* was marked by its presence in Agassiz, Alameda, and Burroughs, and nearly invisible in Bartholdi and Chester, another indication that improvement efforts must go beyond shallow coping if they are to make a difference.

CONCLUSION: Active problem-coping efforts are extremely central in successful implementation. Passive avoidance, procrastinating, "doing business as usual," and shuffling people from job to job do not work, if they are the only strategies used. They must be accompanied by "deep" coping strategies such as vision building and sharing, rolling planning, substantial re-staffing, increasing school control over the environment, empowering people, and redesigning the school organization.

How Good Coping Works

We've seen that deep coping is better. We think that this follows from certain assumptions held in our more successful sites. They tended to treat the school organization not as a "given" or something to complain about, but as something to be *changed*, redesigned. They were also willing to "go outside the frame" and entertain unusual ideas for improving things, such as the self-esteem training program for faculty and students at Agassiz. A further look at the cases also suggests two additional principles: assertiveness and problem-appropriateness.

Assertiveness

It was also clear from the cases that our more successful sites were proactive about coping. They *never* "did nothing," and they very rarely postponed action — usually only when a "holding action" was required.

■ For example, Agassiz principal Cohen deliberately postponed attention to the more difficult problem of teacher resistance to program changes until he could, in effect, buy credibility through serious attention to school order and safety through a strong discipline-guidance mix, pushed by three assistant headmasters.

But at moderately successful Burroughs, and less successful Bartholdi and Chester, passive approaches to coping were more frequent.

■ For example, though the cabinet and steering group meetings at Bartholdi were often chaotic and sometimes conflictful because people had few skills of meeting management, nothing was ever done to rectify this (through training or coaching, for example).

Problem-Appropriateness

A careful look at the linkage between problem type (more to less tractable) also turned up a clear finding. More successful sites were able to key the depth of their coping strategies to the difficulty of the problem. In metaphorical terms, they did not carry out major surgery when a band-aid was needed.

■ At Agassiz, for example, problems of staff attitudes (skepticism, reluctance to invest time) were handled by people shuffling: assigning a clearly interested teacher to cluster work, and inviting voluntary participation from others. No effort was made to mount a large-scale persuasion or training effort.

This problem keying may also help to explain our survey finding that schools where a wide range of coping strategies was used were more effective. It's also relevant that our more successful case study sites were likely to use a mix of technical, political, and cultural interventions (as we saw at Agassiz), while less successful ones were characteristically more focused on technical, and sometimes political, strategies.

■ At Chester, though cultural norms (such as "don't rock the boat") and strongly held beliefs ("we are not good finishers") were a major barrier to implementation, it was rare to see any cultural coping methods at all. The only one tried (putting program goals on a school banner) had almost no impact.

It's also noteworthy that problem-appropriate coping in *individuals* follows a similar pattern, according to Roth and Cohen (1986). They divided coping into "approach" and "avoidance" categories, and in reviewing a large number of studies found that healthy individuals tended to use "avoidance" strategies such as denial or postponement when they seemed appropriate, but were also capable of strong "approach"-oriented strategies such as active knowledge-seeking, careful planning, and taking responsibility for action, when the problem required it.

CONCLUSION: Careful problem-sensing and deliberate coping efforts are the hallmark of success. Non-assertive coping strategies, such as ignoring, denying, or pushing off problems, usually don't work – though there are times when deliberate denial or postponement may be wise. Using a *wide range of coping efforts, matching* them to the difficulty of the problem at hand, leads to success.

WHAT LEADS TO BETTER COPING?

It is unlikely that exhorting ourselves to be better copers will accomplish very much. But there were some factors in our survey and case data that definitely seemed to lead to better coping.

A Clear Vision

In the survey, we found that stronger consensus about the plan for improvement (that is, a shared "vision") was related to better coping. Specifically, 67 percent of those schools where the planning process resulted "to a great extent" in a school-wide consensus about the goals for improvement carried out wide-range coping. In schools where the consensus had occurred to "some" or "a little" extent, wide-range coping happened for only 21 percent. Similar findings occurred for "a shared understanding by all staff of the school's problems," and "strong teacher commitment to implementing the program."

A clear vision increases confidence in making active coping decisions. Furthermore, a history of reaching agreement on a plan builds trust and the ability to make joint coping decisions. Even more basically, the vision permits people a quick reminder of what the intended activities were, and enables coping in ways consistent with the original intent.

■ A negative example comes from Chester, where there was little if any shared vision. The program had been mandated from the central office, and was not discussed or "owned" by the faculty or even the administrators. Thus shallow coping (delaying, avoiding) was frequent — as a method of successfully avoiding the pains of implementation.

Awareness

Better coping in our cases relied very heavily on steady awareness of what was going on in the change program. That meant regular monitoring of problems — of course — but more importantly, remaining carefully aware of which coping strategies were used, noting their consequences, learning from those consequences, and re-coping.

■ In Bartholdi, for example, the coordinator was severely overloaded, and the program director was ill and could devote little serious time to orchestration. Furthermore, the program was running into problems with vested interests around the school. These problems were repeatedly noticed and bemoaned, but not until the decision was made to appoint a well-respected department head as director did the lesson come clear: Coordination requires both time and power. From that point on, progress was more substantial at Bartholdi.

In this sense, good coping rests on routines for personal and organizational learning (Abbey-Livingston & Kelleher, 1988; Hedberg, 1981; Lowy et al., 1986), such as empowerment of key groups, good information flow to managers, encouragement of self-reflective action, and provision for "organizational memory" to protect good operating procedures, norms, and values.

Sustained Effort

It was also clear that good coping was most likely in sites where planners and implementers assumed that substantial effort, continuously available, should be devoted to problem sensing and coping. We have already discussed this under "The Importance of Minding the Store," and simply re-emphasize it here. The survey found that the amount of "strong support" received from administrators, staff, and community during implementation was strongly related to good coping. Specifically, 72 percent of high-support schools had wide-range coping, while only 41 percent of low-support schools had good coping. There was a similar finding for the sheer amount of the key administrator's time spent on the program: 67 percent for those spending over a quarter of their time, and 41 percent for those spending less. (See also Table C.7, Appendix C.)

Assistance

Good coping was strongest in sites that used large amounts of sustained, need-responsive assistance. This came clear in the survey, where we noted that external assistance, like the two factors just mentioned, was strongly related to coping. The finding here was strong: 87 percent of schools with high levels of external assistance (top third) did wide-range coping, while only 35 percent of low-assistance schools (bottom third) coped well.

It appeared that assistance helped coping in two ways: (a) it suggested useful alternative coping strategies to deal with the steady flow of problems; and (b) it enhanced the capacity of administrators and teachers to manage change and cope more effectively.

■ In Agassiz, for example, the principal got strong assistance from the school's business partner, New England Telephone, not only on specific program ideas, but also on personal capacity improvement (the self-esteem, motivation, and goal-setting program), and on change management skills (participatory planning, self-evaluation, and supervisory functions).

Mobilizing Through Structure

Finally, our cases showed that "deep" coping itself improved later coping. Strategies such as setting up new coordinating roles or groups to steer implementation, redesigning the schedule to permit work on change efforts, or redesigning organizational structure or procedures appear in turn to mobilize a wider range of coping efforts. That is in part because of the empowering effects involved, in part because more resources can be focused on problems, and in part because existing structures are often a kind of "energy sink" leading to overload and hopelessness. Deep coping, to the extent it involves serious capacity-building and redesign efforts, is also a strong step toward institutionalization of the change program.

■ Here we can point to the well-developed MIRT team at Alameda, whose members took central and continuing responsibility for staff development during the first years of the change effort. In subsequent years this function was shifted and built directly into the school's operating departments, while MIRT team members, along with SIP council members and department chairs, worked as a large steering group of "Key Planners" to manage all change efforts in the school.

CONCLUSION: "Go thou and cope better" is not a useful commandment. Rather, better coping is more likely when certain pre-conditions have been worked out. These include a coherent, shared vision; a stance toward coping that stresses learning from experience; strong support for implementation efforts; adequate time and energy set aside for coping through regular meetings; use of external assistance to expand the coping repertoire and extend skills; and deep coping itself – as a way of mobilizing further good coping through durable structures.

CONCLUDING COMMENT

As we have seen, effective coordination and orchestration of the ins and outs of implementation are tasks taking a good deal of time and energy by a person or group with "a license." Implementation of change generates a very substantial number of problems over and beyond those of regular school life. It's important to look actively and carefully for problems, and to treat them as serious occasions for corrective action, not blaming or defense.

Avoiding, denying, or postponing problems rarely works. The trick is to assess the difficulty, "tractability," and importance of the problem, and cope with it appropriately. More often than not, good coping requires depth—going to the root of the problem, and building personal or system capacity, or redesigning the school organization—rather than taking a "business as usual" approach or simply trying harder.

Better problem coping happens when there is a clear, shared vision of the change program and strong support for it, when serious energy is devoted to coping as such, and when external assistance is welcomed. Finally, good coping itself leads to better coping in the future, through the development of stronger coping structures.

NOTES

1. The resource difference between survey and case study sites, as we saw in Chapter 3, was substantial: Case study sites had considerably more than the average survey site.

2. The measure of coping range added up the number of different coping methods used in the school, drawn from a checklist that included 22 items such as "train staff to be trainers," "involve outside consultants," "try to increase consensus about program goals," "designate a program coordinator role," "transfer staff who did not support the project," and the like. The range of responses was from 1 to 21, and the median score was 11.

3. Recall that Bartholdi, by late 1986, was considered a "C" or less successful site, and then called Caruso by us. Two years later, implementation had gone a good deal better, and we moved it to the "B" category.

12

Leading and Managing Change
What Does it Take?

We've come to a pause point in our journey in and around our survey data, through and across our five case study sites. What does it all add up to? What does it mean for people faced with the daily task of improving urban high schools?

We see little point in laboriously re-summarizing the conclusions we have reached along the way—the reader can refresh memory by scanning through the CONCLUSION boxes and our concluding comments in each chapter. We certainly do not want to conclude with exhortation, knowing as we do that it represents "shallow coping" that will not solve the problem faced by school people reading this book: How do we use its findings in our own settings?

Furthermore, as researchers of an extraordinarily complex process, we do not feel like offering much sage advice. The people we watched and talked with as they struggled to turn their schools around have our admiration, along with our knowledge that as professionals, they were way ahead of anything we could do if we were put in their position.

Finally, we are convinced that a narrow "rules for change" model of what to do to improve urban high schools is just unworkable. Leadership and management of change, as we have seen repeatedly during this book, are matters of dealing with uncertainty, complexity, turbulence, and the cussedness of many different people. Narrow blueprints will not work. As Fullan (1982) points out, the issue is developing "a feel for the process," and "learning to get better at change."

But we can perhaps point to some implications of what we have found. Given what we came to understand and have reported in this book, what might it mean in action terms? And what are some of the problems that might come up along the path between understanding our findings and using them productively?

We want to speak directly to the core audience of this book: administrators and teachers in big-city high schools and district offices who care enough about school improvement to be doing something about it.

Concerned citizens, politicians, business partners, university teachers and researchers, state department staff and policy makers, and others can listen in, but we are talking to those closest to the school improvement action. We believe with McLaughlin (1987) that implementation is a problem of the smallest unit. That means the school within its district context. Policy and directives framed outside the school ultimately stand or fall by what is actually done, day to day, by teachers, administrators, and students.

FROM KNOWLEDGE TO ACTION

How might people working to improve urban high schools use the knowledge we've arrived at in our study? Elsewhere (Miles, 1987) we have proposed that at least five issues are involved in getting from knowledge to action.

1. *Clarity*. The knowledge must be understood clearly — not be fuzzy, vague, or confusing.
2. *Relevance*. The knowledge is seen as meaningful, as connected to one's normal life and concerns — not irrelevant, inapplicable, or impractical.
3. *Action images*. The knowledge is exemplified in specific actions, clearly visualized. People have an image of "what to do to get there."
4. *Will*. There must be motivation, interest, action orientation, a will to *do* something with the knowledge.
5. *Skill*. There must be actual behavioral ability to *do* the action envisioned. Without skill, the action either will be aborted or won't really follow from the knowledge.

We believe that the ideas in this book are reasonably clear (though clarity really has to be worked out in the eye of the beholder). And we further believe that a reasonable degree of relevance is likely, exactly because of the concrete action images that come from our case studies. These images, too, have to be made "real" by the reader for his or her own situation.

But the weak points are still to come. Many research-to-practice efforts founder on these questions. First, *will*. Do you really want to do it? This is such a primitive, old-fashioned, even trite question that we often don't even ask it of ourselves. People in schools often complain that nothing can be done, that all power resides elsewhere (in the union, in the board, in the budget, in the schedule, in the central office, in the principal, in the department heads). Yet in our study we have repeatedly seen action taken on near-intractable problems when someone, simply, decided to act. Triteness to the rescue: "When there's a will, there's a way." Where does will come from? That's mysterious, but it comes partly from sheer courage and assertion, partly from believing that one's actions can make a difference, and partly in turn from some prior success.

Questions of *skill* are also often ignored. Knowing *that* X is a workable action you want to take is very different from knowing *how* to deliver X. The paths of educational improvement are strewn with examples of behavior that no one knew how to deliver: the team teaching project where no one knew how to get good group decisions; the clinical supervision program where principals had no practice in how to give effective feedback; the science inquiry project where teachers persisted in their use of closed-end questions; the comprehensive planning project that assumed that supplying people with forms to be filled in was enough.

Furthermore, many people think that skill can be developed through reading, explanations, or watching videotapes. It can't. Improving skill requires *doing*, practice, getting feedback, reshaping the doing until the action makes sense, is smooth, and gets you where you want to be. Most people know this about skiing, tennis, and golf, but don't consider it in relation to the behaviors involved in educational change. Good skill-development models (for example, that of Joyce & Showers, 1983) often don't get used when it comes to day-to-day school improvement work. People either minimize their skill lacks, or assume they don't need practice and coaching.

With this outline of knowledge-to-action requirements in mind, let's turn to the knowledge we've developed in the book.

Using the Findings

In the rest of this chapter, we will review our major findings on what it takes to really improve big-city schools, look at some of the implications, then comment on some of the will and skill issues that are typically involved. We'll cover in turn issues of context, planning, vision building, resources, and problem coping.

The Context

Our basic findings here were that turbulence is the norm, and that school improvement is most successful when schools and their districts are actively engaged with each other, but with few strict rules and much autonomy for the school in choosing change goals and strategies. The school's own history of past innovation, the staff's cohesiveness, and their willingness to look forward rather than reminisce about a "golden age" all can help, along with a reasonably coherent school organization.

IMPLICATIONS. District offices will have to learn to rely more on their working relationships with schools to steer a course through the turbulent waters, and less on rules and mandates. When there is pressure, it had better be accompanied by plenty of support. Schools have to have room, a good deal of local decision power, *and* help with the problems they face. That means a well-coupled relationship, not a distant one.[1]

Schools, on the other hand, while keeping a wary eye on the district to build the relationship, and get and protect the power (and resources) they need, must also address their own internal contexts. Weak cohesiveness, cynicism about past failures, or disgruntlement about the present non-golden period need to be addressed directly early in the improvement process, not avoided.

ISSUES OF WILL. Central office people often worry that schools already have a lot of *de facto* power, and that empowering schools will just lead to chaos (read central office powerlessness). There is often a zero-sum view (more power for them means less for us — when real empowerment usually expands the pie, with more coherent control on everyone's part). Also, once something like school-based management is launched, district staff may not be tenacious enough in staying with the effort to make it work. Or they may just abandon schools to their own devices, which is not at all the point.

People in schools, for their part, sometimes feel unwillingness to stick their necks out, ask for the autonomy they need, bid for the type of working relationship that will get things done. It's safer to blame "downtown" than to take responsibility for working things through with the central office. And it's also easy to avoid taking a square look at the school's own internal context, or doing some direct work on less-than-optimal conditions. (Getting organization development technical help here is useful.)

KEY SKILLS. The needed skills of empowerment are not easy to learn, because power is so central in organizations. Essentially, one needs to take active initiative without shutting others out — and to support others' initiative without becoming maternal/paternal. It can help central office people to realize that they are not necessarily sharing or delegating decision power over every aspect of school life.

Even where clear school powers are spelled out, many unforeseen issues appear. The key skill is clear decision *allocation* (this one is non-negotiably ours; I will decide this one, but need your advice; that one belongs to the school; this one we should discuss and decide jointly in a principals' meeting; that one is properly a board decision). Coaching helps (yes, central office people can use coaching).

The skills of relationship building between previously unequal partners are not minor and cut both ways: how to build trust and supply/receive help if the history is one of rules and control/compliance/avoidance?

On the school side of the relationship, key skills include assertiveness (how to ask for what's wanted directly, without aggression, game playing, or blaming); and how to negotiate effectively when resources are scarce or there are competing claims. Assertiveness training, as well as training in negotiation and conflict resolution for principals and department heads (since the same issues appear internally when school-based management is under way), is money well spent.[2]

Planning

We found that an evolutionary stance works best, with plenty of early action (small-scale wins) to create energy and support learning. Broad and multiple goals work better than limited, specific ones. A gradually emerging vision, built out of successive and parallel "change themes," helps bring coherence. Planning is the first point where real empowerment takes hold, and works best through a cross-role group of people who may not normally work together.

IMPLICATIONS. In many respects evolutionary planning is more "natural" than the tightly rational, highly specific blueprints administrators have been urged toward in the past. Still, a dictum like "do, then plan" is at first glance hard to tie in with "build a shared vision," and sheer sloppy opportunism may be hard to ward off. It's also clear that good evolutionary planning requires careful and regular monitoring of what's happening as action goes forward. Simple, low-cost methods of staying in touch are crucial.

ISSUES OF WILL. Evolutionary planners have to learn to live with ambiguity, and fight off the tendency to premature closure—or pressures from others to "give us the answer." The risk is to oscillate between too tight planning and timelining on the one hand, and laissez-faire drifting on the other ("We'll just have to take it one day at a time."). Taking a regular look at change themes and the emerging vision helps. Furthermore, fears of loss of control or chaos can lead to a loss of will to really empower others.

KEY SKILLS. Since evolutionary planning is not done in a vacuum, but typically by a newly formed cross-cutting group, there is a cluster of skills involved: communicating openly, building trust with each other, making joint decisions, learning from experience. Seen at the small-group level, exactly the same sorts of skills we've discussed in relation to school-level empowerment also apply: initiative taking, support without falling into the "parent" role, decision allocation. We can also note some cognitive skills: how to draw well-founded conclusions from data on the progress of the effort, and how to derive sensible action steps from the conclusions. Both intensive "retreats" and an at-the-elbow process consultant can be of great help as the planning/steering group develops.

Vision Building

Our findings were that broad, ennobling, feelingful, *shared* images of what the school should become are an important feature guiding successful improvement; they may either emerge from or lead to smaller "change themes," many of which may develop as a response to outside mandates or pressures. Gaining real ownership of visions by school staff is critical, and requires serious time investment, patience, and empowerment for success.

IMPLICATIONS. As with evolutionary planning, a "blueprinted" approach to vision is unlikely to be successful, and people who doubt their own charisma need not worry that they are missing some magic ability to paint an inspirational picture of an achievable, highly desired future. Visioning is a joint process; hope depends on successful and optimistic interaction between people.

ISSUES OF WILL. Will looms very large in vision building. Many people experience fear and uncertainty about the future, because "it cannot be known." (Many consultants have found that asking people to look *back* on the future, as if it had already happened, is very helpful. An example: "It's October 6, 1995. The governor's office has just cited this school as one of 10 outstanding schools in the state. Write the citation.")

Furthermore, people often stop themselves from vision building by doubting themselves and their ability to be "out front," leading, making a commitment. And they weaken the power of their visions by taking present structures and procedures as "givens," not as things to be transcended.

KEY SKILLS. Here we can point to the skill of "going outside the frame," thinking laterally and creatively. A closely associated skill is the ability to design, invent new structures and procedures. (A useful sourcebook of ideas and techniques here is Koberg & Bagnall, 1976.)

The struggles of the classic hero, or Don Quixote's delusory quests, are not good models for vision sharing. The basic skills of collaboration are key. Visions can't be shared without direct, joint work on decisions that matter, or without the ability to support and encourage others in dreaming.

Resources

Essentially, we found that getting a "floor" of funds (from $50,000 to $100,000 annually for several years) is needed for serious change efforts. Such funds may be "add-on," or come from unallocated resources in the normal budget. A strong proportion of funds needs to go to external assistance and internal coordination. Scanning actively for a broad-based view of resources (time, the right people, services, educational programs and materials, and "intangible" support and influence) in support of a vision makes for success, when accompanied by assertive, imaginative negotiation to get what's needed. Building permanent internal resource structures (for example, cadres, coordinators, program managers, steering groups) is also important.

IMPLICATIONS. Although money is a "master resource" used to buy other resources, it is equally important to think of assistance and internal coordination as "multiplier" resources. Intense, sustained, focused assistance, and careful coordination will often determine more than anything else how well funds are spent in the service of implementing change. Good assistance and coordination will lead to better decisions on staffing, educational practices, and materials—and to a more productive process. Thus program managers need to do a careful diagnosis, looking thoughtfully at the program and the people doing it; assess their needs for training, consultation, and support; and locate appropriate helpers.

ISSUES OF WILL.   One of the biggest is facing up to the fact that changes cost money, and confronting a second fact: Powerful others may lack that realization, and may have to be persuaded, converted, or even bypassed. Resource finding and getting take a large amount of tenacity, hanging in there, persisting against obstacles.

A second big issue is false pride and mistaken feelings of self-sufficiency. The basic feeling that "we can do it ourselves" is sometimes reinforced by a mistaken belief that our school system is unique, and ideas from elsewhere won't work. Assistance seeking has to be seen as a sign of intelligence and strength, not of weakness.

KEY SKILLS.   Negotiating skills, "getting to yes" in Fisher and Ury's (1981) terms, loom very large. They can be learned with guided practice. A less focused but equally important skill is the "garage sale junkie" stance: the ability to scan regularly and automatically for whatever looks good and fits with the vision.

Here too the skill of "going outside the frame" is rather crucial, not only in reworking existing resources in creative ways, but looking in odd places for what you need.

In the special case of assistance resources, key skills are those of how to broker the right assistance to needy parts of the improvement program; how to develop a clear contract with assistance givers, especially outsiders; and how to design and strengthen internal assistance capacity. ("No training without training trainers" is a useful motto.)

Problem Coping

Here we found that problems during school improvement efforts are multiple, pervasive, and often nearly intractable. But dealing with them actively, promptly, and with some depth is the single biggest determinant of program success. "Depth" means thinking structurally, or in terms of capacity building, rather than in a "business as usual" or "push a little harder" or "fire fighting" style. Don't just fight off the alligators one by one; drain the swamp, and teach people to keep it drained.

IMPLICATIONS.   Because coping is so central, it pays to become aware of one's own typical coping style — and the styles most frequent in the school as a whole. Reviewing recent problems, what was done about them, and whether they stayed solved can be very illuminating. It also helps to routinize problem scanning (for example, beginning meetings with a "worry list"), as well as solution generation (always getting a range of brainstormed alternatives before deciding on one) and follow-up (reviewing consequences of each past coping effort).

ISSUES OF WILL. Passivity and denial are the main enemies of good coping. Doing nothing (or its partner, procrastination) rarely works unless done deliberately with good reasons. Pretending or convincing oneself that the problem doesn't really exist, or will go away, is also a way to stop effective coping in its tracks.

Here too refusal to "go outside the frame" can have bad consequences. A dogmatic preference for low-risk, incremental coping (sometimes expressed as fear of seeming "too radical") means that the "deep" coping required for difficult, persistent problems won't happen.

KEY SKILLS. One is the ability to locate and state problems as natural occurrences, without blaming anyone, arousing defensiveness, or implying a pre-determined solution. (See Miles, 1980, pp. 170–171, for a learning exercise.)

And, as we've seen repeatedly, creativity, invention, and design skills are critical in generating coping alternatives that go deeper than "trying harder," go to the roots of the problem, and build others' capability for future problem coping.

Our comments on our findings, and the issues of will and skill involved, show the limits of what can be done with words on paper. Still, we believe it's important to push words and ideas as far as we can, remembering that they shape beliefs about what is possible in school reform, and the actions that will bring it about.

The message of this book is: We know that high schools in our big cities can be turned around, because we've seen it happen. And we know with some confidence *how* and *why* it happened. We hope our reflections will be useful in supporting the energetic efforts we know are going on in hundreds of high schools across the country. That is where the action is, and we applaud it.

NOTES

1. This discussion deals only with the main issues we found critical in district–school relationships. For a full and helpful discussion, see Patterson, Parker, & Purkey (1986). See also Hill et al. (1989).

2. For further helpful material along these lines, see Block's directly written book *The Empowered Manager* (1987). Helpful work on conflict resolution appears in Cole (1983). The technical skills of actually managing local school budgeting are not simple ones. Caldwell & Spinks (1988) have described some very useful methods.

Appendixes

References

Index

About the Authors

Appendix A
Case Study Methods

This Appendix describes the methods we used to produce our five case studies: how we planned them and selected sites, how we collected and analyzed data, how we revised and verified case reports, how we did our cross-site analysis, and how we produced the final reduced case reports in this book. We are doing this to follow Miles and Huberman's (1984) call for careful methodological accounts of qualitative studies.

PLANNING

Because efforts to fund our study took nearly 18 months, we had ample time for careful planning. Given the generally well-developed conceptual status of research on implementation and change, and our own familiarity with schools, we opted for a well-structured approach to the case studies.[1]

Conceptual Framework

Figure A.1 shows a simplified block diagram of the conceptual scheme for the study. (It was used to guide the survey as well as the cases.)

We wanted to describe the contextual influences in and around the school, the improvement program itself, the assistance provided, the actual events and processes during implementation, the problems and barriers encountered, and how they were dealt with. Naturally, we wanted to assess the overall quality of implementation, and the outcomes achieved.

Within each of the blocks, we named a series of specific variables, drawing from our own prior studies of school improvement, and those of others. For example, in the outcomes block, we listed interim out-

Figure A.1 Conceptual Scheme

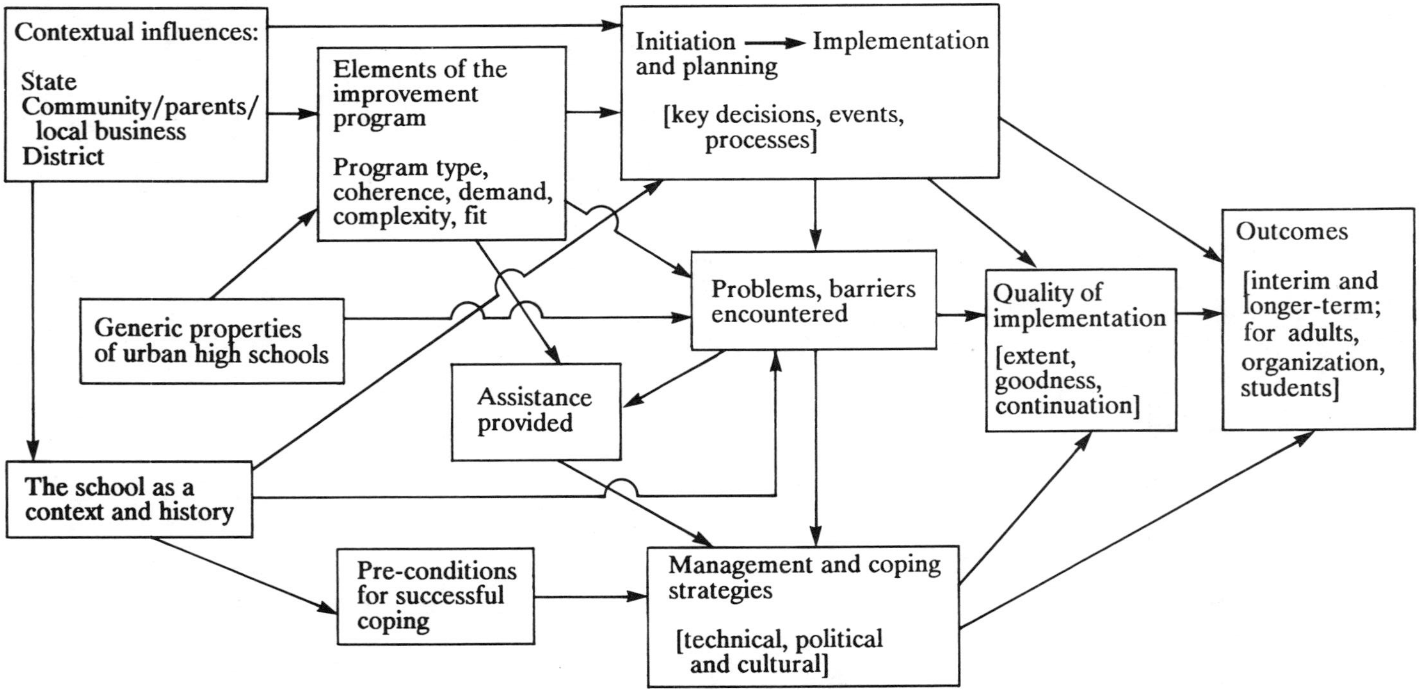

comes such as ownership of the program and increased collaboration; longer-term "adult" outcomes such as teacher skill and methods mastery, and image of the school in the community; and student outcomes such as achievement, behavior, retention, employment, and further education. We did not try for a tight or well-defined conceptual framework, but wanted to be as mindful as possible of what *might* be important in our sites.

Research Questions

In parallel with the development of the conceptual framework, we developed a set of nine *descriptive* research questions and five *explanatory* research questions, aimed at probing the arrows in Figure A.1. They are shown in Figure A.2.

Plans for Data Collection

The principle we followed was to drive the data collection by the anticipated product. We did not generate a standard interview or observation guide, but asked each site researcher to collect the data needed to produce a well-defined case. Each case study report was expected to run about 40 pages. They would be very focused, and make use of displays intermixed with text. The structure of the cases was to follow the research questions.

The originally planned rough sequence and tempo of data collection are shown in Figure A.3.

We expected to do a minimum of three two-day visits spaced over the school year. In fact (see below), somewhat more time was involved, and one-day visits also happened.

Outlining the Case Studies

With the conceptual framework and research questions in mind, we then outlined what we believed the case study products should look like (Figure A.4).

In addition, an extended case outline fleshed out things more fully, and included specifications for each of 13 "displays," which were usually large matrices summarizing qualitative information in systematic, focused form (see Miles & Huberman, 1984, for rationale). For example, a display under section IV.E of Figure A.4 listed typical problems encountered during implementation, and showed the technical, political, and cultural coping strategies used to deal with them.

Figure A.2   Working Research Questions

These are sorted into descriptive questions (1,2,4,5,6,7,9,11,13) and causal or explanatory questions (3,8,10,12,14). They were addressed by both survey and case studies.

1. What does the local *context* look like (state, community, district, and school)?

2. What are the *elements of the improvement program* that is initially chosen or locally developed?

3. What influences the *elements of the improvement program*? Sources may include the local context, and the properties of urban high schools.

4. What was the basic *chronology* of events, during the periods of initiation/ planning, and of implementation? What roles did key actors and groups play?

5. What were the basic features of the *planning/implementation process*? These include its goals, its costs in time and money, the fit of the program to school and teachers, changes and adaptations made, and the social processes involved (inter-action, influence).

6. What *barriers, problems, and dilemmas* were encountered during planning/ initiation, and implementation? These may be "inherent" in the nature of high schools and the improvement process, or conditioned by the local context.

7. What *management and coping strategies* were employed to deal with the barriers/problems/dilemmas? Which are technical, which are cultural, and which are political in nature?

8. What influences or causes *management/coping strategies*? We may look at the barriers or dilemmas, and at the assistance provided.

9. What *assistance* is provided to the school to deal with the barriers/dilem-mas/problems? What are the sources of assistance, external or internal to the schools, and its nature, intensity, adequacy?

10. What influences the amount and type of *assistance* provided? Sources may include specific elements of the program, its general demandingness, and the barriers/dilemmas/problems encountered.

11. How well *implemented* is the program, in terms of extent, quality, thorough-ness, and likelihood of continuation?

12. What *explains or causes good implementation*? How do key implementation events, the barriers/problems/dilemmas, and the coping strategies employed lead to this quality?

13. What are the *outcomes* of the program? These may be interim, or longer-term; they may be seen for the adults involved, for the school as an organization, and for students.

14. What *explains or causes successful outcomes*? Causes may include particu-lar program elements as they show up in specific implementation events, the quality of implementation attained, and the coping strategies employed. Interim outcomes may also cause longer-term outcomes.

Figure A.3 Timing of Data Collection

	Res. Q.
VISIT 1	
Entry, locate key actors in school and district context description	1
Program elements	2
Contextual influences	3
Beginnings of chronology	4
VISIT 2	
Chronology, dynamics of planning and implementation (try to visit some meetings)	4,5
Problems/barriers; coping; influences on these	6,7,8
Assistance and what influences it	9,10
Quality of implementation; outcomes	11,13
VISIT 3	
Recheck quality of implementation and outcomes	11,13
Explanations of implementation and outcomes	12,14
Follow-up on assorted leads and loose ends	

SELECTION OF SITES

In a proposal written during the summer of 1984, we defined criteria for choice of sites, beyond the obvious one that the schools should be secondary, and located in an urban setting. We sought schools that

- were implementing effective schools activities focused on classroom-level interventions.
- were successfully grappling with the dilemmas and requirements of implementation (not "excellent" schools, but ones committed to improvement).
- had some probability of real "success," as measured by improvement in effectiveness indicators such as student achievement.
- were not initially "outstanding" in any way — that is, were typical urban secondary schools on a current trajectory of improvement.
- were located so as to minimize travel costs.

We expected that the selection of final candidates from a larger pool would also increase the diversity of the sample along several dimensions:

Figure A.4   Abbreviated Case Outline

A Beginning Note: Case Methods and Data

  I. The Context
     A. The school: An overview
     B. The community context
     C. The school district
     D. The state context (SEA and legislature)
     E. The school: A more detailed picture
     F. Pre-conditions for change

 II. The Improvement Program as Planned: An Overview

III. Why This Program?

 IV. The Story of Planning and Implementation
     A. Chronology
     B. The process of planning and implementation
     C. The problems
     D. The assistance provided
        1. Sources, types, and adequacy
        2. Why this assistance?
     E. How problems were dealt with
        1. Managing and coping strategies
        2. Why these strategies?

  V. The Program Implementation Effort
     A. Overall program extent and quality
     B. Prospects for the future
     C. Why implementation occurred as it did

 VI. The Results
     A. Interim results
     B. Longer-term results

VII. Why These Results?

VIII. Lessons for Improving the Urban High School

- Racial mix of students.
- Presence of at least one junior high/middle school.
- Degree of state support for school improvement.
- Geographical spread (Northeast, Southwest as a minimum, to contrast older vs. newer cities and contracting vs. expanding/stable economies).

As we moved toward final selection, two added criteria appeared:

- Non-reliance of the site on a "charismatic" principal (we wanted to examine implementation dynamics without resorting to the familiar bromide "the principal is key").
- Active interest of a funding agency in attention to a particular city or school. (This occurred in Cleveland and in New Jersey.)

Access

We used nominations from state departments, city districts, school improvement programs, and funding agencies to focus our search. When we found a small pool of promising candidates that met our criteria, we carried out exploratory visits to see whether the school would be interested in participating.

For these visits, and for later contacts during data collection, we developed a two-page brochure about the study. In brief, it

- Outlined the need for understanding the *process* of becoming effective: "How do you get there?"
- Described the plan for the case studies, the survey, and the "administrative guidelines" we expected to produce.
- Explained that researchers would spend seven to nine days over the year talking to administrators, teachers, and students about the history and progress of the change effort, and visiting meetings, training sessions, and classrooms.
- Laid out ground rules: no passing on of information received to anyone else in the site; individual and school identities protected; case study draft checked for accuracy with people in the school before anyone else sees it.
- Discussed possible benefits for the school: insight and ideas about the improvement effort, along with copies of all case studies, the survey report, and the guidelines.
- Specified probable time investments (typically an hour or two for most individuals, more for key people), and indicated that participation for individuals was voluntary.
- Identified the researchers, with vitae, and sources of funding.

In general, local school discussions went well. In all cities multiple candidates were considered, and final decisions reached relatively promptly after exploratory contacts.

The final sample of schools is reviewed in Table 3.1, Chapter 3.

DATA COLLECTION AND ANALYSIS

In this section we detail the extent and nature of our actual contacts with sites: how, when, and what kind of data were collected; we also outline our data analysis methods.

Site Contacts

Site visits, carried out alone (or, in two sites, by partners), normally included interviews with administrators (both school level and central office), teachers, counselors, and students; observations of meetings and classrooms; and much informal observation of events in halls, cafeteria, and offices. Interviews were not structured, and typically lasted a period or an hour. Researchers normally took notes during interviews unless "off the record" requests were made (this was rare). The notes were usually extended or fleshed out afterward, during coding. Researchers also collected a wide range of program-related documents, from attendance and achievement records to student newspaper articles, program plans, and assorted memos. We also spoke with salient external representatives (foundation, state department, and business people, for example).

Agassiz had two researchers (Karen Seashore Louis and Tony Cipollone) who, because of their physical proximity to the school, could do many brief visits. They spent a total of approximately 10 days at the school during the school year, and formally interviewed 25 people (administrators, program staff, teachers, students, and technical assistance givers), did a group interview of teachers, and had many briefer individual contacts during general observations. Interim phone calls also provided added data. Interviews of the superintendent, other key staff members at the central office, and individuals associated with the Boston Compact were conducted by Cipollone and Eleanor Farrar, as part of another research project (Farrar & Cipollone, 1988). Most key informants, both at the school and in the district, were interviewed several times over a year-and-a-half. The school was also visited in the fall of 1988 by Cipollone, who was then also involved in another study of the Boston Compact. Documents included newspaper reports, teacher guidebooks, prior studies of the school, and official school district data.

Alameda's researcher (Sheila Rosenblum) visited the school 3 times, for a total of 11 days. She did 67 interviews, observed eight classes, and attended six meetings, of administrators and of the SIP council. There were over 60 documents, including SIP plans and proposals, brochures, staff development flyers, school newspapers, meeting agendas, schedules, and parent communiques.

Bartholdi's researcher (Matthew B. Miles) visited the school for seven days during the year, and the assistant superintendent's and central office for a day. There were 51 interviews with administrators, key staff, and teachers, and a student classroom group interview. About two-thirds of interviewees were seen two to three times. Formal meetings of four planning and coordination groups were observed. There were 23 interim phone calls. Documents totaled 78, ranging from attendance reports to minutes of meetings, class lists, handbooks, the school newspaper, and program updates.

At Burroughs, the researcher (Eleanor Farrar) visited the school and district for 11 days spread throughout the year. She carried out 65 interviews, with the principal (many times), the vice-principal (twice), 27 of the 36 academic teachers, plus a few special-purpose teachers, and two guidance counselors. Nine core team teachers (included in the number above) were interviewed twice. At the district office she interviewed deputy and assistant superintendents. Her external interview contacts included staff of the Henry Harman Foundation, a Cleveland *Plain Dealer* reporter, and a state department of education deputy superintendent. She attended three school meetings and observed three classes. Documents collected included Foundation guidelines, proposals, year-end reports to the Foundation, district statistical reports, reports of the desegregation monitoring team, and E2 and staff training materials.

At Chester the researchers (Matthew B. Miles and Sheila Rosenblum) visited the school on eight days during the year; on three of these days both researchers were present. There was a total of 75 interviews with central office administrators, school administrators, supervisors, teachers, and state department of education officials, and a group interview with student leaders. Repeat interviews were typical for administrators and supervisors. There were 65 documents, including attendance reports, minutes of meetings, class lists, memos, handbooks, the school newspaper, and program reports and updates. Meetings observed included those of the school cabinet, administrators and supervisors, and departments; training sessions; and a student leadership class.

Data Analysis

The raw field notes were directly *coded* by the site researcher, without being transcribed. Then the researcher reviewed the field notes for coded sections, entered data directly into displays using a word processor, and wrote accompanying analytic text, within the pre-existing outline.[2] After a first visit, naturally, there were plenty of "DK's" (don't know) and missing data. Many research questions had only partial answers. The draft cases were circulated to other project staff members, and a "project partner" commented on them; this advice and the missing data needed provided the targets for the next round of data collection.

In successive rounds of data collection, this procedure was iterated until data collection, and the fully analyzed cases, were complete.

CASE REVISION AND VERIFICATION

Near-final versions of the cases were sent to several key people in each site. They were asked to correct errors of fact, and to suggest alternative interpretations to those in the case. This was done in all sites, and was accompanied in Bartholdi, Burroughs, and Chester by meetings to discuss the case as well. Alternative interpretations were incorporated either in text or as footnotes. The final versions of the cases ran from 69 to 102 pages, and are cited in our reference list as follows:

Agassiz — Louis & Cipollone, 1986
Alameda — Rosenblum, 1986
Bartholdi — Miles, 1986
Burroughs — Farrar, 1987b
Chester — Miles & Rosenblum, 1987

THE PRESENT CASE REPORTS

We prepared a revised outline for the cases for this book, and produced cut-down versions of all five cases. The original authors also carried out follow-up visits to each site during the late spring of 1988 to produce an "Epilogue." They asked about major events that had occurred in the preceding two years, including personnel changes; how the school had changed; how the improvement effort stood; people's explanations as to why the current state of implementation had occurred; what the results of the program had been; and why those results had taken place. Drafts of these Epilogues were included in each case. The overall case length now ranged from 29 to 38 pages, or about 30 to 40 percent of the original length.

Each case report was once again reviewed with key site personnel, who made suggestions for correction and improvement. Using these suggestions, the final drafts were produced in consultation with the original authors.

CROSS–SITE ANALYSIS

When the original case drafts were largely done, the project staff carried out preliminary cross-case analysis in a series of meetings, on such themes as the effects of historical context, reasons for the choice of program, problems encountered, coping strategies, and key variables influencing implementation. Data from each site were entered in cross-site displays to permit drawing conclusions. Some of these preliminary findings were reported by Miles (1987).

The analysis had more power than we had expected, because the sites were not equally successful. As we have already indicated, Agassiz and Alameda were generally successful in implementation and outcome, Burroughs and Bartholdi somewhat less so, and Chester least. Thus we could compare phenomena across the five sites with some sense of their contribution to implementation success.[3]

During the summer of 1987, staff members individually carried out cross-site analyses on a series of topics, drawing conclusions across the five sites on the topics of program goals, state and district contexts, change process overview, program chronology, degree and quality of implementation, problems encountered, coping strategies, assistance provided, outcomes, and a model of good implementation.

These analyses were integrated into an "administrative guidelines" document, and relevant data from the survey were incorporated. (Most case-derived conclusions received confirmatory support, and none were directly contradicted.) The document was entitled *Lessons for Managing Implementation: [Improving the Urban High School: A Preliminary Report]* (Miles, Louis, Rosenblum, Cipollone, & Farrar, 1987).

The analysis for this book extended the preliminary report, relying on comparisons across the A-B-C cases, and on correlational, regression, and cross-tabulation data from the survey.

NOTES

1. The rationale for this pre-structured approach is discussed more fully in Miles (1989).

2. Displays were not used in the Burroughs case.

3. Bartholdi, in 1986, was seen as less successful, and called "Caruso" to symbolize its C-level status. By 1988 we considered that its success had become more substantial.

Appendix B
Survey Research Methods

Although the primary data source of the project on which this book is based was the five case studies, the survey was an important vehicle to test whether the findings that emerged from the cases were supported by a larger representative sample of big-city high schools seriously involved in improvement efforts. The survey was viewed as critical, as previous studies of large-scale change in urban high schools have not explored the *process* of improvement, but only program characteristics and impacts (Purkey, Rutter, & Newmann, 1987).

DEFINING A UNIVERSE AND SAMPLE

The goal of the survey was to get a complete sample of all high schools located in cities with a population of 75,000 or more (1) that were not serving special populations (examination or special schools for dropouts); (2) that were implementing a comprehensive change program affecting the entire school and based on the research findings from the effective schools literature (Kyle, 1985; Purkey & Smith, 1983); and (3) that showed visible signs of improvement. However, we knew from the Wisconsin analysis of high school improvement programs[1] that only approximately 780 urban high schools had any kind of school improvement program at all, while approximately 430 had a "comprehensive" program using criteria that included adherence to the principles underlying the effective schools research.[2] The Wisconsin study also found that principals as respondents were very likely to report programs that were hardly visible (for example, less than 50 percent of the teachers in the school were aware of the activity).

Our budget did not permit interviewing both teachers and principals, or the kind of extensive screening and replacement procedures necessary to locate such a small universe within a larger group using random sampling techniques (the estimated total number of urban high schools is 1,260 according to Purkey, Rutter, & Newmann, 1987). Reputational sampling was therefore chosen. Three key groups were contacted for referrals that met our criteria: (1) developers of effective schools programs who were listed in the Effective Schools Program Directory (Miles & Kaufman, 1985); (2) staff of the Council of Great City Schools who were knowledgeable about improvement efforts in the major cities (where development is more likely to occur within the district office); and (3) staff responsible for selecting the schools that were identified by the Ford Foundation as "improving" in their high school recognition program. We explained our initial criteria, emphasizing that we were not looking for "excellent" schools, but *improving* schools that initially had not been high-performing. The total number of nominated schools was 279.

Issues of confidentiality do not permit us to discuss specific cities in the sample. However, it is interesting to note that quite a few major cities in the United States had no schools at all in the sample; further telephone calls to verify this were made, with the same results. While a few districts had programs that involved all schools, in most districts only a few schools were nominated.

Comparison of Urban High School Sample and the High School and Beyond Sample

We located only 279 schools by reputation, as compared with 430 in the Wisconsin sample. This difference is probably attributable to (1) our stricter criteria for city size (75,000 as compared with 50,000), and (2) our requirement that schools have implemented the program for at least one year, and show real evidence of improvement as a result of the program according to an outside observer.

SURVEY DEVELOPMENT

A 27-page predominantly close-ended survey instrument consisting of 435 items was developed using the same conceptual model that guided the case study data collection.[3] The instrument was pre-tested on October 11 and 12, 1985 by three professional interviewers who were staff members of the Center for Survey Research at the University of Massachusetts/Boston. Ten pre-test telephone interviews were conducted, and minor revisions were made in the instrument and procedures.

DATA COLLECTION

A briefing of the larger interviewer staff (nine interviewers and one supervisor) took place on October 22, 1985, and data collection continued until January 16, 1986. All interviews took place by telephone, usually after setting up a specific appointment with the principal. In some cases, interviews were conducted with other administrators in the school, if they were designated by the principal as the person most knowledgeable about the effective schools/effective teaching program in that school. The average length of the interview was 50 to 60 minutes, including "short interviews" with schools that were not eligible for the study. Some lasted for as much as two hours.

Response Rates

Four schools were eliminated because we could not locate addresses or telephone numbers for them. The response rate for the remaining 275 was 90.2 percent, including 213 interviews with schools that were implementing a program, and 35 shorter interviews with schools that were not eligible; that is, they were not involved in an improvement program based on effective schools and effective teaching principles.[4] Of those not interviewed, 14 (5.1%) refused (usually citing "time pressures" rather than lack of interest in the survey), while 13 (4.7%) posed serious problems of scheduling, and were eventually eliminated due to time constraints. Details of the sample are shown in Table B.1. Table B.1 summarizes the procedures and numbers of schools involved at each stage.

Many of the schools in the population of 207 that engaged in long interviews had not completed the planning stages of their improvement effort. Most of the analysis reported in this volume is based on an N of 178 schools that were actually implementing a program.

DATA BASE CONSTRUCTION AND ANALYSIS

All completed questionnaires were reviewed by trained research assistants, and entered into personal computers using a data entry program adapted by the Center for Survey Research (the program rejected out-of-range entries). A 50 percent sample of each research assistant's work was reviewed for accuracy by a supervisor. A senior research assistant developed a working data file in the SAS program, and engaged in exploratory and confirmatory scaling to reduce batteries of questions to

Table B.1 Sample Procedures and Survey Outcomes

A. NOMINATION RESULTS	
Total eligible nominees:	
Developers/Ford/CGCS[1]	279
B. SURVEY RESULTS	
Total respondents[2]	248
C. SCREENING RESULTS	
Results of initial screen for eligibility[3]	218
Second screen: planning began in 1984 school year	
or earlier	207

[1]This number includes only schools that met our criteria of being a non-specialized high school, located in a city with a minimum population of 75,000, that was not initially a "high-performing school," and which began working on a comprehensive effective schools program in January 1984 or earlier, with some visible signs of improvement. It excludes all overlapping nominations.

[2]This is a response rate of 88%. Respondents were interviewed on the telephone, and were either the principal or another administrator with responsibility for program management.

[3]School agrees that it is involved in an effective schools program that began after 1981 or was substantially modified by effective schools findings after 1981.

the broader indicators implied by our research framework. This reduced set of 130 variables was then analyzed using simple frequencies, cross-tabulations, and regression analysis.[5]

NOTES

1. This estimate was given to us by R. Rutter and F. Newmann, who analyzed the High School and Beyond data about comprehensive school change, reported in Purkey, Rutter, & Newmann (1987).

2. These estimates were based on an extrapolation from a national sample of high schools.

3. A copy of the survey instrument is available from the authors at reproduction costs.

4. A school was eligible only if the principal agreed that it was involved in an effective schools program that began after 1981 or was substantially modified by effective schools findings after 1981.

5. Further information about the survey is available from Karen Seashore Louis, and a more technical report of the results is in preparation.

Appendix C
Survey Tables and Figures

Here we include tables and a figure drawn from the survey data, as referred to in the book.

Table C.1   Characteristics of the Schools

SIZE

Median average daily attendance	1,540
Median number of teachers	82
Median number of non-teaching professionals	11

PUPIL CHARACTERISTICS

Median percent one or more grades behind national norms in reading	35%
Median percent qualifying for subsidized food programs	40%
Median percent Hispanic	10%
Median percent black	49%
Median percent from white-collar families	18%
Median percent from blue-collar families	55%
Median percent from families where adults are on public assistance	24%

STABILITY

Median percent student turnover within any school year	11.5%[1]
Median percent of faculty within school for 10+ years	50%[2]

[1]Twenty percent of the schools have turnover rates of 20 percent or more, indicating rather high instability.

[2]Twenty percent of the schools are highly stable, with 75% or more of the faculty having 10+ years in the school; another 20% are rather unstable, with fewer than 30% of the staff having 10+ years of experience in the school.

Table C.2 Effective Schools Programs: What Are Their Components in Urban High Schools? (N = 238)

A. CORE COMPONENTS	*Percent*
Improving the school's atmosphere or climate	94%
Creating more structured educational environments	92%
Improving discipline and safety	92%
Creating high expectations for student performance	90%
Increasing teacher classroom management skills	87%
Improving the use of staff development	85%
Increasing consensus on school goals	82%
Increasing parental involvement	82%
Requiring frequent/specific feedback on student progress	80%
B. COMMON COMPONENTS	
Increasing student participation and leadership	74%
Requiring more attention to measuring achievement	73%
Improving working conditions for students	66%
Enlarging the role of the school leader over instructional decisions	64%
C. INFREQUENT COMPONENTS	
Increasing the amount of time teachers spend with students in individual help	44%
Individualizing instruction	35%

Table C.3 Sources of Influence over Program Development (N = 206)

A. DISTRICT	*Percent*
Percent whose program is part of a larger district effort	75%
Percent indicating that district office had "a great deal" of influence over their plan	51%
Percent indicating "some influence"	33%
B. STATE	
Percent indicating that state policies were a "major factor" in some program changes	75%
Percent indicating that the SEA had a "great deal of influence" over the local school plan	22%
Percent indicating "some influence"	30%
C. SCHOOL	
Percent of various groups with "a great deal" of influence:	
Principal	85%
Department heads	63%
Individual teachers	57%
Assistant principal(s)	53%
Parents	42%
Teaching staff as a whole	41%
Departments as a whole	36%
Students	18%
Consultants	18%
Business community members	14%
Unions	12%

Table C.4   Factors Affecting Planning (N = 177)

A. FACILITATING FACTORS	*Percent "Helped"* [1]
Reactions from teachers	92%
Support from district	85%
Level of agreement in district/school on need for action	84%
Staff attitudes about students	70%
Time and energy available from staff	67%
B. HINDERING FACTORS	*Percent "Hindered"*
Problems of time and scheduling (open-ended)	32%
Staff attitudes about students	22%
Time and energy from staff	17%
Previous (negative) experiences with innovation	15%
Poor staff morale (open-ended)	14%
Staff resistance (open-ended)	12%

[1]The response options were (1) helped; (2) no effect; (3) hindered.

Table C.5   Problems with Implementation (N = 158)

A. MAJOR PROBLEMS[1]	*Percent*
Teacher time and energy	46%
Money	42%
(money, resources – open-ended)	19%
Arranging for staff development	29%
Maintaining communication about the project	22%
Constraints of the physical plant	22%
Teacher morale/resistance (open-ended)	20%
B. MINOR PROBLEMS	
Lack of staff skills that were required	58%
Slow progress in reaching goals	57%
Staff disagreement over goals	57%
Maintaining staff interest/involvement	51%
A project plan that was too ambitious	48%
Unanticipated crises detracted from the program	45%
Competing requirements from other change programs	44%
C. "NON-PROBLEMS"	
Conflict with special interest groups	77%
Political pressures/tensions in the city	73%
Conflicts with the district office	66%
Adult–student tensions	65%
Turnover among key personnel in the district office	60%

[1]Major problems are defined as those where more than 20 percent indicated it was a major problem. Minor problems are those for which more than 40 percent indicated it was a minor problem, but less than 20 percent saw it as a major problem. "Non-problems" are those where more than 50 percent indicated it was not a problem.

Table C.6   Outcomes/Effects of Effective Schools Programs

	Implementation 1982 or Before (N=75)	Implementation 1983 or After (N=102)
STUDENT OUTCOMES		
A. *Student Achievement*		
Greatly Improved	35%	17%
Somewhat Improved	63	62
No Change/N.A.[1]	2	22
B. *Student Behavior*		
Greatly Improved	53%	46%
Somewhat Improved	39	43
No Change/N.A.	8	11
C. *Student Dropout Rate*		
Greatly Improved	20%	11%
Somewhat Improved	53	42
No Change/N.A.	26	47
D. *Student Attendance*		
Greatly Improved	51%	30%
Somewhat Improved	40	51
No Change/N.A.	9	19
E. *Student Attitudes*		
Greatly Improved	51%	38%
Somewhat Improved	42	50
No Change/N.A.	6	12
F. *Employment of Graduates*		
Greatly Improved	19%	8%
Somewhat Improved	38	19
No Change/N.A.	42	72
TEACHER OUTCOMES		
A. *Staff Morale*		
Greatly Improved	47%	39%
Somewhat Improved	47	47
No Change/N.A.	6	14
B. *Staff Communication About Education*		
Greatly Improved	51%	29%
Somewhat Improved	43	56
No Change/N.A.	6	15
C. *Staff Commitment to Student Achievement*		
Greatly Improved	60%	42%
Somewhat Improved	39	53
No Change/N.A.	2	5

(continued)

Table C.6 *(Continued)*

D. *Teaching Methods*		
Greatly Improved	42%	20%
Somewhat Improved	57	66
No Change/N.A.	1	14
E. *Teachers' Mastery of New Skills*		
Greatly Improved	35%	10%
Somewhat Improved	61	71
No Change/N.A.	4	19
ORGANIZATIONAL OUTCOMES		
A. *School Image*		
Greatly Improved	65%	52%
Somewhat Improved	30	35
No Change/N.A.	5	13
B. *School Organization to Meet Student Needs*		
Greatly Improved	53%	40%
Somewhat Improved	42	46
No Change/N.A.	5	14
C. *The Way Problems Are Solved in the School*		
Greatly Improved	49%	44%
Somewhat Improved	40	52
No Change/N.A.	9	21
D. *Interdepartmental Collaboration*		
Greatly Improved	42%	35%
Somewhat Improved	49	51
No Change/N.A.	9	14
E. *Student–Faculty Relations*		
Greatly Improved	51%	27%
Somewhat Improved	40	52
No Change/N.A.	9	21

[1]N.A. covers response of "too early to tell."

Table C.7   **Backwards Stepwise Regression of Planning Outcomes, "Ownership" and Assistance on Coping[1] (N = 166)**

	Coping
Consensus	.24**
	(.31)
Quality of Plan	.14**
	(.25)
Sch. Infl. on Plan	—
Amt. of Assistance	.17**
	(.05)
Impl. Support	.35**
	(.08)
Admin. Time	.13**
	(.01)
Project Age	—
Multiple R	.49
F Value	30.76

[1]Standardized regression coefficients; standard errors in parentheses for regression model where F statistic for all variables is significant at .10 or better.

  * = sig. at .05

  ** = sig. at .01 or better

For the reader who may not be familiar with regression analysis, the numbers can be interpreted as the strength of association between two variables, controlling for the effects of the other predictor variables in the table.

Table C.8   Backwards Stepwise Regression of Outcome Variables on Predictors[1] (N = 166)

	Program Outcomes		
	Student Achievement	*Teaching Improvement*	*Organizational Improvement*
Org. Prg. Emphasis			.14* (.15)
Staff Dev. Prg. Emph.		.14* (.18)	
Instruct Prg. Emph.			
Process Emph.			
Magnitude of Change			
Consensus		.14 (.14)	
Quality of Plan		.14 (.11)	
Sch. Infl. on Plan			
Implementation Problems			
Coping	.38** (.05)	.28** (.03)	.37** (.04)
Amount of Assistance			
Support for Implementation	.22** (.05)	.15** (.04)	.22** (.05)
Admin Time			
Year of Implementation	.13* (.24)	.23** (.08)	.13* (.10)
Multiple R2	.29	.44	.37
F Value	22.77**	20.81**	23.61**

[1]Standardized regression coefficients; standard errors in parentheses for regression model where F statistic for all variables is significant at .10 or better.

   * = sig. at .05

  ** = sig. at .01 or better

For the reader who may not be familiar with regression analysis, the numbers can be interpreted as the strength of association between two variables, controlling for the effects of the other predictor variables in the table.

Figure C.1 Pearson Correlations Among Planning, Vision,
and Implementation

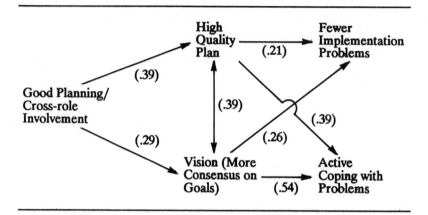

References

Abbey-Livingston, D., & Kelleher, D. (1988). *Managing for learning in organizations: The fundamentals*. Toronto, Ontario: Ministry of Tourism and Information.

Alexander, G., & Louis, K. S. (1989). *Changing teacher and principal roles: A report from Minnesota schools*. Minneapolis: Center for Applied Research and Educational Improvement, University of Minnesota.

Allison, G. (1971). *The essence of decision: Explaining the Cuban missile crisis*. Boston: Little Brown.

Anderson, B., & Odden, A. (1988). State initiatives can foster school improvement. *Phi Delta Kappan, 67*, 578–581.

Anderson, S. G. (1989). The management and implementation of multiple changes in curriculum and instruction. Ph.D. dissertation, University of Toronto.

Austin, G. (1979). Exemplary schools and the search for effectiveness. *Educational Leadership, 37*, 10–14.

Bachrach, S., & Conley, S. (1986). Education reform: A managerial agenda. *Phi Delta Kappan, 67*, 641–645.

Barczek, G., Smith, C., & Wilemon, D. (1988). Managing large-scale organizational change. In *Managing organizational change in the 1990's*, Vol. 16, autumn, 1987, pp. 23–35. New York: American Management Association.

Barnard, C. (1938). *The functions of the executive*. Boston, MA: Harvard Business School.

Beckhard, R., & Harris, R. (1987). *Organizational transitions: Managing complex change*. Reading, MA: Addison-Wesley.

Berman, P. (1981). Educational change: An implementation paradigm. In R. Lehming & M. Kane (Eds.), *Improving schools: Using what we know* (pp. 253–286). Beverly Hills: Sage.

Berman, P. (1985). Next steps: The Minnesota plan. *Phi Delta Kappan, 67*, 188–193.

Berman, P., & Gjelten, T. (1984). *Improving school improvement: An independent evaluation of the California school improvement program, Vol. 2, Findings*. Berkeley: Berman, Weiler Associates.

Berman, P., & McLaughlin, M. (1974). *Federal programs supporting educational change, Vol. I: A model of educational change*. Santa Monica, CA: Rand.

Berman, P., & McLaughlin, M. (1977). *Federal programs supporting educational change, Vol. VIII: Implementing and sustaining innovations.* Santa Monica: Rand.

Block, P. (1987). *The empowered manager: Positive political skills at work.* San Francisco: Jossey-Bass.

Bolman, L., & Deal, T. (1984). *Modern approaches to understanding and managing organizations.* San Francisco: Jossey-Bass.

Boyer, E. (1983). *High school: A report on secondary education in America.* New York: Harper & Row.

Brunsson, N. (1985). *The irrational organization.* New York: Wiley.

Burns, J. M. (1978). *Leadership.* New York: Harper & Row.

Caldwell, B. J., & Spinks, J. M. (1988). *The self-managing school.* London: Falmer Press.

Cetron, M. (1985). *Schools of the future: How American business and education can cooperate to save our schools.* New York: McGraw-Hill.

Chubb, J. (1988). Why the current wave of school reform will fail. *The Public Interest, 90,* 28–49.

Clark, B. (1972). The organizational saga in higher education. *Administrative Science Quarterly, 17,* 178–184.

Clark, D., Lotto, L., & Astuto, T. (1984). Effective schools and school improvement: A comparative analysis of two lines of inquiry. *Educational Administration Quarterly, 20,* 41–68.

Clark, D., McKibbin, S., & Malkas, M. (1980). *New perspectives on planning in educational organizations.* San Francisco: Far West Laboratory.

Clune, W., & White, P. (1988). *School-based management: Institutional variation, implementation and issues for future research.* New Brunswick, NJ: Center for Policy Research in Education, Rutgers University.

Cole, D. W. (1983). *Conflict resolution technology.* Cleveland, OH: The Organization Development Institute.

Corcoran, T. B. (1985). Effective secondary schools. In R. M. J. Kyle (Ed.), *Reaching for excellence: An effective schools sourcebook* (pp. 71–98). Washington: U.S. Government Printing Office.

Corcoran, T. B., Walker, L. J., & White, J. L. (1988). *Working in urban schools.* Washington, DC: Institute for Educational Leadership.

Cox, P., French, L., & Loucks-Horsley, S. (1987). *Getting the principal off the hot-seat: Configuring leadership and support for school improvement.* Andover, MA: The Network.

Crandall, D. & Associates. (1982). *People, policies and practices: Examining the chain of school improvement.* Vols. I–X. Andover, MA: The Network.

Crandall, D., Eiseman, J., & Louis, K. S. (1986). Strategic planning issues that bear on the success of school improvement efforts. *Educational Administration Quarterly, 22,* 21–53.

Daft, R., & Lengel, R. (1984). Information richness: A new approach to managerial behavior and organizational design. In B. Staw & L. Cummings

(Eds.), *Research in organizational behavior, 6*, pp. 191–233. Greenwich, CT: JAI Press.

D'Amico, J. (1982). Using effective schools studies to create effective schools: No recipe yet. *Educational Leadership, 40*, 60–62.

Deal, T., & Rallis, S. (1981). Greenfield Junior High School. In K. Louis, D. Kell, K. Chabotar, & S. Sieber (Eds.), *Perspectives on school improvement: A casebook for curriculum change* (pp. 95–106). Washington, DC: National Institute of Education.

Dentler, R. A. (1984). Ambiguities in state–local relations. *Education and Urban Society, 16*, 145–164.

Dentler, R. A., & Scott, M. (1983). *Schools on trial.* Cambridge, MA: Abt Books.

Donaldson, G., & Lorsch, J. W. (1983). *Decision making at the top: The shaping of strategic direction.* New York: Basic.

Egan, G. (1988). *Change agent skills: Assessing and designing excellence.* San Diego: University Associates.

Elmore, R. F., & McLaughlin, M. W. (1988). *Steady work: Policy, practice and the reform of American education.* Santa Monica, CA: Rand.

Farrar, E. (1987a). Improving the urban high school: The role of leadership in the school, district and state. Paper presented at the annual meeting of the American Educational Research Association, Washington, DC.

Farrar, E. (1987b). John Burroughs Junior High School: The dilemma of school improvement in the cities. Buffalo: Faculty of Educational Studies, State University of New York.

Farrar, E. (1988). Environmental contexts and the implementation of teacher and school-based reforms: Competing interests. Paper presented at the annual meeting of the American Educational Research Association, New Orleans, LA.

Farrar, E., & Cipollone, A. (1988). After the signing: The Boston Compact 1982–1985. In M. Levine & R. Trachtman (Eds.), *American business and the public school* (pp. 89–120). New York: Teachers College Press.

Farrar, E., DeSanctis, J., & Cohen, D. (1980). Views from below: Implementation research in education. *Teachers College Record, 82*, 77–100.

Farrar, E., Neufeld, B., & Miles, M. B. (1984). Effective schools programs in high schools: Social promotion or movement by merit? *Phi Delta Kappan, 65*, 601–706.

Firestone, W. A. (1980). Images of schools and patterns of change. *American Journal of Education, 88*, 459–487.

Firestone, W. A. (1981). *Great expectations for small schools.* New York: Praeger.

Firestone, W. A., & Herriott, R. (1982). Prescriptions for effective elementary schools do not fit secondary schools. *Educational Leadership, 40*, 51–53.

Firestone, W. A., Herriott, R., & Wilson, B. (1987). Explaining differences between elementary and secondary schools: Individual, organizational and institutional perspectives. Philadelphia: Research for Better Schools.

Firestone, W. A., & Rosenblum, S. (1988). The alienation and commitment of students and teachers in urban high schools. *Educational Evaluation and Policy Analysis, 10*, 285–300.

Fisher, R., & Ury, W. (1981). *Getting to yes: Negotiating agreement without giving in.* Boston: Houghton Mifflin.

Frechtling, J. (1982). Alternative methods for determining effectiveness: Convergence and divergence. Paper presented at the annual meeting of the American Educational Research Association, New York, NY.

Friedkin, N. E., & Necochea, J. (1988). School system size and performance: A contingency perspective. *Educational Evaluation and Policy Analysis, 10*, 237–249.

Fullan, M. (1982). *The meaning of educational change.* New York: Teachers College Press.

Fullan, M. (1988). *Change processes in secondary schools: Towards a more fundamental agenda.* Toronto: University of Toronto.

Fullan, M., & Newton, E. (1988). School principals and change processes in the secondary school. *The Canadian Journal of Education, 13*(3), 404–422.

Goodlad, J. (1983). *A place called school: Prospects for the future.* New York: McGraw-Hill.

Haberman, M. (1988). *Preparing teachers for urban schools.* Bloomington, IN: Phi Delta Kappa Educational Foundation.

Hall, G. (1979). The study of individual teacher and professor concerns about innovations. *The Journal of Teacher Education, 27*, 22–23.

Hall, G., & Guzman, F. (1984). *Where is the leadership for change in high schools?* Austin, TX: Research and Development Center for Teacher Education.

Hall, G., & Hord, S. (1987). *Change in schools: Facilitating the process.* Albany: SUNY Press.

Hedberg, B. (1981). How organizations learn and unlearn. In P. Nystrom & W. Starbuck (Eds.), *Handbook of organizational design*, Vol. 1, pp. 3–27. Oxford: Oxford University Press.

Hill, P. T., Wise, A. E., & Shapiro, L. (1989). *Educational progress: Cities mobilize to improve their schools.* Santa Monica, CA: Rand.

Hopkins, D. (Ed.). (1985). *School-based review for school improvement.* Leuven, Belgium: Acco.

Hopkins, D., & Bollen, R. (Eds.). (1987). *School-based review: Towards a praxis.* Leuven, Belgium: Acco.

House, E. (1981). Three perspectives on innovation. In R. Lehming & M. Kane (Eds.), *Improving schools: Using what we know* (pp. 17–41). Beverly Hills: Sage.

Houston, H. (1988). Restructuring secondary schools. In A. Lieberman (Ed.), *Building a professional culture in schools* (pp. 109–128). New York: Teachers College Press.

Huberman, A. M., & Miles, M. B. (1984). *Innovation up close.* New York: Plenum.

Huitt, W., Caldwell, J., & Segars, J. (1982). Monitoring and evaluating the critical dimensions of effective classrooms. Paper presented at the annual meeting of the American Educational Research Association, New York City.

Iacocca, L., & Novak, W. (1984). *Iacocca: An autobiography.* New York: Bantam Books.

Joyce, B. R., & Showers, B. (1983). *Power in staff development through research on training.* Washington, DC: Association for Supervision and Curriculum Development.

Kanter, R. M. (1983). *The change masters.* New York: Simon & Schuster.

Kaplan, G. (1985). Shining lights in high places: Education's top four leaders and their heirs. *Phi Delta Kappan, 67,* 7-16.

Kell, D., & Louis, K. S. (1980). *The role of local action teams in school improvement.* Cambridge, MA: Abt Associates.

Koberg, D., & Bagnall, J. (1976). *The universal traveller: A soft systems guide to creativity, problem solving and the process of reaching goals.* Los Altos, CA: William Kaufmann.

Kouzes, J., & Posner, B. (1987). *The leadership challenge.* San Francisco, Jossey-Bass.

Kyle, R. M. J. (Ed.). (1985) *Reaching for excellence: An effective schools sourcebook.* Washington, DC: U.S. Government Printing Office.

Leithwood, K., & Montgomery, D. (1986). *The principal profile.* Toronto, Canada: OISE Press.

Lightfoot, S. (1983). *The good high school.* New York: Basic.

Lindblom, C. (1959). The science of muddling through. *Public Administration Review, 19,* 79-88.

Lipham, J., & Ranking, R. (1982). *Change, leadership and decision making in improving secondary schools.* Madison, WI: Center for Education Research.

Lotto, L., Clark, D., & Carroll, M. (1980). Understanding planning in educational organizations: Generative concepts and key variables. In D. Clark, S. McKibbin, & M. Malkas (Eds.), *New perspective on planning in educational organizations* (p. 20). San Francisco: Far West Laboratory.

Louis, K. S. (1981). External agents and knowledge utilization: Dimensions for analysis and action. In R. Lehming & M. Kane (Eds.), *Improving schools: Using what we know* (pp. 168-211). Beverly Hills: Sage.

Louis, K. S. (1986). Reforming secondary schools: A critique and an agenda for administrators. *Educational Leadership, 44,* 33-36.

Louis, K. S. (1989). School district policy for school improvement. In M. Holmes, K. Leithwood, & D. Musella (Eds.), *Educational policy for effective schools* (pp. 145-167). New York: Teachers College Press.

Louis, K. S., Chabotar, K., & Kell, D. (1981). *Perspectives on school improvement.* Washington, DC: National Institute of Education.

Louis, K. S., & Cipollone, A. (1986). *The slower you go, the faster you get there: The story of reform in Agassiz High School.* Boston: Center for Survey Research, University of Massachusetts.

Louis, K. S., & Dentler, R. A. (1988). Knowledge use and school improvement. *Curriculum Inquiry, 18,* 33–62.

Louis, K. S., Rosenblum, S., & Molitor, J. (1981). *Strategies for knowledge use and school improvement.* Washington, DC: National Institute of Education.

Louis, K. S., & Smith, B. (1989). Teacher engagement and student engagement: Alternative approaches to school reform and the improvement of teachers' work. Paper presented at the annual meeting of the American Educational Research Association, San Francisco.

Lowy, A., Kelleher, D., & Finestone, P. (1986). Management learning: Beyond program design. *Training and Development Journal,* June, pp. 34–37.

Lukas, J. A. (1985). *Common ground.* New York: Knopf.

Lupo, A. (1977). *Liberty's chosen home: The politics of violence in Boston.* Boston: Little Brown.

March, J., & Olsen, J. (1976). *Ambiguity and choice in organizations.* Bergen, Norway: Universitetsforlaget.

March, J., & Olsen, J. (1986). Garbage can models of decision making in organizations. In J. March & R. Weissinger-Baylon (Eds.), *Ambiguity and command: Organizational perspective on military decision making* (pp. 11–52). Marshfield, MA: Pitman.

McCune, S. D. (1986). *Guide to strategic planning for educators.* Alexandria, VA: Association for Supervision and Curriculum Development.

McLaughlin, M. (1987). Learning from experience: Lessons from policy implementation. *Educational Evaluation and Policy Analysis, 9,* 171–178.

Metz, M. H. (1988a). *Final report. Field study on teachers' engagement project on the effects of the school as a workplace on teachers' engagement — phase one.* Madison: National Center on Effective Secondary Schools, University of Wisconsin.

Metz, M. H. (1988b). Some missing elements in the reform movement. *Educational Administration Quarterly, 24,* 446–460.

Miles, M. B. (1980). *Learning to work in groups: A training guide for educational leaders.* New York: Teachers College Press.

Miles, M. B. (1981). Mapping the common properties of schools. In R. Lehming & M. Kane (Eds.), *Improving schools: Using what we know* (pp. 42–114). Beverly Hills: Sage.

Miles, M. B. (1983). Unravelling the mystery of institutionalization. *Educational Leadership, 41,* 14–19.

Miles, M. B. (1986). Caruso high school: Reaching at-risk students. New York: Center for Policy Research.

Miles, M. B. (1987). Practical guidelines for school administrators: How to get there. Paper presented at the annual meeting of the American Educational Research Association, San Francisco.

Miles, M. B. (1990). Innovative methods for studying qualitative data collection and analysis: Vignettes and pre-structured cases. *Qualitative Studies in Education, 3*(1).

Miles, M. B., & Ekholm, M. (1986). School improvement at the school level. In W. Van Velzen et al. (Eds.), *Making school improvement work* (pp. 123–180). Leuven, Belgium: Acco.

Miles, M. B., Ekholm, M., & Vandenberghe, R. (1987). *Lasting school improvement: Exploring the process of institutionalization.* Leuven, Belgium: Acco.

Miles, M. B., & Huberman, A. M. (1984). *Qualitative data analysis: A sourcebook of new methods.* Newbury Park, CA: Sage.

Miles, M. B., & Kaufman, T. (1985). A directory of programs promoting effective practices at the classroom and building levels, in R. M. J. Kyle (Ed.), *Reaching for excellence: An effective schools sourcebook.* Washington, DC: U.S. Government Printing Office.

Miles, M. B., & Louis, K. S. (1987). Research on institutionalization: A reflective review. In M. Miles, M. Ekholm, & R. Vandenberghe (Eds.), *Lasting school improvement: Exploring the process of institutionalization* (pp. 25–44). Leuven, Belgium: Acco.

Miles, M. B., Louis, K. S., Rosenblum, S., Cipollone, A., & Farrar, E. (1986). *Lessons for managing implementation: Improving the urban high school: A preliminary report.* Boston: Center for Survey Research.

Miles, M. B., & Rosenblum, S. (1987). Chester Central High School: Working against the odds. New York: Center for Policy Research.

Miles, R., & Randolph, W. A. (1981). Influence of organizational learning styles on early development. In J. Kimberly, R. Miles, & associates (Eds.), *The organizational life cycle* (pp. 44–82). San Francisco: Jossey-Bass.

Montgomery, L. (1986). *Improving productivity and quality of work life: An impact study of work redesign at Infocorp.* Ph.D. dissertation, Harvard University, Graduate School of Education.

Morgan, G. (1986). *Images of organization.* Newbury Park, CA: Sage.

National Commission on Excellence. (1983). *A nation at risk: The imperative for educational reform.* Washington, DC: U.S. Government Printing Office.

Neufeld, B., Farrar, E., & Miles, M. B. (1983). *Review of effective schools programs: Implications for policy, practice and research.* Cambridge, MA: The Huron Institute.

Oakes, J. (1987). *Improving inner city schools: Current directions in urban district reform.* Santa Monica, CA: Rand, Center for Policy Research in Education.

Odden, A., & Marsh, D. (1988). How comprehensive reform legislation can improve secondary schools. *Phi Delta Kappan, 10,* 593–598.

Ouchi, W. (1981). *Theory Z.* New York: Addison-Wesley.

Patterson, J., Parker, J., & Purkey, S. (1986). *Productive school systems for a non-rational world.* Alexandria, VA: Association for Supervision and Curriculum Development.

Pava, C. (1986). New strategies for systems change: Reclaiming non-synoptic methods. *Human Relations, 39,* 615–633.

Peters, T., & Waterman, R. (1984). *In search of excellence.* New York: Harper & Row.

Pfeffer, J., & Salancik, G. (1978). *The external control of organizations: A resource dependence theory.* New York: Harper & Row.

Powell, A., Cohen, D., & Farrar, E. (1985). *The shopping mall high school.* New York: Houghton Mifflin.

Public Education Association. (1986). *Effective dropout prevention: An analysis of the 1985-86 program in New York City.* New York: Public Education Association.

Purkey, S., Rutter, R., & Newmann, F. (1987). U.S. high school improvement programs: A profile from the High School and Beyond supplemental survey. *Metropolitan Education, 3,* 59–91.

Purkey, S., & Smith, M. (1983). Effective schools: A review. *Elementary School Journal, 83,* 427–452.

Ralph, J., & Fenessey, J. (no date). Effective schools research: Can we trust the conclusions? Baltimore: Johns Hopkins University.

Riecken, H., & Homans, G. (1954). Psychological aspects of social structure. In G. Lindzey (Ed.), *Handbook of social psychology* (Vol. 2). Cambridge, MA: Addison-Wesley.

Rosenblum, S. (1986). Alameda High School: The big fix. New York: Center for Policy Research.

Rosenblum, S., & Louis, K. S. (1981). *Stability and change: Innovation in an educational context.* New York: Plenum.

Rosenholtz, S. (1989). *Teachers' workplace: The social organization of schools.* New York: Longmans.

Rossmiller, R. A. (1989). *Field study on principals' management of schools to affect teacher engagement.* Madison: National Center on Effective Secondary Schools, University of Wisconsin.

Roth, S., & Cohen, L. J. (1986). Approach, avoidance and coping with stress. *American Psychologist, 41,* 813–819.

Rutherford, W., Hord, S., & Hall, G. (1985). Changing the American high school: Descriptions and prescriptions. Paper presented at the annual meeting of the American Educational Research Association, Chicago.

Rutter, M., Maughan, B., Mortimore, P. & Ouston, J., with Smith, A. (1979). *Fifteen thousand hours.* Cambridge, MA: Harvard University Press.

Schmuck, R. A., & Runkel, P. J. (1985). *Third handbook of organization development in schools.* Palo Alto: Mayfield.

Schön, D. (1984). The crisis of professional knowledge and the pursuit of an epistemology of practice. Paper presented to the Harvard Business School 75th Anniversary Colloquium on Teaching by the Case Method.

Schön, D. (1987). *Educating the reflective practitioner.* San Francisco: Jossey-Bass.

Sedlak, M. W., Wheeler, C. W., Pullin, D. C., & Cusick, P. A. (1986). *Selling students short: Classroom bargains and academic reforms in the American high school.* New York: Teachers College Press.

Sergiovanni, T. J. (1987). *The principalship: A reflective practice perspective.* Boston: Allyn and Bacon.

Sergiovanni, T. J., Burlingame, M., Coombs, F., & Thurston, P. (1987). *Educational governance and administration* (2nd ed.). Englewood Cliffs, NJ: Prentice Hall.

Sirotnik, K. (1983). What you see is what you get: Consistency, persistency, and mediocrity in classrooms. *Harvard Educational Review, 53,* 16–31.

Sizer, T. (1984). *Horace's compromise: The dilemma of the American high school.* Boston: Houghton Mifflin.

Snow, C., & Hrbiniak, L. (1980). Strategy, distinctive competence and organizational performance. *Administrative Science Quarterly, 25,* 315–334.

Steiner, G. (1979). *Strategic planning: What every manager must know.* New York: The Free Press.

Tichy, N. M. (1981). Problem cycles in organizations and the management of change. In J. R. Kimberly, R. H. Miles, & associates, *The organizational life cycle* (pp. 164–183). San Francisco: Jossey-Bass.

Tichy, N. M. (1983). *Managing strategic change.* New York: Wiley.

Vaill, P. (1982). The purposing of high performing systems. *Organizational Dynamics,* Autumn, pp. 23–39.

van Velzen, W. G., Miles, M. B., Ekholm, M., Hameyer, U., & Robin, D. (1985). *Making school improvement work.* Leuven, Belgium: Acco.

Weick, K. (1976). Educational organizations as loosely coupled systems. *Administrative Science Quarterly, 21*(1), 1–19.

Wilson, B., & Corcoran, T. (1988). *Successful secondary schools: Visions of excellence in American public schools.* East Sussex, England: Falmer Press.

Index

About the Authors

Karen Seashore Louis received her doctoral degree in sociology from Columbia University, and has worked in a variety of policy research and academic settings over the past 15 years. She is currently Associate Professor in the Department of Educational Policy and Administration at the University of Minnesota. Most of her research and consulting has focused on how to improve schools through organizational design and development, research utilization, and better planning and implementation processes. Her experience in these areas includes evaluation and research on federal and state programs in the United States, and work on school improvement with a variety of European countries, Canada, and the Organization for Economic Cooperation and Development. She is the author of *Exchanging ideas: a study of knowledge use in educational settings* (1985); *Supporting school improvement* (1989); "Knowledge Use and School Improvement" (*Curriculum Inquiry*, 1988); and "The Role of the School District in School Improvement" (in *Educational policy for effective schools*, Teachers College Press, 1989).

Matthew B. Miles, a social psychologist, has been Senior Research Associate at the Center for Policy Research, New York City, since 1970. Before that he was Professor of Psychology and Education at Teachers College, where he worked from 1953. He has carried out research, development, and consulting in the field of planned change in education for over 30 years, leading major studies of leadership and intensive group training, school organizational renewal, educational innovation, program implementation, design of new schools, and the work of "change agents." He has developed widely used training materials on group skills, "social architecture" (creating new schools), project management, and consulting skills. Miles has consulted with schools, school districts, regional education centers, universities, state departments, and ministries of education in the United States, Canada, Denmark, Norway, Sweden, the Netherlands, Australia, and New Zealand. Recent books he has co-authored include *Innovation up close* (1984), *Qualitative data analysis* (1984), *Lasting school improvement* (1987), and *Assisting change in education* (1990).